(RE)MEMBERING KENYA

Publisher:
Twaweza Communications Ltd.
P.O. Box 66872 – 00800 Westlands
Twaweza House, Parklands Road
Mpesi Lane, Nairobi Kenya
www.twawezacommunications.org

Editorial office: Catherine Bosire
Design: Iris Buchholz
Cover photography: Mbũgua wa-Mũngai
Printed: Dr. Cantz'sche Druckerei,
Germany

© 2010 Twaweza Communications.

ISBN 9966-7244-7-8

All rights reserved.
No part of this publication may be reproduced or utilized in any form or by any means, electronic or mechanical, including photocopying, recording, or by any information storage and retrieval system, without permission in writing from the publisher.

With the support of Goethe-Institut Kenya, The Ford Foundation, Office of Eastern Africa.

Printed on Munken Pure. Munken is a FSC-certified paper. Certified environmental management proves that the used wood comes from exemplary forest management and makes the grade of the demanding, ecological, social and sustainable standards of the FSC label.
For more information: www.articpaper.com

(RE)MEMBERING KENYA

VOL. 1
Identity, Culture
and Freedom

―――

Edited by Mbũgua wa-Mũngai
and George Gona

A project by Goethe-Institut Kenya
The Ford Foundation
Twaweza Communications

Dedicated to Kenya's IDPs, a new category of citizens whose very existence reminds us daily of what we have done and haven't done, can do but haven't, should do and shouldn't do.

Content

9   Acknowledgements
10   Joyce Nyairo, Johannes Hossfeld
      Foreword
16   Mbũgua wa-Mũngai, George Gona
      Introduction
24   Mbũgua wa-Mũngai
      Prescript—Blessings of Bullets: A Survivor's Personal Experience

Identity

32   Pius Kakai Wanyonyi
      Historicizing Negative Ethnicity in Kenya
50   Peter Wafula Wekesa
      Negotiating 'Kenyanness': The 'Debates'
72   Mbũgua wa-Mũngai
      Iconic Representations of Identities in Kenyan Cultures
96   Tom Odhiambo
      Gerontocracy and Generational Competition in Kenya Today: An Observation

Culture

110   Ruth Wangeci Ndũng'ũ
       Socialization and violence: Ideas and Practices in Kenya
126   Sophie Macharia
       Gendered identities: Women and Power(lessness) in Kenya

Freedom

142 Frederick K. Iraki
Cross-media Ownership and the Monopolizing of Public Spaces in Kenya

160 Karambu Ringera
The politics of Media Culture and Media Culture Politics

178 Kĩmani Njogu
Globalized Identity: Diaspora Kenyans and Local Conflict

206 V. G. Simiyu
Intellectuals and the State: A Historical Perspective

Conflict & Reconciliation

224 George Gona
The South African Truth and Reconciliation Commission (TRC): Lessons for Kenya

248 Betty Caplan
Post-script—On the Path of Truth and Reconciliation: A Reflection

256 Notes on Contributors
257 List of papers presented

Acknowledgements

The editors wish to acknowledge with gratitude the International Institute for Education, The Ford Foundation and Twaweza Communications for their support to the project. The audiences that faithfully attended the presentations at the Goethe-Institut Kenya auditorium were a critical part that ensured the success of the undertaking. Acknowledgement is made to Katharina Greven of Goethe-Institut Kenya for organizing the seminars. Not least we wish to acknowledge Catherine Bosire for her patience with the script as well as her commitment to seeing the entire process of putting together the publication come to fruition: *Tumetoka mbali*!

Foreword

This book, mooted under special but depressing circumstances, is the product of collaborative work between The Ford Foundation and Goethe-Institut Kenya. In the season following the violence of the 2007 General Election, the air was thick with the anger of unanswered questions and the tension of questions whose voicing might very well ignite a new round of bloodletting. Sites of public assembly became places that one avoided lest you say something that annoyed the other, or you heard something that released your tenuous hold on an ugly tirade. The Internet and its chat-rooms, list-servs and blogs was a veritable minefield of emotively expressed opinions many of which could not survive the scrutiny of intellectual inquiry. At the heart of all the anger, tension and fear was the simple question: Was the idea of Kenya as it had been conceived in 1963 no longer tenable? If so, what were the alternatives and could any of them be achieved without further pain or ugliness?

Even as the country was hurtling towards calamity a key question began to emerge: Was it possible to try and understand the fuller picture in order to see how Kenyans got to this 'dark moment' in their history? What kind of mark was this that was daily being embossed on the country's history? Was it possible to step outside the charged rhetoric in those heady days after the elections and isolate ideas, patterns and connections between them that might allow one to grasp some aspects of what was unfolding with such fatal force?

With the signing of the National Peace Accord on February 28, 2008 the mist began to lift. But not fast enough. Sites of public engagement were still being guarded with cautious words like:

you can come but don't discuss politics. As public universities re-opened their doors the role of the academic as a public intellectual was not automatically welcome. In the long months of election campaigns and post-election violence some of the academics that had graced television screens, debated on FM airwaves and penned op-eds in the daily press and on list-servs had unwittingly cast a shadow on the neutrality of the public intellectual who was now seen as a tout in search of political patronage and rescue from an unfulfilling life of research and correcting students' scripts. But there was still a balance of questions in the public domain, questions that demanded sustained inquiry and dispassionate analysis. For instance, how had we as a country arrived at this destination of intolerance, ethnic hate, political greed and violent disregard for women and children? With the universities' virtual embargo on political utterances by their teaching staff, who was going to do this work and how would it be done and where would the urgent debates take place in ways that included diverse audiences attentive to the emergent plight of being Kenyan?

In addition to this a second question came up: What were academics saying about events that were unfolding, to whom were they saying it, why and in what fashion? The voice of Kenyan intellectuals who kept a critical distance from the political field seemed to be weak before and during the crisis. The role of the intellectuals in Africa has been enormous (as Ali Mazrui once noted) and this is true also for Kenya. Particularly from the 1970s to the 1980s, but also in the democratization movement in the 90s and up to the 2002 election of the National Rainbow Coalition (NARC), this intervention in the political field—without losing the independence and the grounding in a specialised field of knowledge and culture—was important. But it is also true that right from the peak of the Moi regime (circa 1984) the split between engagement that is grounded in a field different to the political, religious or economic field, and an engagement that loses this critical distance led to a considerable decline in the public status and indeed the reputation of intellectuals in Kenyan society (in a moment of intense international discussion about the general decline of the figure of the engaged intellectual). Fear of reprisals, as well as Government patronage through appointments to prestigious public office, were no doubt factors in the entanglement of some intellectuals with the Moi state. Equally damaging as the criminalization of inquiry was the neglect of universities (especially in the face of IMF dictated SAPs) which led to a dearth of research and an overall decay in institutions of higher learning.

Against this background, conversations between The Ford Foundation and the Goethe-Institut about the reconstitution of the public sphere and the promotion of research and public debate culminated in the formation of "Re-membering Kenya", a lecture series through which we hoped to bring empirical bearing to the myriad theories of Kenya's decay and failure that were circling people's minds, living rooms, internally displaced persons (IDP) camps, offices and political caucuses. "Re-membering Kenya"—the deliberations that were held fortnightly at the Goethe-Institut in Nairobi between June-August and September-November 2008—need to be seen as an endeavour calling for a "scholarship with commitment", *pace* Bourdieu, to engage in an open and respectful exchange, with the aim of deepening our understanding of Kenyan society. Alongside other efforts to document popular experiences of the period, the weight of research and public debate in the Re-membering Kenya circuit was intended to lend educated substance and a culture of informed advocacy to the remarkable work that local civil society groups were doing in variously engaging the election crises.

As Mbũgua wa-Mũngai and George Gona courageously led this effort to bring diverse opinions and varied intellectual traditions and methodologies to a fresh inquiry of what it meant to be Kenyan between 1963 and 2008, Goethe-Institut provided the much needed safe space. It was felt that this was an accessible space in which colonial legacies could be overwritten and put to new uses, donor agendas and the anxieties of media houses and university deconstructed.

Two features are distinctive for (Re)membering Kenya. Firstly the series largely represented a younger generation of scholars that might be disillusioned with the older intellectual generation of scholars(hip). Secondly, and reflecting the education of the younger generation, the idea of currency goes beyond the narrow borders of political theory and is informed by the theories and methodologies of the last 20 years as might be found in cultural studies, deconstruction, postcolonial and gender studies. This is marked by the theme for the first round of this lecture series: Identity, Culture and Freedom.

The premise of this series was that since the idea of Kenyan nationhood was being called to question in both subtle and overt ways then it was necessary to try and come to terms with ideas and practices that citizens have hitherto used to define who they are. Indeed one could even ask: "Is there such a thing as a Kenyan nationhood and how do the people it supposedly defines understand and live by it?" Given that identity—whether civic or otherwise—was a prominent point of contestation during the conflagration alluded to above, coupled with the fact that practices rooted in culture and freedom ultimately shape conceptions of identity, it was necessary that these three key terms be interrogated within a common same framework. Some of the essays in this volume speak to some major issues like ethnicity, the search for a Kenyan identity and social (in)justice that have had a direct bearing on the way Kenyans apprehend their relations amongst themselves especially during crises moments such as the 2005 constitution referendum and the 2007 general election.

At the same time if it is to be accepted that there is a historical bearing to these issues then it is necessary to acknowledge that there are powerful ways through which the nation's history is actively expressed and circulated daily in ways that determine how people view and treat others within the polity. Thus it is critical that questions be asked about language—in private and domestic spaces, in politicians' rhetoric or the mass media—because it shapes thought in crucial ways and this ultimately translates into a range of human relations within culture, the economy, politics and so on. As has been pointed out in this volume, the role of the media in amplifying particular narratives (in themselves acts that are based on institutional politics and cultures) needs to be critiqued in order to see how it mediates and politicizes relationships between those who exercise power and those upon whom it is exercised as well as amongst the 'powerless' themselves. Overall an important question is raised within the following pages: "What next after the drums of war have fallen silent?" In this vein, the matter of Truth and Reconciliation becomes crucial to any attempts to re-member Kenya and thus the need to make a careful consideration of models of truth and reconciliation bodies and the specific contexts in which such bodies have worked. Equally important is the need to carefully assess how to redress the various grievances amongst the victims. Each of the papers presented here—alongside an interview with a former resident of an internally displaced persons' camp and a personal reflection on truth and reconciliation—enable the reader to see the topics covered under the lecture series in a new perspective.

From the perspective of Goethe-Institut Kenya and The Ford Foundation it was not only a question of mandate but a necessity to working towards and providing the context for engaged knowledge and public discourse among and between citizens; because it is these kinds of dialogue that can guarantee citizens' common future. For both institutions, being strongly connected to and rooted in the academic field in Kenya and having a strong focus on public discourse on questions of the Kenyan society, it was necessary in this difficult key moment to be working even more strongly together with our partners in the cultural field and academia, with academicians, artists and activists who engage themselves in the Kenyan society. Our collective prayer was for a season of honest engagement in which dignity could be re-written into the work of local academics and that a record of their own efforts to reconstruct the nation-state an entity aware of its imperfect origins but determined to correct its legacies in order to create equality and social justice could be documented. This endeavour to remember—looking at Kenya from a historical perspective—and at the same time to try to contribute towards bringing together again what has fallen apart must also be seen as a space-clearing gesture; an attempt to entrench a culture of asking awkward and difficult questions, the kind of questions that will keep Kenyans thinking about their role in constructing an equitable society where respect for their fellows is both instinctive and paramount to their definition of self and nation.

Joyce Nyairo,
The Ford Foundation

Johannes Hossfeld,
Goethe-Institut Kenya

Introduction

Ngugi Wa Thiong'o's *Petals of Blood* depicts the residents of Ilmorog—a dusty rural settlement perched upon the escarpment overlooking the Rift Valley— wearied body and soul by an unrelenting drought, and having waited in vain for help from their Member of Parliament, trekking to the city in search of their fugitive Member of Parliament (MP). It is a journey fraught with many risks, personal and collective, but determined to see their effort through to the end, the villagers soldier on to the city of many lights. What is illustrative about this epic journey is not the many things that happen along the way but rather the discoveries that the people of Ilmorog make about themselves, their neighbours and friends and the power-wielding class.

It was a curious coincidence that in the third week of October, 2009, another group of 'villagers' this time placed in actual geographical space, began their journey at Limuru, only now they were marching away from the city, towards Laikipia to take up land that Salome Lenana, seeing that the small church compound at Kīrathimo, Limuru, was no place for over three hundred families to live, had donated to them. They would be following a pattern established earlier in 2009 when a group of IDPs from Nakuru trekked to Ol-kalou to occupy land that they had bought after the government failed to afford them means of transport. According to Martin Kabaī Ndung'ū, the spokesman for the Limuru displaced persons, they had requested the government for transport to Laikipia but their request had been turned down. In the rain the dejected lot of women, children, girls, boys and men trudged along Nairobi-Naivasha highway only to be confronted upon arrival in Naivasha by angry provincial administration officials who demanded to know why these people had not remained where they had come from and waited for the government's help. Both the ineptitude and cruelty of government had been exposed. Indeed a few weeks before, Ekiden, a Community Based Group, had mobilized athletes and popular musicians to take part in a campaign to raise money to help (re)settle the displaced who were languishing in camps. Perhaps in a happy coincidence indicative of the timed nature of government operations that same week the president ordered the Minister for Finance to ensure that money was immediately 'found' to buy land upon which to resettle the victims of the 2007/2008 violence and have the IDP camps closed down in two weeks. Displaced persons have learnt a mode of engaging government: the October 2009 march was replicated on February 17 2010, when a group attempted to trek over 200 kilometres from Olkalou to Nairobi to voice their grievances to the President. The march was violently broken up by the police officers outside Gilgil Town (*Daily Nation*, "IDPs protest march halted" February 18, p. 72). The irony of the situation is that it takes Kenyans tired of government inertia and lack of vision about pressing problems to jolt officialdom into righteous indignation and promises of action. It therefore seems that internally displaced persons—in the first instance driven to that state because the political class couldn't settle quarrels amongst themselves in a civil way—only become a problem to be solved urgently not because there is any sense of moral and civic duty towards such persons but *only* because their presence and visibility embarrass those in power. This remains true today as it was in Ngugi's fictional Ilmorog as Kenya's ghosts, past and present, burst into life to haunt Kenyans. If there is anything that proves right Cyprian Ekwensi's assertion that "this thing called nation-building is not sugar" (*Survive the Peace*) then it is Project Kenya.

General official indifference to citizens' plight—not just the fate of those Kenyans at Kĩrathimo but also that of the ones "forgotten" in the open behind UNHCR tents at the Eldoret Show ground, Naivasha, Total/Mau Summit, Mawingo, those others who exist in camps such as Miotoni and Sawmill Camps (Molo) Sawmill, at the mercy of NGOs like the Danish Refugee Council, the thousands who live under tents at Maai Mahiu, Kikopey, Pipeline, Burnt Forest and other camps all over the Rift Valley, various transit camps near rural townships and which mediate the space between the bigger camps and the village, the thousands who, once they were displaced, fled to other parts of Kenya where they were "absorbed" by local communities, those despairing in a refugee camp in Uganda—is difficult to comprehend, and cannot be justified. And yet, insulting as it might seem, there are the ever-present calls for even such displaced/violated people to think about their Kenyanness. However, beyond the situation of these displaced persons whose circumstances are highlighted here because their festering wounds and scars are more than anything else the most visible reminder of the missteps that we have taken as a country, it is incumbent for us to ask how we got onto that road in the first place and, even more importantly, what can be done to ensure that Kenyans don't trek down that road of shame and pain again. Beyond politicians' rhetoric and histrionics when attempts are made to account for and even to legitimize Kenya's state, what are the subtle issues that led citizens to their present circumstances? Can a sober examination of the issues at hand be achieved?

Going by sentiments expressed in various fora, particularly in printed media, there has been growing concern that academics had abdicated their role of offering informed direction about the course of events in the country particularly before the 2007 general elections. What is worse, it was clear that academics allied to the various political parties took highly partisan and narrow positions, some of which not only negated the spirit of nationhood by actively calling for Kenya's dismembering but also justifying hatred against particular communities. Naturally, questions began emerging about the role of education in creating and fostering a sense of civic duty. Thus, with support from The Ford Foundation and Goethe-Institut Kenya was born a public lecture series in the heady days of early 2008 to bring together academics and the general public to dialogue with one another about critical matters arising from the pitiable situation into which the country had descended. The idea was to build greater clarity of issues related to memory, identity and citizenship in the nation building project in Kenya. By drawing on the past and building links with the present the lecture series has been an attempt to seek a deeper understanding of the challenges facing Kenya.

For four months between June and October 2008, local academics and the public engaged in discussions on critical national issues within the framework of the (Re)membering Kenya: Identity, Culture & Freedom Public Lecture Series that were supported by The Ford Foundation and hosted at the Goethe-Institut Kenya, Nairobi. The broad objective was to tap into scholars' understanding of what went wrong with events surrounding the 2007 elections and, even more crucially, their analysis of how the country's history had cut a sure path for those tragic events. While it was generally apparent in public discourse that the causes of the election-related violence could be linked to key aspects of Kenya's past as well as contemporary history, it was felt that the various aspects of these debates needed to be laid out for interrogation in a systematic fashion so as to enable a more objective assessment of Kenya's state of affairs. It was hoped that placing academics at the forefront of such engagements with the public would at least shape discussions on the matters at hand by offering some contemplative leadership. Thus, where academics were at that point being criticized for their perceived failure to play a robust enough role in national debates, and sometimes being seen as acquiescing bad governance, the lecture series became a way of trying to get scholars to re-engage meaningfully with the Kenyan public.

Key areas that were debated include: ethnicity and its ramifications, the politics of identity and identity formation in Kenya, the land question(s), truth and justice commissions and the lessons Kenyans could learn from the South African experience, media and politics, gerontocracy and generational competition and the gendered nature of Kenyan politics and national life. Kakai's paper grapples with the question of negative ethnicity which goes by the tag of "tribalism" in everyday Kenyan life. Tracing the evolution of the term tribe within the work of colonial administrators he points out that what people, academics included, have failed to appreciate is that the term tribe is of little or no analytical value whatsoever in contemporary Kenya. Devised to enable colonial policing, it is now deployed by politicians as a glib rhetorical device for marshalling support for narrow causes. The unfortunate consequence of all this is that Kenyans have always been manipulated around ethnic alliances and causes rather than ideological principles as was clearly shown in the 2005 referendum on a new constitution. The civil service has also been ethnicized in ways that make absolute mockery of the term 'civil'. But even as it is hoped that a new constitution might redress some of the problems to do with ethnicity, it must still be asked why extant laws that forbid discrimination on this basis under the present constitution are not enforced.

On his part, Wafula calls to question assumptions that are often made in discussions of 'Kenyan identity'—"what is that?" he asks and proceeds to show how Kenyans could very well be living a lie. Aware that identity is at once malleable and formulated in contingent situations, the author examines prevailing discourses on how to craft a national identity. Examining the historical origins of the Kenyan 'nation', he finds that at different times Kenyanness is a forced construct, forged as it were by people with different imperatives at any given time. However, Wafula points out that as an ethical and philosophical doctrine Kenyanness can indeed inspire the citizenry in particular positive ways in attempts to fulfil certain goals. Definitions of identity produced by the state must entertain the fact that its citizens, whatever their similarities, have differences that can never be wished away.

Staying with the question of identity, Mbũgua's paper interrogates the uses to which iconography in Kenyan cultures enables the state to reproduce desired identities at the same time as citizens, especially through popular culture iconography, produce their own. The state's identity, being heavily gendered, is geared towards the centralization of patriarchal authority and in this regard the pre-eminent practice of having elder's councils playing a critical role in Kenyan politics is examined. This inevitably leads those who feel unrepresented by the state's identity icons to fashion their own representational strategies especially from the field of popular culture.

Language is a complicated mode of representation which in post 2007 election Kenya has been used to slant particular stories and phenomena. New vocabulary has been invented to mask the essence of particular realities. 'IDP 'has become linguistic shorthand that erases the individuality of persons by lumping them with others and presenting them as the responsibility of the UNHCR, the Red Cross and other humanitarian relief agencies. Language also lies. For instance, to repeatedly state that there was such a thing as post election violence (PEV) legitimizes the idea that the 2008 atrocities were perpetrated purely because of the elections, a line of thought that is clearly vacuous given its refusal to acknowledge historical facts. It bears pointing out that even as far back as the 1940s, Gĩkũyũ who had bought land in Kisii were being violently evicted from their holdings. At another level 'compensation' has become the plank upon which all sorts of demands, ranging from the reasonable to the patently ridiculous, are placed at the feet of government; it matters little that a good number of people making such claims have no moral justification for doing so. It has also become a fad to invoke 'historical injustices' even when it is no longer clear what the term refers to. Language's critical role in socializing individuals into violence is the subject of discussion in Ndũng'ũ's paper. The violent events of 2007/2008 occurred within a context in which citizens had become so much exposed to propaganda in the media and language that presented violence as 'normal' and therefore an accepted/expected aspect of everyday life. Through cultural behaviour, stereotypes, jokes, and insults among other methods, othering becomes a regular notion with which to think about difference. At home, work, school or places of leisure, Kenyans purvey ideas that legitimize brutality against perceived others through subtle and glaring means. Politicians have been particularly adept at using, and therefore making fashionable, forms of language that encourage and justify violence against opponents.

How have Kenyan women responded to the fractured world around them? Macharia's paper examines the gendered nature of Kenyan politics and discusses the role that women's organizations such as KANU'S *Maendeleo ya Wanawake* have played. As she demonstrates it is possible for women's agenda to be conscripted to that of male politicians to detrimental effect. But women have been getting smarter as seen in their adoption of strategies that enable them to navigate the public spheres of work and school in ways that enable them to lead fulfilling lives beyond the confines of the otherness of a male dominated world. Personal choices often have to be balanced against ethnic and gender bias but in the end narratives abound about women who have fruitfully put to practice the idea of fluidity that is constantly invoked in discussions of identity.

The media has been substantially berated for its role, real or perceived, in the events of 2007/2008. That the media control a formidable amount of knowledge is not in dispute; but to what use is the knowledge presented in the media applied? Answers to this question are dependent on a set of inter-related factors; ownership of these media, which is the subject of Iraki's paper, and media culture, the topic to which Ringera's paper speaks. In both cases, the fact that Kenyan media is predominantly male-owned means that major stories that emerge from the media are told from particular political and gender perspectives. These dynamics significantly affect both the content of news stories as well as the ways in which they are relayed. Ultimately, the question arises as to whether this situation is conducive to the telling of narratives that can positively influence the search for Kenyan nationhood. At another level, Njogu's paper demonstrates how diaspora Kenyans used virtual media—internet chat rooms and e-mail—to actively summon their kinsmen resident in Kenya to dismember the country. Ethnic bigotry was a key feature of these interactions in which, unfortunately, even highly educated academics blithely took part and in the end one wondered what kind of identity these diaspora Kenyans were encouraging. However, virtual media is a double-edged sword because for all the negative things that it is seen to have facilitated, the internet also played an important role in getting the Kenyan story out into the world; sometimes people were rescued from situations of grave danger because an sms was sent *via* the internet to a website hosted abroad that was coordinating logistical support for such persons. Indeed but for the intensity of the coverage of the Kenyan situation in various media, not least on cyberspace, it is doubtful that the mayhem would have attracted as much interest from the rest of the world as it did. A useful contrast here is that the pathetically scant attention in world media that Rwanda received during the 1994 genocide guaranteed the deaths of hundreds of thousands in a short span of time.

There is a key lesson to be drawn from the discussions that were generated when the papers collated in this volume were presented at the Goethe-Institut Kenya; the audience at these fora has been particularly engaging and has offered much thought provoking input for these papers. There was consensus developed amongst participants that the 2007 elections' debacle was merely the cusp of momentous crises to do with among other issues poor governance, law and order, parliament's abdication of its role in ensuring accountability of the Executive, dilemmas of identity and socio-economic marginality. It will certainly help if Kenyans discuss the present state of affairs with their eyes firmly fixed upon history in order to frame matters within their proper context as well as interrogate specific questions more critically. In this regard it is noteworthy that the lecture series' reflections have spurred discussions in other spaces (within civil society organizations, among activists and in newspapers) where the public continues to expand on the theme of (re)membering Kenya along different trajectories. Hopefully a broad range of citizens will continue contemplating and deploying the lessons learnt from the 2007/2008 crises.

But it is also necessary to point out that Kenya isn't out of the woods yet and that honest self-reflection is a critical part of (re)membering the country. Looking beyond the first round of the lecture series at the political inertia around matters of reform as outlined in Agenda IV of the National Reconciliation Accord that the president and the prime minister signed in February 2008 it seems clear that there are forces and individuals still actively bent on dismembering Kenya. Even though the physical barriers that were thrown into place early in 2008 to cut off particular areas from the larger entity of the nation might be gone, there exist internalised psychological obstacles and perceptions of otherness that are daily summoned for the purposes of buttressing divisions of the state and detracting from the idea of a common nation-building project. In everyday situations, for example, ethno-cultural stereotypes have become a critical means through which these points of fracture are apprehended, interrogated and disseminated. The reality is that the issues under contestation during the period immediately after the elections remain unresolved and continue to polarize citizens; *the dismembering of Kenya continues unabated in various guises*. Vigilance is necessary just as ultimately the need to keep exploring ways of bridging some of the existing sharp differences amongst Kenyans and thereby re-membering Kenya remains. It is hoped that the reflections offered in the papers contained in this volume will provoke further discussions about crucial questions around which Kenya is defined and that in turn affect citizens' relations with both the state and with one another. Perhaps one day all the disillusioned IDPs who have loudly and repeatedly stated that they see no use for 'serikali' (government) in their lives will be persuaded of the need to see themselves as Kenyans once again. These essays are offered to anyone who is interested in exploring ways of ensuring that Kenyans will never again have to be subjected to forced treks in the rain and to die of pneumonia along the way or to live in flooded tents and to be shot by police officers for demanding food and protection.

Mbũgua wa-Mũngai   *George Gona*

Prescript—Blessings of Bullets: A Survivor's Personal Experience

INTERVIEW BY MBŨGUA WA-MŨNGAI

The stories of violence, anger, greed, and often pure hatred based on one's ethnicity that were repeatedly relayed as I drove through the scarred beauty of the Rift Valley landscape alerted me to the fact that many people were searching for both healing and justice which unfortunately they also quite realistically knew might never be achieved.

One warm afternoon in 2008 21-year old S was in a throng of internally displaced persons who were demonstrating against non-delivery of relief food that the government had promised them. Instead of food a special delivery arrived by way of a Kenya Police bullet to the lower shin of S's right leg. This interview took place in her father's house in a village deep in the Rift Valley. The house itself is not much—mud and wattle papered over with old newspapers, the many holes that rats have made out of the papers (even the current MP's face on a frayed calendar hasn't been spared!) a potent and constant reminder of the many ruptures in this family's life. Broken things—over a tiny cabinet a disused old thermal tea flask hangs over a wall clock that stopped sharply one day or night at ten minutes past six—abound in this household, but in equal or perhaps even greater measure one detects the family's yearning to patch their lives back together. The memories contained in the following interview are one such effort.

Q: *(To the daughter after she unhesitatingly lifts the leg of her jeans pants to reveal a three inch long, two-inch wide scar permanently seared into the smooth skin of her body)*: How did you end up at the internally displaced person's camp?

(The father interjects): It is a long story. It has many flights, turns and scares in between. But we are still here, even if it means setting down our roofs and having to remove the recently nailed-down iron sheets for re-use in the next location of refuge. I mean they would have wanted us dead but look, despite the hardships of the days, we are still moving on. It began in 2006 after the referendum when we were violently evicted from Matunda Farm, at Keringet in Kuresoi.

(Mother, smiling wistfully): They say there is nothing you can't laugh about, but this story defies laughter. You should have seen *mzee* here frantically removing the brand new iron sheets from the roof that had barely been in place for a month. We had heard from our neighbors that the Gĩkũyũ would be evicted from Matunda, but we didn't think it would happen. Or that it would happen that fast. I wish you had seen us in those moments of madness... We sent our daughters to run off with the grand-children as we were left behind to gather together whatever we could. And then the cattle! Those ones are another story. You can imagine forcing unwilling cattle to run in an unfamiliar direction *(laughs)*! Then mzee left me with the stubborn cows and he went off to see where the other men were so they could plan what to do in self defence. I moved on determinedly but my scariest moment was when I had to pass by a group of Kalenjin youths standing by the path, watching me come up, saying nothing.

I knew I was dead so I decided to just go on anyway. What options did I have? They could have killed or raped me, but they just looked at me and the cattle, perhaps content in the fact that we and our animals were leaving the area, which was their intention in the first place—to drive us off. If I had turned back towards home then I am sure they would have done something bad to me.

Father: When we fled we were given temporary sanctuary at my mother-in-law's, and then my wife was invited to occupy a small portion of her sister's land. I had my own land at Keringet but now I am a squatter on my in-laws' property. It is but a tiny piece of land which cannot support my large family. So when in 2007 my sister in-law asked us to send S to live with her we gladly accepted. S has a child with whom she moved to her aunt's place.

s: At the church we were told by the chairman of the IDP group to go to the camp to fill in registration forms and collect relief food. It was about three O'clock and the chairman asked us to go to the DC's office to enquire about the delay in food distribution. Before we got to the DO's office he arrived in his official Land Rover and told us he was going to the DC's office to inquire about the matter. None of us was allowed to talk to the DO. Some members of the group branched off towards the DO's office while the rest of us begun walking towards the main road.

Before we got to the main road a Land Rover filled with police officers sped past us and blocked our advance. They alighted and begun shooting, forcing us back.

Q: In what direction were they shooting?

s: Some were shooting in the air, but there was one who was shooting directly at us. We were forced to scamper...opposite the school, there is a slight decline which gets marshy. It used to be bushy but I recently noticed that the area has been cleared. That is where I was, all of us were fleeing, when I was shot. I experienced a slight pain in my leg and I assumed that I had just been scrapped by a stick. But when I looked I saw two holes. I had been shot. I couldn't move. I fell. Other people in the crowd saw that I had been shot but since the shooting was still going on they first ducked for cover. Then the shooting stopped after a short while. They finished and went. Some three men came to my rescue. They picked me and carried me over quite a distance from the marshes to the main road. They flagged down a private motorist who without fuss agreed to take me to hospital. Just then, the police Land Rover came back. The officers saw I had been shot but they said nothing. They just drove off.

Q: Did you see who had shot you?

s: No. There is no way I could have seen that. We were a huge crowd, and in any case we were fleeing and there was no way you could have looked behind to see who was shooting.

Q: Did those who assisted you retrieve the spent bullet with which you were shot?

s: They collected many bullets. I don't know who eventually kept them.

Q: Were you asked for a P3 form before accessing treatment at the health facility?

S: No. I was just given first aid and I was then taken to the district hospital. It was dark when we got there and I was informed that I needed to be taken to the theatre urgently.

Q: How long were you in hospital?

s: I stayed at the hospital for three weeks. I left sometimes in April.

Q: Did any government official come to see you all this while that you were hospitalized?

s: Only some CID officers from the local police station came two days after I had been admitted to record a statement.

Q: That was all you ever heard from the police? Have you ever heard anything from any other official quarters?

s: That was it. They left, but when I went back to my aunt's home, some people from a human rights organization came to take a statement from me. I haven't heard anything either from them since.

Q: How long was it before you were able to walk again?

s: After being discharged from hospital I was required to go back for follow-up clinics. Often I would miss these check-ups because we had neither the bus fare nor the means of transport to the hospital. I remember we were even contemplating removing the cast on my foot ourselves because when we were eventually able to go to hospital to have it removed the staff demanded a bribe from us before they could remove it. Finally there was this Kamba man who took pity on me and my aunt and he agreed to do it. What I remember vividly and in shock is that his colleagues—imagine, they were Gĩkũyũ like me—were insulting him for having agreed to do what in the first place was his job! That was in May 2008. But even after that I couldn't really walk and it wasn't until January 2009 that I was finally able to walk haltingly on my own.

Q: What have you been doing in terms of earning a living since you got better?

s: Not much. You realize that now I can't walk long distances, and my leg often goes very cold and all the time I have to be warmly dressed. I can't carry heavy load and that severely limits what I can do. When I was unwell my cousin took care of my baby and in August 2008 my parents came for us. Now I get along by doing whatever light work that I can. My life will never be the same again.

Q: Did you ever get to know who shot you?

S: (*Her voice drops to a barely audible whisper*) I was told by those who were in the demonstrating throng with me that I was shot by a Kalenjin female officer. But you never know, maybe she wasn't the one that shot me.

Q: If this officer was presented to you and you were told, "This is the person who shot you," what would you say?

S: (*With a slow headshake, voice trailing off*). I can't ever bring myself to face her. But if I could bring myself to speak to her I would only tell her that God avenges the weak. If she had hit me elsewhere with her bullet, may be I'd be dead. God is good I am not dead. Yes. I leave her to God.

Q: What if she said she was just doing her job and that she was ordered to shoot at trouble makers?

S: I would have nothing to say to her.

Q: Has anyone ever come asking you to forgive and reconcile with this officer who shot you?

S: Nobody has come and I am not expecting anyone anyway. I leave her to God.

After the interview we went for lunch in one of the nicer establishments in a town along the way to Nairobi. We noticed that revelers were seated in two distinct groups, with an unoccupied table clearly separating them, and it was evident that there was something effected about the laughter that was occasionally heard in this bar. They conversed nervously in Kalenjin and Gĩkũyũ. When one group comprising seven men left, someone from the other group stated matter-of-factly: "*they* are the ones." I didn't bother to ask who 'they' meant or what they were supposed to have done given that the weight of the statement was loaded with accusations. I assumed that one was supposed to instinctively know the 'who' and the 'what' of the statement, something that no doubt is repeated in different permutations all over Kenya, even in places that were quite distant from the actual theatres of the 2007/2008 violence. The atmosphere was damp and charged with suspicion, something that brought a ring of hollowness to current invocations of 'reconciliation' and 'forgiveness.' Something here reminded me of the magnificent unoccupied two-storey building perched in a lonely crouch on a ridge overlooking Molo town across the road from the Raiply factory. According to local lore, residents defecated in the house when it was newly completed because the owner, a politician, had insulted them. Unless the Rift Valley is cleansed of the various acts of desecration that have repeatedly occurred in predictable cycles, the province's breath-taking landscapes might never be habitable.

The stories of violence, anger, greed, and often pure hatred based on one's ethnicity that were repeatedly relayed as I drove through the scarred beauty of the Rift Valley landscape alerted me to the fact that many people were searching for both healing and justice which unfortunately they also quite realistically knew might never be achieved. There was palpable anger, for these survivor's wounds run deep. Thus, contemplating the many shiny corrugated iron roofs which have been recently put up and that dot the deceptively serene Rift Valley scenery especially in places that were most affected by the 2007/2008 violence, one must wonder whether this ugly newness that assaults the eye because of its sharp contrast to its surroundings, a shininess that seems to exist without any good reason, is indicative of a convinced fresh start or merely a forced papering over of things. Driving back to Nairobi through heavy rain, I couldn't help wondering about all the families all over Kenya (and those who fled to exile in Uganda) that daily persist in spirited efforts to patch together souls and livelihoods that have been shattered, like S's shin, by the actions of others 'mightier' than themselves.

Immense gratitude is owed to individuals who facilitated this interview on October 17 2009

Identity

Historicizing Negative Ethnicity in Kenya

PIUS KAKAI WANYONYI

—William Ochieng, 2008.

One word seems to drive our national fate. Tribalism. If the December (27, 2007) elections were hijacked, we all blamed it confidently on tribalism. In any case, the most spectacular consequences—the violence that rocked the entire country—seemed to pit certain tribes against others.

The preceding quotation, extracted from the magazine section in *The East African* foregrounds the importance of the topic under discussion. In our intervention, we seek first to situate the origin of the concept 'tribalism', what our study about the Kenyan peoples' pre-colonial history tells us about ethnicity and how the colonial situation impacted on the nature of ethnicity in Kenya. Second, the discussion will then focus on post-independence manifestations of ethnicity in the Kenya state. This second part will attempt an analysis of how the three successive post independence regimes in Kenya have worked towards the deconstruction or otherwise of the Kenya state.

The Genesis of 'Tribe' and Ethnicity

Various authorities have attempted to situate the origins of the terms 'tribe' and 'ethnicity'. We first examine the origin of 'tribe' before turning to 'ethnicity'. William Ochieng (2008, pp i, iv and v) posits that 'tribe' owes its origin to ancient Rome. It comes from the Latin word *tribus* (plural—*tribi*) which originally referred to one of the political entities into which the Italian peoples were divided as satellites of Latium (today's Lazio) the area across the River Tiber in which Rome was built. These peoples' culture and language were called Latin.

Ochieng further explains that as the Roman Empire expanded, *tribus* came to be applied also to the non-Italic peoples of Europe, North Africa, Asia Minor (today's Turkey) and Southwestern Asia. This means that originally a tribe had nothing to do with blood, culture and language of a community.

There is yet another angle in which tribe is understood. According to Ochieng, this second perception dates from about 500 years ago when Western Europe began rising to the position of world hegemony. Going by this second perception, tribe is a group of individuals with a common blood heritage eking out a living at a very low level of socio-economic formation. These views on the second meaning of tribe echo Mukaru Ng'ang'a's position. Ng'ang'a writing in 1994 argued thus:

> 'The word tribe is *trubutus*, that is tributary, or third rate. Julius Caesar, the Roman Emperor, used it when he conquered and colonized people. The Roman conquerors distinguished themselves from their colonized people particularly through language. The conquered people's language was called 'vernacular' from the Latin word *'vanaculus'* (Mukaru Ng'ang'a, 1994 p.1).

Ng'ang'a in the above quotation places the term ino the Kenyan context by highlighting the argument that the British after conquering Kenya, classified the indigenous people as *'tribes'* (slaves) and the languages they spoke were classified as vernaculars which by inference meant the languages of slaves. The two sources above affirm the fact that, *tribe* and its derivative *tribalism* are pejorative terms. One wonders why our colleagues have continued using the offending term in reference to various Kenyan communities. Indeed, one would expect the offending terms to be allowed to go into the archives to be replaced with more positive concepts.

In relation to the foregoing it is necessary to attempt an understanding of the term *ethnicity*. Ahmed Imatiaz (1999 p. 63) states that the term *'ethnic'* is derived from the Greek word *'ethnikos'* which originally meant heathen, pagan, gentile, non-Jewish and non-Christian. However, the pejorative implications of the term have diminished and in their place the positive aspects seem to have assumed prominence. Hence the word 'ethnic' and its derivative 'ethnicity' are more positive[1] than 'tribe' or 'tribalism'. Indeed Archie Mafeje (2003, 55) points that in social science discourse, 'ethnicity' as a concept is presumed to be less offensive or more respectable than terms like 'tribalism' which got associated with Africa in Western minds.

In addition, he distinguishes between an 'ethnic group' and an 'ethnic category' by using parallel distinctions made in classical sociology between a 'social group' and a 'social category'. According to classical sociology, 'social groups' are characterized by necessary patterns of social interaction. For instance a lineage, an association, a political faction or a religious sect fit into that characterization. In contrast, while characterized by a common identity, a 'social category' exhibits no necessary or regular patterns of interaction. Hence, 'ethnic groups' like 'social groups' exhibit regular patterns of interactions whereas 'ethnic categories' do not despite the latter being a common identification entity. This fact means that people within an ethnic entity may indeed blend into its neighbouring ethnic entity without having a distinct cultural-linguistic boundary. This is especially clear when one studies the population settlements in various parts of Kenya in the pre-colonial era. For that matter, I will use the term ethnic category instead of ethnic group.

Ethnicity in pre-colonial Kenya

In the construction of Kenya in the pre-colonial era one is compelled to visualize interactions by members of different ethnicities in the geo-political space of what later came to constitute the Kenyan state. Studies carried out among the various pre-colonial people of Kenya seem to affirm the existence of porous boundaries separating members of different communities. As a result almost all present day Kenyan ethnic categories derive their existence from a sociocultural medley in which members of one dominant category assimilated those from minor groups.

The history of the migration and settlements of the Kenyan communities testifies to the heterogeneous ancestry of these Kenyan people. Indeed Ogot (quoted by Atieno Odhiambo, 2002 pp. 30–31) contends that the inhabitants of the interlacustrine region of East Africa commingled for a millennium within the region creating systems of production, exchange and redistribution which were predicated on local identities rather than specific Bantu or Nilotic language, culture and ethnic communities.

In demonstrating the interminglings, Atieno-Odhiambo argues that fifty three clans that inhabit Luoland and speak Dholuo came from different traditions, cultures, languages and ethnicities. The Walowa also known as Abalalo came from Uganda and eventually dispersed into Yimbo, Alego and north Mara, in Tanzania. The Abaludhi clan of Luoland came from Bunyala while the Abaxgaro clan fled into the Abasamia sub-ethnic group of the Abaluyia.

In general Atieno-Odhiambo's thesis is that the present-day Luo-speaking community is a result of a multiplicity of interactions between various components of the plains and highland Nilotes as well as Bantu speaking communities. This same reality exists among the Abaluyia. As is demonstrated by Were (1967) and later researchers among the Abaluyia, the eighteen sub-ethnic communities are as a result of heterogeneous origins. Some of these members originated from the River Lake, Highland and Plains Nilotic as well as other Bantu speakers.

The same is true of the Agĩkũyũ of Central Kenya. Muriuki (1974) submits that the Agĩkũyũ represent a fusion of many different ethnic elements. These elements include the Gumba, Maasai, Athi and the Okiek.[2] Members from these communities were absorbed either as a result of conquest, seeking asylum as refugees or through intermarriage and being offered land by their in-laws from these other communities. These assimilated communities have enriched the Agĩkũyũ culturally and linguistically. For instance, all names of wild animals, trees and the three initiation generations of Chuma, Maina and Mwangi age-sets were borrowed from the Thagicu. By and large this intermingling of various elements to constitute ethnic groups as Ogot pointed out above applies to many other Kenyan peoples such as the Kalenjin, Maasai, Samburu, Meru, Akamba, Abagusii, Abakuria, the Oromo, the Somali and the Mijikenda. As a result, one cannot talk about a pure ethnic group. By the time colonialists arrived in Kenya these linguistic and cultural interactions[3] were already in progress. Upon establishing authority over their subjects, however, colonial administrators radically transformed the inter-ethnic relations including the nature of intermingling. The following sub-section briefly addresses this issue.

The impact of colonialism on ethnicity

As the above section intimates, various ethnicities intermingled freely and even ended up assimilating elements of foreign communities into dominant ones. As a consequence ethnicity was a mere sign of identification. Membership was fluid. The colonial situation however introduced a colonial state proffering a different social milieu altogether. Rodney (1989, p. 244) correctly points out that one of the prominent features of the new set up was the negation of freedom imposed by the imperial presence on the colonized peoples. Colonial forces achieved this by introducing new authoritarian policies, administrative values and practices, all of which were aimed at benefiting colonialists to the disadvantage of the colonized people. To be colonized, Rodney has argued, is to be removed from history. Fanon (1968, p. 37) articulates the intricate process colonialists indulge in to create their world. He points out that the colonial world is a dual one that parcels groups as belonging or not belonging to a given race, species, or religious creed.

What has been described above also applied to the British whom since the 1880s colonized Kenya, first through the Imperial British East Africa Company, and by 1895 through the British government itself. In their process of governance, the British divided the then British East Africa Protectorate—which after 1920 became the Kenya Colony—into administrative boundaries to suit their colonial interests. Among other consequences of these boundaries was the denial of freedom of movement and association to the indigenous people. To further make this limitation real the colonial administration introduced identity cards ('*Kipande*') bearing details about the holder. These included the name of the holder, his ethnicity and his employer.

The history of the kipande in Kenya is traceable from 1915 when the registration ordinance was passed. The ordinance aimed at obtaining a steady flow of labour to European establishments, constant payment of taxes by Africans and apprehension of Africans who refused to work on European farms. It required every male African of sixteen years and above to carry a kipande wherever he went (Kakai, 1993, p. 160).

The kipande was by law required to be kept in a metallic container and tied around the neck of the holder at all times for identification. Failure to obey the requirement meant a stiff penalty to be meted out to the victim. This ordinance, however, was inefficient until 1919 when the Governor's labour circulars urged government officials up to the level of chiefs to compel Africans to work for whites. In a way, these identification cards helped to rigidify ethnicity. No wonder, in the recent post election violence, goons used the same tool to identify individuals' ethnicity and either vented violence on them or spared them as the case demanded.

Ogot's previously cited quotation vividly portrays this divisive and discriminatory colonial policy that rigidified ethnicity. He argues that, 'they (European colonialists) created the colonial states and gave them names, often with scant attention paid to indigenous historical antecedents. There was a category of colonial boundaries which could for lack of a better word, be referred to as segregation boundaries. These included "White Highlands", "Native Reserves", "Outlying Districts" and "Closed Districts".' (Ogot, 2000, p. 16) Ogot further argues that Europeans monopolized fertile parts of the Kenyan highlands while other European settlements were planted in border areas in order to separate and isolate different African groups from one another. For instance, buffer zones of European settlements were established between the Kipsigis and the Gusii, the Kipsigis and the Nandi, the Kipsigis and the Luo, the Nandi and the Terik (Nyang'ori) and between the Kikuyu and the Maasai. In a way, this strategy which in itself was part of a grand scheme by European colonialists to divide Africans so as to rule and oppress them, weakened the pre-colonial intermingling which existed among many communities. The strategy also helped to intensify and fossilize ethnic consciousness amongst the different communities and ended up promoting the feeling of exclusiveness and eventually planted the seeds of ethnocentrism and the urge for ethnocracy.

It wasn't only in border areas that the separation and isolation of different ethnic categories took place. Even on individual European-owned farms the same strategy was employed as Nobel Laureate Maathai Wangari (2006, p. 22) points out. She explains that on settler Neylan's farm for instance the labour force was drawn from diverse local communities. They included Luo, Kipsigis and Kikuyu workers. However these same communities could not live in close proximity to each other. Each community kept to the category of jobs assigned to it. The Kikuyu worked in the fields, the Luo laboured around the homestead as domestic servants, and the Kipsigis took care of the livestock and milking. These workers also lived separately. Thus a Kikuyu village was separate from a Luo one which was in turn separate from a Kipsigis counterparts'. In a way this practice contributed to the emergence of specific ethnic stereotypes and at the same time perpetuated interethnic exclusivity.

As it can be discerned, the establishment of an ethnic consciousness amongst Africans is to a large extent a creature of the colonial period. However Africans did not readily acknowledge and appropriate it. They defied this strategy and embarked on forming trans-ethnic political parties. For instance in 1944, the formation of Kenya African Union (KAU) drew membership from many parts of the country. Among the leading figures of KAU were Walter Odede, Achieng Aneko and Oginga Odinga from Luo Nyanza while Joseph Otiende, John Adala and W.W.W. Awori were from Luyialand. John Kebasso was from Gusii whereas Kiptoo Arap Chirchir represented Kalenjinland. Mwinga Chitasi was from Mombasa and Woresha Mengo hailed from Taita (Bogonko, 1980, p. 40).

However, the Mau Mau uprising caused the banning of KAU and it took some time before the colonial administration allowed the formation of provincially based political parties. The nomination and election later in 1957 of African representatives to the Legislative Council (Legco) they began following a provincial pattern. For example Oginga Odinga represented Central Nyanza while L. G. Oguda was the South Nyanza representative. The two regions were, just as they are at present, predominated by the Luo, Abagusii and the Abakuria. Daniel Toroitich Arap Moi on the other hand represented Rift Valley which comprised of mainly the latter day KAMATUSA (Kalenjin, Maasai, Turkana and the Samburu) while J. Muimi represented the Akamba. Masinde Muliro represented the Abaluyia, Ronald Ngala the coastal communities of the Mijikenda while the Central Province groups were represented by B. Mate (Bogonko, *ibid* p.182). In 1957 one could argue that it was only Tom Mboya who was elected in a cosmopolitan and multi-ethnic constituency of Nairobi (Kakai, 2004, p. 5).

The realities of the colonial situation however only served to heighten African nationalists' awareness of the bigger and oppressive colonial situation. For instance Bildad Mwaganu Kaggia and General China were some of the foremost leaders among Kenyan African ex-world war II returnees from foreign countries who began the agitation for independence. They focused their attention to the removal of colonialism physically, politically, economically and psychologically. For these ex-world war II soldiers, territorial rather than ethnic nationalism shaped their worldviews. Indeed the African ex-soldiers wondered why the colonial government could not settle them in Kenya highlands as was done to white ex-soldiers who were allocated land in places like Trans Nzoia and Uasin Gishu (Kenyanchui, 1992, p. 117).

Hence the fight for independence took mainly a trans-ethnic and racial struggle. Whether through political parties of the time or religious movements, outward provincial or ethnic characteristics of these entities did not constrain their preoccupation from the broader national and trans-territorial concerns. Even Kenya African National Union (KANU) and Kenya African Democratic Union (KADU) largely concentrated on national independence even if the internal dynamics of these parties had some ethnic trappings.

It is true that since KADU was composed of largely smaller ethnic categories, they advocated for an ethno-regional kind of federalism that would operate in post-independence Kenya. This system would bequeath to each ethno-regional entity—*jimbo* (singular) and *majimbo* (plural)—control over land, primary and secondary education, taxes for local use, a police force and a local government. In proposing this type of governance, KADU stalwarts have been accused of majoritarian phobia. This meant that KADU was afraid of being under the leadership of larger ethnic categories of Kikuyu and Luo who were dominant in KANU.

Unlike KADU, KANU advocated for unity and centralism (*umoja*). Its members favoured a strong central government. Ironically in an attempt to draft a constitution which would reflect their dreams the KANU leadership looked for constitutional advisors from India (Mr. B. Malik) and USA (Mr. Thurgood Marshal) both of which had federal governments. KANU's central government would control all important organs of the executive, the legislature and the judiciary among others.

As a result of the constitution that was brokered during the Lancaster House talks an accord was reached and a quasi-federal constitution was drafted to usher Kenya to independence in 1963. The first post-independence leadership aware of the existence of profound ethnic sensitivities as it embarked on a nation-building project. To what extent this project has reduced the sharp ethnicity of the colonial divide and rule policy is what the following sub-section will address.

Independent Kenya and 'Nation-Building'?
As indicated in the preceding paragraph the first government of independent Kenya had an onerous task of uniting the many areas of Kenya into one nation; a

nation-state in which all people were equal before the law without any discrimination based on race, ethnicity, colour or creed. This task required a lot of tact given that the north eastern region, predominantly occupied by the Somali ethnic categories, wanted to secede and join the Republic of Somalia (Bogonko, 1980, p. 262). The strategy brought into focus efforts which would improve relations among the roughly forty-two ethnic entities as well as among the many religious groups and unite them under shared political and economic systems. Success in achieving such goals lay in devising an appropriate ideology. We examine below the measures post independence leaders took to realize what we see now as having been an elusive dream.

Walter Oyugi (1998 p. 29) contends that the majimbo constitution adopted on the eve of independence provided room for political conflict between KANU and KADU. Given that the two major parties were made up of majority ethnic categories (KANU) and minority ethnic counterparts[4] (KADU) the stage was set for ethnic competition in politics. Between 1963 and November 1964, the conflict between the KANU government and the only opposition party, KADU, led to areas which were predominantly KADU being denied funds from the central government to run regional (majimbo) governments. As a result ethnic communities in KADU areas vented their anger upon the Kikuyu and Luo communities that were predominant in KANU. Towards late 1964 the frustrated KADU dissolved and joined KANU for the sake of unity and development (Oyugi, ibid).

However, KADU's disbandment only marked the end of one phase in the ongoing inter-ethnic suspicion and tensions. In the place of the inter-ethnic struggles which were previously camouflaged in party outfits, now the struggles that took place under the *de facto* one party state became brazenly crude. Specifically the two former allies the Kikuyu and the Luo became opponents largely because their leaders Jomo Kenyatta (Kikuyu) and Oginga Odinga (Luo) had ideological differences. These differences reached their climax in 1966 when Odinga quit KANU and together with Bildad Kaggia (a Kikuyu of leftist inclinations formed a socialist oriented party, Kenya People's Union (KPU). About one fifth of the members of parliament (MPs), the majority of whom were Kikuyu and Luo, supported KPU (Ogot, 1999, pp. 280–281). This party opposed the conservatism and western orientation of the KANU leadership. In addition, it aimed at replacing the persistently ethnic basis of politics with a cleavage based on ideological, class or socio-economic grounds.

Nonetheless, through the fifth amendment to the Kenyan Constitution all 29 MPs who had defected to KPU were forced to resign their parliamentarian seats and seek a new mandate from the electorate. The amendment compelled other MPs to withdraw the support for KPU. As a result, the eleven (Nasong'o, 2005, p. 20) MPs who won in the by election on KPU were mainly from Nyanza. The resulting by-election of 1966, also referred to as the 'Little General Election' therefore ended up ethnicising KPU. Those who vied in Central province were branded as traitors and therefore denied votes which would have enabled them serve out their terms in parliament. That ethnicisation of what was otherwise a healthy ideological debate sadly marked the premature end of among others Bildad Kaggia's lively contributions in parliament.

Ethnic animosity between the Kikuyu and the Luo reached a violent turn in 1969 with the assassination of the flamboyant Tom Mboya. Mboya, the Secretary General of KANU and Minister for Economic Planning and Development was from the Luo[5] community whereas his alleged assassin, Nahashon Njenga Njoroge, was a Kikuyu. News about Mboya's assassination raised ethnic emotions to a crescendo in Nairobi and Nyanza. Riots in Kisumu resulted in several deaths.

According to Ogot (2003, p. 233) Mboya's death united the Luo under the leadership of Jaramogi Odinga. It also united the Kikuyu through the compulsory oaths which the community members were forced to take at Gatundu to ensure the presidency remained among their community. One might then argue that Kenyatta's remaining years in office were marked by tension among the bulk of the Luo and Gĩkũyũ populations. This would be interpreted to mean that Kenyatta's years in office helped to reinforce the colonial legacy of divide and rule instead of creating national unity.

This is clearly evinced by the conduct of members from other communities and the way they fitted in this Kikuyu—Luo axis. Oyugi (op cit. p. 297) argues that they learnt to devise linkages that enabled them to survive the Kikuyu-Luo tensions. A kind of court system of governance emerged which enabled various ethnic and other interest groups to pay visits to the 'court' at Kenyatta's home in Gatundu or in the Nakuru or Mombasa state houses for special favours.

Yet we still had sober politicians who considered the nation-building project viable. They include the flamboyant and populist J.M. Kariuki who together with Mwai Kibaki were perhaps the only two prominent Kikuyu politicians to go and bury Tom Mboya at his Rusinga Island home. This latter category includes the leftists who joined the radical Kenya People's Union even at a time when interethnic stakes were very high. It is this crop of national leadership who upon Kenyatta's death in 1978, constitutionally provided an avenue for the then Vice

President Daniel arap Moi to succeed him peacefully. But did President Moi re-energize the nation-building project?

When Moi assumed power in 1978, he opted to leave the structure of power undisturbed between 1978 and the general elections of 1979. During those elections, there were serious political intrigues which were employed to engineer the defeat of many establishment politicians. Moi got an opportunity to form his own team for the first time while at the same time he avoided antagonizing the Kikuyu some of whose members still held strategic positions in various ministries and parastatals.

Nonetheless after the abortive coup of 1982 Moi systematically began dismantling Kenyatta's ruling clique and established his own (Nasong'o, 2005 p. 22). He appointed into his cabinet a significant number of members from hitherto marginalized communities such as the Maasai and the Somali as well as many of his Kalenjin people. Among the Kikuyu, he appointed those who were previously not within the mainstream of Kenyatta's government (Oyugi, op. cit. 299).

Gradually, but systematically, Moi entrenched himself and appointed members of his ethnic group into strategic positions which were previously held by the Kikuyu during Kenyatta's reign. During the later part of 1980, he outlawed "ethnic-based" organizations including Gikuyu, Embu and Meru Association (GEMA), The Luo Union, The New Akamba Union and the Abaluyia Welfare Association as well as ethnic-based football clubs.

According to Moi he wanted only one 'ethnic group' known as 'Kenya'. Looked at from the sloganeering point of view one could argue that under Moi, ethnic issues were repressed. But as later years would reveal, ethnic-based practices in government never disappeared. They were manifested in various political pronouncements and policies. At the political level, Moi also encouraged politicians to make visits to State House to pledge loyalty to him. This was very much like Kenyatta. In terms of his policies the District Focus strategy that was introduced in 1983 and the introduction of quarter system during selection of students into provincial schools are examples that demonstrate ethnic manifestations of Moi's government strategy.

District Focus aimed at transferring development strategies from provincial level to district level. Given that most of the districts are conceived around specific ethnic or sub-ethnic communities, one might conclude that the District Focus for rural development further reinforced 'ethnicism'. This conclusion can equally apply to the quarter system in secondary school selections of students.

The system gave more opportunities to students from around the school locality and allowed admission of only a quarter of students who hailed from outside the province. As a consequence young people who previously qualified and got admitted to good schools outside their provinces were, under Moi's era, constrained to learn mainly within their provinces. This strategy, while encouraging communities to invest more in constructing new and well equipped secon-dary schools, also adversely affected the nation-building approach.

How far this statement is true came to light during the crusade for the reintroduction of multiparty politics. Reintroduced in December 1991, (Nyanchoga et al. 2008 p. 37) multi party politics gave rise to the formation of many parties foremost amongst which were Forum for Restoration of Democracy-Kenya (Ford-Kenya), Forum for Restoration of Democracy—Asili (Ford-Asili) and Democratic Party of Kenya (DP). In December 1992, these parties together with KANU participated in the general elections whose results shocked many people.

Godfrey Muriuki's (1995) sentiments may reflect the general feeling amongst many analysts. He argued that despite their pretensions to the contrary Kenyan political parties had a rude shock in the 1992 general elections especially because they had denied the ethnic character of their parties. KANU was largely supported by the Kalenjin, Ford-Kenya by the Luo while Ford-Asili and DP had the Kikuyu and their GEMA cousins for supporters (Muriuki, 1995, p. 19). This trend was repeated in varying degrees in 1997. Every major political party received its greatest support from among the community of the party leader. Hence the ambition to cement a stable and trans-ethnic Kenya has many hurdles in its path. This is especially so with the politico-ethnic violence that has always emerged during election years.

It could be the need to reduce the dangers of over reliance on parties based on ethno-regional support that persuaded politicians to start what came to be known as 'cooperations', 'partnerships' and 'mergers' as happened between Moi's KANU and Raila Odinga's National Development Party (NDP) between 1998 and 2002 (Badejo, 2006, pp. 182–205). The effort at least broadened Moi's influence in the KANU-NDP zones during the five years before the two politicians differed over the Moi succession struggle.

During this struggle for supremacy in the post Moi era, a similar alliance brought Mwai Kibaki's DP, Charity Ngilu's Social Democratic Party (SDP) and Michael Wamalwa's Ford-Kenya together. The 'big three's' alliance known as National Alliance Party of Kenya (NAK) scheduled meetings to cement their party leadership as they strategized on how to defeat KANU in the 2002 general elections. It is to this NAK that Raila and his dissatisfied KANU colleagues defected from KANU, after having formed a loose alliance known as the Rainbow Alliance which soon after morphed into a political party known as Liberal Democratic Party (LDP). The LDP then joined and further strengthened NAK at the expense of KANU. The new alliance was known as National Rainbow Coalition (NARC) which was registered as a political party. This winning coalition comprised DP, Ford-Kenya, LDP, SDP and other smaller parties whose membership was drawn from among the Kikuyu, Luyia, Luo, Kamba, Mijikenda, Maasai and Kalenjin among others. In this situation, NARC was a viable model for downplaying ethnicity and fighting against the national vices that were arguably embodied in KANU.

NARC leadership allegedly formulated a memorandum of understanding (MOU) whose articles included the setting up of the office of an executive Prime Minister (PM) once the party won in the general election. Given NARC's trans-ethnic base, its members resoundingly trounced KANU and other minor parties. Thus on December 30th 2002 NARC's presidential candidate, Mwai Kibaki was sworn in as Kenya's third President. Within the first months, the NARC leadership endeavoured to honour some of its campaign pledges. Kibaki appointed into his first cabinet members from all the eight provinces of Kenya.

But as Murunga and Nasong'o 2007, (p. 9) argue, in less than two years, after being elected, Kibaki abandoned the MOU and with it, the power sharing arrangement it promised. He also marginalized LDP allies and invited politicians from the opposition KANU and Ford-People into his cabinet.

Looked at from a political party point of view, LDP meant little. But when one understands that its stronghold was in Luo Nyanza then the aspect of ethnic sentiments is discernible. The sentiments were even more pronounced in the 2005 public debates on the entrenchment of the position of the executive PM into the proposed new constitution. Whereas LDP heavyweights from the coalition pushed for the introduction of the PM's slot into the new constitutional draft, political heavy-weights from the Mount Kenya region (Kibaki's stronghold) rejected the project arguing that having two centres of power was counterproductive[6]. In the run-up to the November 21 2005 national referendum, campaigning for or against the proposed constitutional draft (also known as Wako draft) was largely influenced by ethnic considerations as opposed to the actual articles in the draft constitution. The ethnicization of this campaign was such that apart from the Mt. Kenya region, perhaps very few other regions voted

'Yes' for the draft. The overwhelming majority voted for 'No' not to the constitution but to an ideology of anti-Kikuyuism that had coalesced amongst the 'No' supporters. As a result, the draft was rejected not necessarily because of its clauses, but because of ethnicity.

Defeat of the Wako draft led to the sacking from the Kibaki cabinet of those LDP Ministers who had opposed the draft. Consequently, the LDP together with colleagues from other parties which were opposed to the draft and therefore voted 'No' reassembled and formed the Orange Democratic Movement (ODM) as their platform in preparation for the 2007 general elections.

Orange was the symbol that the Electoral Commission of Kenya (ECK) chose for those who were opposed to the Wako draft while the Banana signified those who approved of the draft. Hence the resounding victory by the Orange group in the referendum was perceived to be a precursor of the December 2007 general elections. Therefore, ODM was hence oppositionist and in some quarters perceived to be promoting an anti-Kikuyu agenda. It could be for this reason that no parliamentary aspirants from the heartland of Central Province won a parliamentary seat on an ODM ticket.

On the other hand, supporters of the incumbent after a series of discussions settled for Party of National Unity (PNU) as the vehicle through which President Kibaki was to defend his seat. The pitched battle fought between ODM and PNU, punctuated by frequent opinion polls which revealed a near neck to neck outcome not only excited the political campaigns but also inadvertently excited ethnic sentiments. Thus when on December 27th 2007 voters turned up to vote for their preferred civic, parliamentary and presidential candidates, both local and foreign observers were quoted as declaring the event as one with the highest voter turnout ever witnessed in Kenya.

Once December 27 was over and the results began trickling in, the anxiety, anguish and agony seemed to reach breaking point with every passing day as the nation waited for the announcement of who their new president was going to be. When finally the results were announced over the Kenya Broadcasting Corporation (KBC) Television on December 30th 2007 it was like unleashing a bottled up genie which swiftly moved to wreak havoc especially in Nairobi, Rift Valley, Nyanza and Western provinces.

As news about the clashes, butchers, destruction and expulsions reached the public, it emerged that the over forty four odd years' effort of nation-building were largely wasted! Kenyans had degenerated into 'tribal' or ethnic hatred against compatriots. As a result, when common sense prevailed, over 1,200 people had been butchered, 350,000 displaced, thousands more injured and billions worth of property destroyed (Nyanchonga et. al, op. cit pp. 61–62).

The preceding pages have discussed manifestations of ethnicity in the political arena. But it is also argued that ethnic favouritism operated in appointments in the civil and public service offices. Several scholars and political commentators have highlighted ethnicity in the dishing out of jobs, funds for projects, institutional equipment among many other favours. For instance Oyugi (op. cit, p. 305), commenting on the early post independence years, argues that replacement of expatriates by Africans meant in practice that the benefits would be confined to only those ethnic categories that had received formal colonial education. Hence the Kikuyu, Luo, Luyia and to some extent the Kamba benefited. Of these categories Oyugi argues, the Kikuyu and the Luo were the first beneficiaries in the formative years.

However, after the exit of the Luo from KANU, they lost their favoured positions and also joined those communities that complained of 'tribalism' in the civil service. Dominic Odipo (1999, p. 8) argues that in 1974, as Kenyatta was aging, his kinsmen used the opportunity to appoint to senior civil service positions their relatives without giving consideration to merit. For instance he points out that in the Finance Ministry and related institutions, at the Kenya Ports Authority, in the Ministry of Defence with the exception of the Armed Forces Command, in the Office of the President among others, senior positions were held by persons from the Kikuyu community. In fact of the eight Provincial Commissioners (PCs) four came from Central Province. Godfrey Muriuki (1979, pp. 39–44) clearly points out the Agĩkũyũ's disproportionate visibility in key civil service and parastatals jobs. Nonetheless, Muriuki also clarifies that the Kiambu Kikuyu were the most favoured.

What is true about the public service during Kenyatta's era can also apply to Moi's era. It has been pointed out that the Kalenjin under Moi unfairly enjoyed a relatively greater advantage in receiving job allocations, funds for projects, equipment for schools, recruitment into certain training institutions among many other privileges when compared with other communities in Kenya. For instance, in 1997 a concern was raised in the National Assembly about why thirty-five out of sixty five District Commissioners (DCs) were Kalenjin when this ethnic category is not even among the top three in numerical strength (*Sunday Nation*, September 19, 1997, p. 2).

Kibaki's first term in office (2003–2007) did not depart from the norm. Though attempting to balance job allocations to various ethnic groups in his coalition government during the first two years, events that followed the referendum tell a different story. As Karuti Kanyinga (2006 pp. 385–393) points out, among the Permanent Secretaries (PS) Kibaki appointed more Kikuyu and Meru PSs or about 34% of the total number of these officials. In actual figures, Kanyinga argues, out of twenty-five permanent secretaries, eleven were either Kikuyu or Meru communities. The numbers from other main ethnic categories was roughly about three each except the Abaluyia who had about two. This imbalance in favour of employees from Mt. Kenya was reflected in other government departments and the foreign affairs office.

In terms of DCs when Kibaki took over on December 30th 2002, the Kalenjin had 30.4% of the total DCs. But by 2006 the share of the Kalenjin holding positions as DCs had declined to about 12% while that of the Kikuyu had increased to 23%. Perhaps this decline among the Kalenjin partly explains why they overwhelmingly voted against President Kibaki and his PNU team during the December 27, 2007 general elections.

The question of land offers another factor that has stoked ethnic feelings especially in the vast and multi-ethnic Rift Valley province. In this expansive province what exploded into inter-ethnic violence after the announcement of the December 27 2007 presidential election results has a long history. Unlike in other provinces where when white settlers occupying indigenous communities' land departed on the eve of independence and gave room for the indigenous people to settle, in the Rift Valley the case was different. Here, the vacated land did not directly revert to the indigenous Maasai and Kalenjin communities. Instead, Kenyatta's regime enabled other communities especially the Kikuyu, Luo, Luyia and Gusii to acquire land either through private purchases or political handouts (Kakai, 2000 pp. 164–166). The indigenous and largely pastoralist communities resented this settlement by other ethnic categories on what was considered ancestral land. By the late 1960s, the numbers of especially the Kikuyu in Rift Valley had increased at the displeasure of the Rift Valley Maasai and Kalenjin. The two communities felt the Kikuyu were receiving preferential treatment in the resettlement of landless people under the Land Transfer Scheme started by the colonial government on the eve of independence (Oyugi, op. cit, pp. 307–308). The government ignored these protests forcing the Kalenjin to organize resistance against further settlement.

Indeed what climaxed into the December 2007/January 2008 violence had been as a result of gradual build-up of inter-ethnic resentment. As the number of people increased and the inelastic parcels of land became scarce politicians in the expansive Rift Valley, especially from among the Maasai and Kalenjin took the opportunity to condemn those they perceived as 'foreigners'. The Nandi did this through the 'Nandi Hill Declaration' of 1969 and in 1975 there was confrontation between the Kikuyu and the Kalenjin in Londiani, and later the Nandi and Luo fought over land. In 1980 the Nandi and the Luyia fought over the same land issue and with the reintroduction of multi-party politics, every election year since 1992 has witnessed inter-ethnic violence in the Rift Valley among other provinces.

Conclusion
How might one describe the architecture of ethnicity in Kenya? The paper has argued that as a symbol of identity, ethnicity is old and harmless. We have traced the genesis of the term 'tribalism' from ancient Europe pointing out that initially it was a geographical or political unit. Later the term began referencing people. When imperialists made use of it, the terms tribe and ethnicity referred to the colonized. The same colonialists used it to divide and lord it over the colonized.

Nevertheless with time the term ethnicity was positively employed to simply identify people without any discriminative innuendo being embedded in the term. It is in this light that every one of the three presidents of the Republic of Kenya has relied on it in his effort to forge national unity. But the paper has also shown that in trying to forge this unity, the leaders, as they allocated resources, jobs, land parcels, among other privileges, developed an element of favouritism, bias and outright disregard to any serious sensitivity to the feelings of the many elements from other ethnicities. This ethnicity-bound governance has damaged the nation-building project and reinforced ethnic sentiments.

In a way the sad situation the country finds itself in at present is attributable partly to Kenya's poor leadership. If the top leadership could look for a way in which ethnicity is not abused at the expense of compatriots, then perhaps ethnicity would be a boost to national diversity. It might be concluded that the emergence of coalitions can be a good pointer that indeed the political class can fight ethnicism and thereby reinforce national unity. If along the same lines, a good constitution which addresses social injustices can emerge out of ongoing review efforts and be properly implemented, negative ethnicity can gradually be tackled. But as things stand at the moment, nation-building may continue being a real challenging task.

Notes

1 It is emerging that 'ethnicity' has been used in two main senses i.e positive and negative ethnicity.
2 Sometimes 'Okiek' is also spelt as 'Ogiek'.
3 Interaction could be peaceful or conflictual.
4 The Abaluyia though not a minority, were divided in such a way that some supported KANU while others supported KADU.
5 Tom Mboya was from the Suba community but was widely understood to be a Luo. Even he himself was captured in the Hansard in the early 1960s declaring that he was a Luo.
6 Following the 2007/2008 violence, the National Mediation Team introduced the Prime Minister's slot which was subsequently entrenched in the current constitution.

References

Ahmed, I. (1999). 'Ethnicity And Identity Politics.' In (eds.) Imatiaz Ahmed, Zimitri Erasmus and Bishnu Mohapatria' *CODESRIA Bulletin, Nos. 3 & 4*. Dakar: CODESRIA.

Atieno-Odhiambo, E.S. (2002). 'Historicising the deep Past in Western Kenya' in (ed.) Ochieng' W.R. *Historical Studies And Social Change in Western Kenya*. Nairobi: East African Educational Publishers.

Badejo, A.B. (2006). *Raila Odinga: An Enigma in Kenyan Politics*. Lagos and Nairobi: Yintab Books.

Bogonko, S. (1980). *Kenya: 1945–1963*. Nairobi: Kenya Literature Bureau.

Fanon, F. (1968). *The Wretched of The Earth*. New York: Grove Press Inc.

Kakai, P. (2004). 'Ethnicity And Politics'. A Paper presented at the Historical Association of Kenya Conference.

Kakai, P. (2000). 'History of Inter-Ethnic Relations in Bungoma, Mt. Elgon and Trans Nzoia Districts, 1875–1997.' PhD Thesis. Kenyatta University.

Kakai, P. (1993). 'Social Concepts in The Initiation Rituals of The Abatachoni: A Historical Study' M.A. Thesis. Kenyatta University.

Kanyinga, K. (2006). 'Governance, Institutions and Inequality in Kenya' in *Readings On Inequalities in Kenya*. Nairobi: Society for International Development.

Kenyanchui, S.S. (1992). 'European Settler Agriculture' in (eds.) Ochieng' W.R. and Maxon R.M. *An Economic History of Kenya*. Nairobi: East African Educational Publishers.

Maathai, W. (2006). *Unbowed: A Memoir*. New York: Anchor Books.

Mafeje, A. (2003). 'Multi-Party Democracy And Ethnic Divisions in Africa' in (eds.) Bujra A. and Adejumobi, S. *Breaking Barriers. Creating New Hopes: Democracy, Civil Society and Good Governance in Africa*. Addis Ababa: DPMF.

Muriuki, G. (1979). 'Central Kenya in The Nyayo Era' in (ed.) Clough M. *Africa Today: Kenya After Kenyatta Vol. 26*. Michigan: University of Michigan Press.

Muriuki, G. (1995). 'Some Reflections On Cold War Africa and After' in (eds.) Munene, M. et al. *The United States and Africa*. Nairobi: East African Educational Publishers.

Muriuki, G. (1974). *A History of The Kikuyu: 1500–1900*. Nairobi: Oxford University Press.

Murunga, G., & Nasong'o, S.W. (2007). 'Prospects For Democracy in Kenya' in (eds.) Murunga G.R. and Nasong'o S.W. *Kenya: The Struggle For Democracy*. Dakar: CODESRIA.

Nasong'o, S. (2005). *Contending Political Paradigms in Africa*. New York and London: Routledge.

Ng'ang'a, M. (1994). 'Democracy in A Multi-Party Society.' A Paper Presented at a Conference in Nairobi.

Nyanchoga, S. (2008). *Constitutionalism And Democratization in Kenya*. Nairobi: CUEA.

Ochieng', P. (2008). *The East African*. May 26 – June 01, 2008.

Odipo, B. (1999). *Sunday Standard*, January 10, 1999.

Ogot, B. (2000). 'Boundary Changes And Invention of Tribes' in (eds.) Ogot B.A. & Ochieng' R.W. *Kenya: The Making of A Nation: 1895-1995*. Maseno University, IRPS.

Ogot, B. (1999). *Building On The Indigenous*. Kisumu: Anyange Press Ltd.

Ogot, B. (2003). *My Footprints On The Sands of Time*. Kisumu: Anyange Press Ltd.

Oyugi, W. (1998). 'Ethnic Politics in Kenya' in (ed.) Okwudiba Nnoli *Ethnic Conflict in Africa*. Dakar: CODESRIA.

Rodney, W. (1989). *How Europe Underdeveloped Africa*. Nairobi: Heinemann Kenya.

Sunday Nation (1997). September 19.

Were, G. (1967). *A History of The Abaluyia of Western Kenya*. East African Publishing House.

Negotiating 'Kenyanness': The 'Debates'

PETER WAFULA WEKESA

*A patriot is a person who loves his country.
He is not a person who says he loves his country.
He is not even a person who shouts or swears
or recites or sings that he loves his country.
He is one who cares deeply about his country
and all its peoples.*

—Barrack Muluka.

*Far from eulogizing 'Kenyanness' as a concept,
there is the need to appreciate the varied nature
of the ethnic identities found in Kenya and their
contribution to the national identity question.*

—Peter Wafula Wekesa.

Two related events readily come to mind when mention is made of the concept 'Kenyanness' and more so in regard to the more recent history of the Kenyan nation state. These events, happening in the year 2004, form an important context for reflecting on the theme of this paper. The first event relates to the activities surrounding the 'Week of the National Focus' (4th–11th December 2004) whose purpose as envisaged by Alfred Mutua, the Kenya government spokesman, was to 'instil a spirit of patriotism and enhance a general pride in who we are as Kenyans'. The event, which was to be re-enacted annually was meant to re-socialize Kenyans from all walks of life into reflecting on their achievements since independence and cultivate the spirit of togetherness and dedication to the country, Kenya. It was noted that Kenyans in general do not identify themselves as Kenyans first, but rather as people from different regions of origin. Therefore it was assumed that a sense of national pride was lacking. The overall theme of the event was dubbed, *'Najivunia kuwa Mkenya'* (I am Proud to be Kenyan). On the whole, several government and non-governmental departments and agencies were marshalled into the great plan of making this idea a success. To a casual observer, the greatest impact of this event was easily discernible in the numerous advertisements in the press, bumper stickers and banners in several social places among other public places.

The second event is the search for the Kenyan national dress that begun around mid 2004. The idea behind this event, like the 'Najivunia kuwa Mkenya' one, was to instil a sense of patriotism and cultivate the spirit of togetherness in Kenyans as well as showcase the country as an important tourist and investment destination. In this event several versions of attire that could be turned out into Kenya's national dress were displayed to the public. After months of deliberation and work by the nine member national dress design team what was envisaged as the national Kenyan garment was finally unveiled. The basic attire for women was to be a two-piece costume, comprising a wrap-top and wrap bottom. The blouse was short-sleeved, and was adorned with a red, vertical ribbon on its front. Going under this was a long, wrap-around skirt that descended loosely to the ankles. Like its top piece, the skirt was white with a full-length red strip on it. The men were only to have a top piece and hat. Made from *Kikoi*, like that of the ladies, the men's shirt or jacket featured a collar that was patterned to three symbolic front slits. According to the designers, the slits symbolised the three legged stool or the three stone fire place that are common in Kenya. The men's and women's attire, together with the accessories, were meant to bring out the wearers' Kenyanness.

Looked at from the context of the year 2004 and the pomp and glamour that accompanied the two events highlighted above one would be vindicated, in spite of the numerous critiques, to imagine that Kenyans were indeed on course towards attaining the state of 'Kenyanness'. Today, only five years down the line, however, few Kenyans can remember that such events actually took place, leave alone the fact that one of the events was meant to be annual. The issue of who is Kenyan and what it means to be Kenyan seem to have faded away as soon as the events wound up in 2004. This paper seeks to reflect on the issue of 'Kenyanness' from the historical hindsight of general debates informing nationhood and cultural identity. In the following section our focus is to specifically try to understand the meaning of the concept 'Kenyanness' and engage its contextual relevance.

'Kenyanness': a tenuous concept?
The short-lived campaign to instil patriotism among Kenyans through 'Najivunia kuwa Mkenya' and also develop the Kenyan national dress poignantly illustrates the difficulty of defining the concept 'Kenyanness' and expressing it with relative unanimity. It also poses serious problems in terms of the debates surrounding the concept of nationhood in general and 'Kenyanness' in particular. To be sure the general debates and critiques surrounding the two mentioned events opened a new space into reflecting on what it meant to be Kenyan.

Reading the various articles in the mainstream media on the two events, it was obvious that the 'Najivunia kuwa Mkenya' project, just like the final products of the Kenyan national attire were hotly disputed, generally ignored and thus promised bleak future prospects in terms of memory. While the organizers of the two events belaboured to explain the rationale behind them, it emerged, at least from the point of view of the critics, that the campaigns made little or no sense to a great many Kenyans. Reading through the articles by Barrack Muluka, Macharia Gaitho and Kwendo Opanga[1] one got the sense that the problem with the two events was two-pronged. On the one hand, the problem was more about the messenger (in this regard Alfred Mutua and the government that was sponsoring the events) than the message. The main point here was that if the events were meant to instil a sense of patriotism in Kenyans, then there was nothing to celebrate and identify with, and the campaigns were therefore premature at best. The argument was that given the many perceived wrongs the government had committed to its citizenry, any association with the events would be interpreted as lending support to the government.

A second issue regarded the publicity stunts associated with these two events. Critics argued that if 'Kenyanness' meant love for one's country, then there was no justifiable reason for perching on rooftops to shout about it. Barrack Muluka[2] particularly quoted Chinua Achebe to state that "a patriot is a person who loves his country. He is not a person who says he loves his country. He is not even a person who shouts or swears or recites or sings that he loves his country. He is one who cares deeply about his country and all its peoples". If this is true, critics opined, why then would the government go out of its way to mount such publicity campaigns over the events in question? Is it a case of the *'Chema chajiuza na kibaya chajitembeza'* (the good thing/item sells itself [in the market) while a bad one needs to be advertised] as the Swahili adage goes? As Muluka bluntly put it, "Mutua (government spokesman) should know that patriotism is not about putting useless stickers on bumpers".

The debates situated around criticism of the events are significant in trying to understand 'Kenyanness'. The concept in essence has more to do with 'being Kenyan'. The term's association with patriotism therefore makes sense to the extent that it relates to one's association and love for Kenya. However being patriotic is not failing to see what is wrong with/in Kenya and speaking up about it; it is doing so and also giving credit where it is due. Although one may not therefore be happy with many aspects of Kenyan life, there is always a tight an association between an individual and the country where one is born or whose citizenship one chooses to keep. There is in this regard a similarity between 'Kenyanness' and Kenyan nationhood. The concept nation in its broader context refers to a considerable group of people united by a common culture, values, standards and political aspirations and occupying a definite territory and having a sense of common identity (see Anderson 1983, Smith, 1986 and Hobsbawn 1992). Such a group sharing the foregoing characteristics is said to have a common nationhood.

'Kenyanness', like Kenyan nationhood, could therefore be considered as an ethical and philosophical doctrine that aspires or inspires Kenyan people into the love for the country. This doctrine, which could form a starting point for the ideology of nationalism, is informed by the fact of a shared identity as well as other attributes including a common descent, language, culture, religion and a territorial boundary. From this broad formulation it is easy to understand why one internet site with a theme under the title 'Kenyanness' claims to be "dedicated to the Kenya nation's culture and identity as expressed in its peoples lifestyles, ethnic groups, languages, media, academia, politics and food with the objective of evaluating what it is to be Kenyan" (see www.mashada.com). This makes it possible, with the benefit of hindsight to reflect, as Henry Indangasi does, on the "Kenyanness of Kenyan Literature' (Indangasi 2003) or the 'Kenyanness' of Kenyan songs, clothing, cultures and so on.

Looked at from a definitional point of view 'Kenyanness', or Kenyan nationhood as we will interchangeably use the terms in this paper, one already envisages an attempt at homogenising anything Kenya. From the debates that emerged about the two events that we have alluded to above, it becomes obvious that 'Kenyanness' as a concept is viewed differently by people and could, perhaps, be a tenuous concept. From an analytical point of view, it is not possible to approach or present anything Kenyan as a homogenous entity given the diverse nature and historical experiences of Kenyans. From a political point of view there also seems to be a disconnection between what is presented as Kenyan and what it is actually Kenyan. We will return to this point shortly as we examine the 'lie' of 'Kenyanness'. What might be stated clearly at this point is that 'Kenyanness' is a contested typology within the various class structures that inform contemporary Kenyan realities. In short, while one group (obviously the elite) exalts loudly its 'Kenyanness', the other group views this as part of a continuing strategy to consign them into poverty and deprivation. In a sum, the latter category resents or even does not care about the whole public talk behind 'Kenyanness' (see Odhiambo, this volume). This in reality has been behind the whole debate on what 'Kenyanness' is and should be. For now we turn to discussion on 'Kenyanness' and assess its significance to the broader issues surrounding Kenyan nationhood.

Living the Lie: Kenyan nationhood or ethnihood?

One of the most striking features of current debates on the Kenyan nation emerges from the events of the disputed 2007 presidential elections and the resultant violence that claimed approximately 1,200 lives and left thousands injured, displaced and billions worth of property destroyed.[3] The nation is still currently agonizing over the resettlement of thousands of people displaced from their homes during the violent aftermath of the 2007 elections. Prices of food and other essential commodities have skyrocketed and social inequality is threatening the social fabric of the nation. More disturbing has been the rise of several militia gangs including *Mungiki, Sungusungu, Saboat Land Defence Force, Taliban* among many others. The key question that comes to mind as one reflects on these events is what has happened to the Kenyan collective spirit. Even more useful is the question whether that Kenyan collective spirit was there in the first place. Why would Kenyans turn against each other with such vengeance yet they claim to be patriotic and committed to the cause of their 'motherland'? My submission is that, perhaps, we have been living a lie.

At the centre of this lie has been the contested terrain of the national 'community'. Put simply we claim to be Kenyans yet, perhaps, we are not. As a human cultural and social community, Kenyans, it seems, have not espoused a shared bond and a common cultural identity. This cultural identity, as Stuart Hall (1994:393) has argued, needs to be appreciated at two levels. On the one hand it could be seen in terms of a shared culture, a sort of collective one true self, hiding in the many other, more superficial or artificially imposed selves, which a people with a shared history and ancestry hold in common. In this regard our cultural identity ought to reflect common historical experiences and shared cultural codes which provide those identifiable, as Kenyans with stable, unchanging and continuous frames of reference and meaning, beneath the shifting divisions and vicissitudes of our cultural history. On the other hand, as the same Hall argues, cultural identity ought to recognize that, just as we have many points of similarity, there are also critical points of deep and significant differences which constitute what we really are or rather—since history has intervened—what we have become. In this second sense cultural identity pays attention to the ruptures and discontinuities that characterize the various levels of interaction over place, time, history and culture (see also Njogu, this volume). We cannot therefore, in this regard speak for long or with exactness about a unitary experience or identity without acknowledging its other side that is subject to the continuous transformative processes of history, culture and power.

Perhaps, without belabouring Hall's succinct exposition on the levels at which cultural identity might be interpreted, it is already easy to see, given the violence that engulfed the country in 2007/2008 that Kenyans have hardly appreciated or lived within these two levels. Cultural identity cannot be appreciated or interpreted without paying attention to specific historical milieu defining the emergence and transformation of a people. Such an identity is not a fixed essence at all lying unchanged outside history and culture. It has its histories, and these have both material and symbolic effects. Their past according to Hall, continues to speak to us. But it no longer addresses us as a simple factual 'past', since our relation to it, like the child's relation to the mother, is always already 'after the break'. It is always constructed through memory, fantasy, narrative and myth. Cultural identities are points of identification, the unstable points of identification or suture, which are made, within the discourses of history and culture (Hall, 1994:395).

A critical question that emerges from the foregoing analysis is whether our knowledge about the dynamic and diverse nature of our cultural identities that inform our historical realities as a people is ever reconsidered. As Barth (1969:9) has observed cultural identities vindicate the reasoning that there are aggregates of people who essentially share a common culture, and have interconnected differences that distinguish each discrete culture from all others. Since culture is nothing but a way of describing human behaviour, it follows that there are discrete groups of people, i.e. an ethnic unit that corresponds to each culture. The differences between cultures and their historic boundaries and connections, the constitution of ethnic groups and the nature of boundaries between them thus represent a key element in the debates on nationhood generally and Kenya-hood in particular.

What then has been the Kenyan lie? Is it that we choose to live in ignorance of our history or we have been made to live in that ignorance? The answers to these questions certainly bring us to address the concept of 'Kenyanness' and the various myths and symbols upon which the concept has been constructed. These myths and symbols, to a greater extent, have been central in defining the levels of negotiation through our nationhood. There is a sense in which one may argue that the ambivalent and contradictory nature in which discourses around 'Kenyanness' have been framed, especially within the 'nationalistic' perspective, is such that we choose to or are made to live in ignorance of our history. The key questions that arise then is which history and who chooses that we remember or ignore certain histories? This problem can be interrogated within discussions of memory in Kenya.

'Kenyanness': History and memory reconsidered

In their book, *In search of a Nation*, Maddox and Giblin (2005) have made an argument, based on the experience in Tanzania, that the construct of a nation in much of Africa has remained alien to its people. As implied in the title of the book, most people in Africa have essentially been engaged in a futile search for a nation. These are not the only authors to reflect on the contradictory nature of nationhood in Africa and specifically on the link between the state and the community. Scholarly writings on Africa implicitly posit a division between state and community. For instance scholars such as Mamdani (1996), Scott (1998) and Herbst (2000) among others portray African states, failed or otherwise, as alien and alienating for the communities over which they rule. In particular, Mamdani argues that because the postcolonial state draws its legitimacy primarily from the urban society and modernity, its rural people remain more subordinated subjects rather than citizens endowed with democratic rights. The key question to reflect upon, however, is whether there is need for a coalescence of both the community and the state. While this question is often answered in the affirmative, the contradictory nature in which the state has managed to alienate the community has hardly been conceptualized. This, in our view, has to be understood within the context of history and memory.

The manner in which the discourses on 'Kenyanness' have been presented reflects the 'state-centric' perspective whose general objective has been a struggle to appropriate historical memory to a nationalist project whose ultimate goal is the struggle over power. The ways in which people remember and articulate what they remember about their past and the choices informing such articulations has been a central component in debates around and about 'Kenyanness'. As Thelen (quoted in Nyairo, 2005) has argued, since people's memories provide security, authority, legitimacy, and finally identity in the present, struggles over the possession and interpretation of memories are deep, frequent and bitter. The possession and interpretation of memories on 'Kenyanness', within the nationalist discourse, as we argue, masks the historical reality defining our dynamic and diverse experience.

In his reflections on memory and the post colony, Werbner (1998) has distinguished between official or state discourses of remembrance and memorialisation, and the memory work that emanates unsolicited from the general public. This distinction exposes us to the realization of the duality of understanding memory and to a greater extent raises the issue of whose historical memory forms the central component in the construction of the past. Indeed, the key concern with this observation has to do with the control and ownership of social memory, of those structures and sites through which social memory is carried and maintained. Since a historian is mainly interested in knowledge and perceptions of the past in order to chart the relevance of that past to the present, the need to understand the sites and structures through which memory is constructed and maintained is primary. Specifically in regard to the question of 'Kenyanness' what is more problematic is the view that there exists a usable past which must form a component part in the recurrent quest for the many possible futures. This past certainly is one that is officially acclaimed.

The control of a society's memory–the regulation of what is remembered, how it is remembered as well as what is ignored or erased-is a valuable tool for maintaining and legitimating political power. According to Thelen (Quoted in Nyairo, 2005), there is need for us to question the similarities and differences between memories constructed by marginalized groups (and within marginalized forms) and those memories that belong to larger, officially recognised enterprises. The idea here is not the designation of certain versions as erroneous and the upholding of others as more factual and correct, but rather to appreciate that memory work can never be total or complete. According to Nyairo (2005) memory, like a broken mirror from which we glean only partial images or shards, must be read as only being capable of constructing in parts. Because memory is partial, it brings with it error which sometimes comes because memory is also necessarily about forgetting. Indeed as Nyairo (*ibid.*) further argues, the critical point to ponder in ignoring the 'erroneousness' nature of memories is the individual's, or the society's reasons for constructing their memories in a particular way. The key function of social memory is the establishment of shared memories, the insistence on shared experiences in the past, which works to bind communities in the present (Thelen quoted in Nyairo 2005).

Shared memories and experiences of the past between individuals define their collective unity within a given community. This in essence qualifies the argument that part of the function of memory is the building and shaping of individual identity in the present (Hall, 1994). To this end, gaps and ellipsis, erasures and suppressions of certain events in the past become imperative if the objective of remembering the individual in the present has to be achieved. What is particularly important is the fact that different communities are differentiated from one another through their modes of remembrance and inclinations towards differences in identities. As Odhiambo and Lonsdale (2003) argue, these differences may be articulated through customs, religions, cultures, traditions and lifestyles. However, as the authors emphasize, in whichever ways these differences are articulated, they reaffirm the centrality of state power as a key condition for civilized co-existence in multi-ethnic and multi-lingual contexts (Ibid. p. 5). What is at stake according to these authors is the question of the existence of a national identity to control that state power, not least to combat the globalizing forces that would erode the ability of states to mediate between the world's losers and winners.

The point to be emphasized from Odhiambo and Landsdale's elaboration above is the centrality of state power in reaffirming the invention of the nation and the coordination of the various components within its boundaries. Through state power, officially endorsed histories have tended to be the stories of the status quo that favour the unique entities of each nation as opposed to the manifest multiple realities that exist within those states. As has been argued "all states that claim to be nations have skeletons in their cupboards, stained with fratricidal blood" (Ibid, p.1). In any analysis of the evolution of the state therefore we need to make a distinction between officially-sanctioned histories and those that emanate from other multiple components within the state. There is need to recognize that nations are comprised of multiple, varied and even contradictory constituencies that have a multiplicity of dimensions arising from the gender, generation, class and ethnic identities of participants. We turn now to examine the pre-colonial, colonial and post-independent historical record in order to see how, through state power, official histories that emphasize 'Kenyanness' have come to define the Kenyan collective experience.

Gleaning through the 'Kenyan' pre-colonial historical record

Strictly speaking, 'Kenyanness' as a concept makes little sense beyond the independence history of the country. Yet, in an attempt to reconstruct the country's history, most analysts, mainly operating from a nationalistic orientation, erroneously locate the concept and particularly the people 'Kenyans' to the pre-colonial and colonial periods. It is true that the name of the country, Kenya, as a signifier of a specific geopolitical space begun to evolve with the British declaration of a Protectorate. This followed the processes of scramble and partition where European powers drew boundaries to divide the various African territories among themselves and establish colonial rule.

The pre-colonial period however occupies a special place not only in the history of Kenyan communities but specifically in the evolution of Kenya as a country and 'Kenyanness' as an ethical and philosophical ideology. Since the term relates to 'being Kenyan' the ways in which various Kenyan peoples become part of this process are significant. Thus, the appropriate starting point in examining such a process of becoming is the analysis of the people's pre-colonial history. This history precedes the European scramble and partition politics and the colonial construction or invention of Kenya as some scholars have put it (see Mudimbe, 1988). It relates to individuals and to the various ethnic communities as well as to the social, economic and political structures that have somewhat come to mould individual and collective experiences.

Knowledge on the various Kenyan communities in the pre-colonial period has been enriched by a multiplicity of sources including oral traditions, archaeology, historical linguistics and cultural anthropology. According to Ogot (2002), the historical portrait of the present Kenya from the earliest times to about 500 AD is scanty. Although archaeological researches have yielded substantial data, a number of questions still remain unanswered especially in relation to socio-cultural developments in the region. What we know, according to Ogot, is that modern humans emerged 40,000 years ago, and that by about 20,000 years ago, the present Kenya had entered the late Stone Age which was marked by the development of microlithic technology.

In regard to the specific cultural and linguistic groups inhabiting the country in this pristine period, evidence has also been scanty although linguists, the work of historians and archaeologists has made significant contributions towards filling up the gaps. What seems clear is that Kenya was not demographically empty, at least before the onset of the first phase of migrations. It was inhabited by a number of hunter-gatherer populations who could be credited with the earliest forms of stone technology. These populations are part of the Khoisan hunter-gatherers who traversed Eastern, Central, and Southern Africa and included the Okiek or Dorobo or Sirikwa as they have variously been called (Ehret 1998; Were, 1972; Mwanzi, 1977; Ogot, 2002). Clues also indicate that the people's economy was simple and hunter-gatherer based while their technology was based on stone and wood.

It is from these hunter-gatherer populations that the earliest immigrants into the present Kenya came. Archaeological and linguistic evidence has suggested that the first cultivators and herders in Kenya were Cushitic speakers and they settled in the area between 3000 BC and 300 BC (Ehret, 1998). They are said to have preceded the Bantu and Nilotes in present Kenya had dominated the region up to 1500 AD (Ogot, 2002:23). Apart from transforming the region into a demographically vibrant entity they had, together with their great influence on the pristine hunter-gatherer communities begun converting the area into a complex contact zone.

The period between 500 AD–1000 AD witnessed a second wave of immigration into the region by pristine Bantu speakers. Their arrival into Kenya ushered in several social, economic and political transformations. Together with the autochthonous populations and the earlier Cushitic immigrants, this area begun to evolve as an ethnically complex region where the various groups interacted with each other. And although some scholars including Huntingford (1944) attest to the fact that the Bantu were a dominant group both numerically and in language, diverse elements from the other groups continued to have an influence on the region's socio-cultural and economic set up.

The arrival of Nilotic speakers in the region marked an important phase in the interactive history of the present Kenyan. The autochthonous populations, the Cushites, the Bantu and the Nilotic-speaking groups interacted with each other fighting, trading and inter-marrying and thereby influencing each other's societies and economic practices. The period from 1500 AD to the late 19th century has continued to receive enormous historical attention. Pioneer scholars including Ogot (1967), Were (1967), Muriuki (1974), Ochieng (1974), Mwanzi (1977) and Aseka (1989) among others have enriched our historical knowledge on individual communities that occupy present Kenya. Like in the earlier periods, studies within this period have emphasized the fact that present day Kenya was already an ethnically complex region characterized by varied communal interactions by 1500 AD. These interactions were constantly altering the social, economic and political entities of the communities in the region. Through the historical process of encounter and interaction, there were evolving ethnic communities that were neither definitive nor pure but hybridized in nature (Ochieng', 1974:44). This process of interaction was already underway even by the time colonialists were arriving.

So far pioneering historical studies have successfully demonstrated a number of things the first of which is that the coming into being of Kenya pre-dates the histories of the country's present day inhabitants. Second, the ethnic composition of the present country Kenya is as a result of a crystallization of many centuries of interaction between the various peoples. These interactions were not only peaceful, resulting in intermarriages, trading and other cultural exchanges but were also, sometimes, conflictual in nature. In this context therefore there can be no basis for talking about definitive or pure community but hybrid entities of sorts. Third, on the basis of available data, especially that from historical linguistics, it may be concluded that Cushitic speakers preceded Bantu and Nilotic speakers in the peopling of Kenya.

Clearly, pioneer scholars whose studies have formed the basis of analysing historical developments in present Kenya have different motivations for conducting research on individual communities. First there appears to be the reality that within the period under study, the intense processes of communal interaction in the region was ushering in the emergence of ethnicity and ethnic consciousness. Ethnic consciousness is construed to be the feeling of a people as a social community with definite identities. It became necessary therefore for research to try and track down this vital aspect of history from the focal point of view of individual communities. Secondly and perhaps related to the preceding point was the new "independence" mood in Kenya which, together with the opening up of new sources of historical inquiry necessitated an in-depth analysis into the history of various peoples. This was deemed necessary for purposes of trying to understand national development. Especially with the acceptance of oral tradition as an important source of African history, each Kenyan community's history, they argued, had a part to contribute to the country's overall history.

Whereas the overwhelming contributions of the pioneer "individual community" based studies have been noted and appreciated, a number of criticism have also been raised. For example, because of the hybridized nature of the pre-colonial, colonial and present Kenya, there is an intrinsic difficulty in focusing studies on a single ethno-linguistic group as a unit of analysis. In view of the enormous comingling alluded to above, it is evident that the continuity and survival of any people as a social or political unit hardly depended on its purity. Rather in the opposite sense, it depended on its ability to accommodate and assimilate diverse elements (Ogot, 2002:26). For instance, the pristine communities including the Cushites, the Bantu and the Nilotes through the historical process of interaction evolved varied institutions that are equally hybridized and differentiated. As such, given that ethnic consciousness is a continuous process, we see evidence of numerous ethnicities and sub-ethnicities arising from the original "proto" groups. Analysing the latter groups distinctly within separate spaces and polities is therefore in itself problematic. Through their long history, the groups have not only altered their spatial locations, but also their social, economic and political realities through the various permutations of socio-cultural elements and processes. At best the pioneer studies perhaps succeeded in solidifying the ethnic divisions that could have been diffused within the diverse experiences of the different Kenyan peoples. In short therefore most of these pioneer studies fall prey to the statist nationalistic agenda of nation building. We now turn to examine this nationalistic project with specific reference to studies on the history of the colonial period.

'Kenyanness' as a nationalist project: the colonial period

Historical discourses informing our understanding of 'Kenyanness' or Kenyan nationhood have often been couched within the state-centred approaches whose main preoccupation has been with nation building. Nationalism, understood as an ideology that holds that nations are the fundamental units for human social life, has been portrayed as the main force behind the evolution and transformation of nations and communities. The claim that the nation is the only legitimate basis for the state and that each nation is entitled to a state has motivated many studies on nationalism with the sole purpose of showing how individual ethnic entities have contributed to the national grid. In Kenya most studies on colonial history have encapsulated various regional and ethnic issues and themes and their relationship to the national.

Theoretically, such studies have de-emphasized the positive aspects of the cross-cultural evolution of ethnic consciousness that had clear links to identity formation processes whose history predates the colonial period. Such cultural forces are usually conflated with the divisive forces of ethnicity and often projected as undermining the process of nation-state formation (Mustapha, 1992). The modernization theorists see cross-cultural linkages as anachronistic forms of ethnicity that were bound to disappear in the face of the modernity of the new nation, Kenya. On their part dependency theories tend to concentrate on external constraints on the Kenyan state while neo-Marxist theories concentrate on the class structure of society, and often consign ethnicity to the realm of 'false consciousness'. Even in contexts where ethnic nationalism is studied systematically, the point of departure is on the unifying needs of the nation-state, rather than the inter-ethnic integrative possibilities and constraints offered by the actual historical dynamics of ethnic groups. Thus dominant intellectual paradigms have helped boost the nationalist agenda at the expense of any others.

Doornbos (1991:64) has drawn our attention to the practical limitations of the state-centred approaches to the study of ethnic consciousness and ethnicity in Africa. The author observes that in the urge to political unity the tendency of many states has been to negate ethnic, regional and cultural diversities rather than recognize them as building blocks in the construction of a civil society. The result has been often a facade of seeming unity at the cost of many unsettled wounds and suppressed or unacknowledged identities. Tragically in the long run, the state project had no meaningful or alternative sources of cultural inspiration to draw upon, leaving it in the end without a vision in the face of impending crisis and disintegration. To see 'Kenyanness' from point of view of a narrow nation-building project negates cross-cultural identities that go beyond the state and which could meaningfully be harmonised within broader inter-ethnic dynamics.

The case of the Abaluyia of western Kenya might be used to elaborate this argument. The history of the Abaluyia, like that of other Kenyan communities points to a remarkable heterogeneity in ethnic composition that go beyond the geographical confines of present western Kenya. Due to the historical interaction between the Abaluyia and the neighbouring non-Abaluyia ethnic groups a hybridized ethnicity has emerged over the entire region contiguous to the present areas of the Abaluyia. The fact that the Abaluyia are not a homogeneous population need not be over-emphasized. Although they constitute about 18 sub-ethnic groups, they have emerged as a cultural entity through several centuries of assimilation and consolidation of peoples of diverse backgrounds (Were, 1967:60).

What seems clear and uncontested is that the Abaluyia did not have a common name for themselves and each sub-ethnic group had its own institutions for settling various social, economic and political problems specific to their people. This seems to have been the state of affairs by the time the groups were settling down between the 12th and 18th centuries and also before the coming of the outsiders including Arab/Swahili traders and later European colonialists in the 19th century. In the context of the Bantu of North Kavirondo from which Abaluyia as a name later emerged, this categorization was convenient in two respects. First, it was not the region in square kilometres that mattered, but rather that the people's nature, compounded with possible similarities in language and culture, would pose few problems to the colonial administrative objectives. Secondly, and the Abaluyia's territorial confines of North Kavirondo overlapped without necessarily coinciding.

Over the years, Abaluyia as a term began to emerge as an alternative name to the pejorative one, 'Bantu of North Kavirondo'. According to Wagner (1949), Abaluyia as a concept began gaining ground towards the late 1920's and early 1930's. It emerged as a reaction against the term 'Kavirondo' which had been superimposed upon the people by Swahili traders and later by Europeans. Abaluyia as a term also seems to have emerged as a concept meant to express unity and solidarity of the various groups as members of an emerging ethno-nation. Osogo (1966) has pointed out that the term 'Baluyia' had both cultural and political implications. Culturally, it was meant to coalesce the various sub-ethnic groups into a cultural entity given the unifying possibilities inherent in their language. Politically, however, Abaluyia as a term was meant to bring together a grouping of related communities. This unity was necessary for political reasons during the colonial period and especially after the Second World War. Indeed, it was in 1940 that the word Baluyia received substantial recognition, when Abaluyia Welfare Association was founded (Osogo, 1966). To crown it all the numerous groups in the North Kavirondo district adopted the name Abaluyia in 1943.

That the colonial period was central to the social, economic and political transformation of Africans' lives cannot be gainsaid. These transformations and the attendant African anti-colonial initiatives varied from one location and Kenyan ethnic community to another. As products of the colonial divisive policies, these initiatives from inception were characterised by the badge of ethnicity for they, by and large, attended to interests that were perceived to be of immediate concern to their ethnic constituencies. In cases where such associations tended to widen their geographical scope and demands by threatening to constitute rallying bases to challenge authority, colonial authorities moved swiftly to domesticate those demands and to institutionalise forums for articulating grievances within specific localities. This served the purpose of creating and sustaining division and discord among the various communities, a strategy that resonated with the colonial state's agenda of denying the local population any united constituency that would have constituted a formidable challenge to its dominance over society. Like all authoritarian institutions, the colonial state thrived on division, hate and oppression.

From a state-centric point of view, territorial distinctiveness and national consciousness have been among the key defining features in the formulation of ideas on ethnicity and nationalism. They have informed debates about Kenyan nationhood. Informed by the reality of the increasing expressions of ethnicity in many post-colonial African societies and the need to offer a critique of ethnicity, this line of thinking has yielded many historical studies. Hobsbawm and Ranger (1983), Anderson (1983) and Smith (1986), have clearly shown that ethnic consciousness was a product of historical experience, and hence its creation and elaboration was a proper subject of inquiry for historians. The link between ethnicity, nationalism and national identity needs to be methodologically revisited. The central theme to be emphasized is the idea that nationalism is a relatively recent creation, specifically in response to the upheavals of the industrial revolution and the evolution of modern bureaucratic states (Hobsbawn and

Ranger, 1983). In demystifying nationalism it has to be demonstrated that nationalist mythologies are historically contingent creations that ignored diversities within ethnic identities. Smith (1986) in trying to trace the link between ethnicity and nationalism specifically identifies two positions. On the one hand are what he calls 'primordialists' or 'perennialists' who conceive of ethnic identity in static, primordial or essentialist terms. On the other hand are the 'modernists' or 'instrumentalists' who conceive ethnicity in a situational, contextual and subjective sense. In his view, ethnicity is something more than situational; and it is not merely a matter of fleeting or illusory time and context.

'Kenyanness' and the national community: the independent state

At the centre of the popular statist discourses on 'Kenyanness' has been the question of the national community which we alluded to earlier. The need for independent Kenyan leaders to construct a national community among the multiple ethnic entities had to be reconfigured within institutional frameworks in existence at the time of independence. The most important frameworks they revolved around the politics of the Kenya African National Union (KANU) and the Kenya African Democratic Union (KADU). The national community was deemed to share a collective existence characterised by a unified past and a manifest joint destiny. The way in which both KANU and KADU conflated into one entity represented the earliest effort by the state to construct a national community. The purpose of this section is to reflect on the significance of the statist dilemma in its agenda for the construction of a national community and the implications of this to the broader issue of Kenyanness.

As Lonsdale and Odhiambo (2003) have observed, national imagination always follows the state. Within the Kenyan context in particular, the efforts towards the construction of a national community were on course following the country's attainment of independence in 1963 and its subsequent incorporation into the international system. Through this process the state became the sole agent of change within its separate juridical and territorial bounds. As Ojo (1985) emphasizes, since a nation is merely an ethnic group that has a common heritage, language, culture and a sense of common identity, its distinction from other nations depended on its occupation of a definite territory and enjoyment of legal sovereignty. The state, he further observes, is a body of people politically organized under one government with sovereign rights and recognised by other sovereign states as having a legal status. The main elements of the state are geography, people, government and sovereignty (Ojo, 1985; Ajomo, 1996:38).

At independence, therefore, the Kenyan state acquired exclusive sovereign rights in the international system to act within its territory without being subjected to any legal control by another sovereign state. Possession of sovereignty conferred upon the country the total jurisdiction on the utilization of the strength of its people and resources in whatever manner it wished, without regard to any political authority inside or outside the national territory (Ojo, 1985; Okoth, 2002). The government was to make and enforce laws of the state, decide and carry out the state's policies, both domestic and international, and conduct official relations with other states operating in the international system. In terms of its various peoples, each ethnic entity within the Kenyan geopolitical state was subject to the social, economic and political transformations in the country. The relations between and across each ethnic community was expected to reflect the country's primary active role in the diplomatic, political and military affairs of its people (Okoth, 2002:281).

Thus, the process of creating sovereignty and a national community not only influenced the nature of nationhood but also sanctified the centrality of boundaries as a means of differentiating the Kenyan national community from others. In any case, the existence of boundaries is an experience in difference, one manifested in accounts of self and other identities, in rules of interacting with different groups and in ways of thinking about differences. The different ethnic groups were thus conceived within the nationalist project of the country. As Benedict Anderson (1983) has argued, such ethnic groups, or nations as he calls them, were 'imagined political communities', imagined as both inherently limited and sovereign. To Anderson, a nation was imagined because the members of even the smallest nation would never know most of their fellow members, meet them, or even hear of them, yet in the mind of each lived the image of their communion. The nation is imagined as limited because even the largest of them has finite albeit elastic boundaries beyond which lie other nations. No nation, Anderson asserts, imagines itself to be coterminous with mankind. A nation is imagined as sovereign in the sense that each one of them imagines itself to be free from all the others. Finally, a nation is imagined as a community because, regardless of the actual inequality and exploitation that may prevail in each, the nation or ethnic group for that matter, is always conceived as a deep, horizontal comradeship.

The relevance of Anderson's observation to the Kenyan context lies in the challenge posed to the new leaders in their effort to weave together a national as opposed to an ethnic consciousness. As Nasong'o (2005) has argued, a nation simply became a psychological bond that joined a group and differentiated it, in the subconscious conviction of its members, from all other groups in a most vital way. Factors that accounted for the collective national psychology were related but not limited to the subconscious belief in a group's separate origin and evolution. After the state's formation, according to Odhiambo and Lonsdale (2003:1):

> ...its schools can teach a standard language, its sergeant-majors shout it to the conscripts on parade grounds. Peasants can thus be turned into citizens. Invented common festivals and subsequent long histories of political compromise may together combine, but not always, to create a patriot culture with a past to be proud of.

According to Barth (1969), when defined as an ascriptive and exclusive entity, the nature of continuity of an ethnic or national group is clear. It depends on the maintenance of a social boundary, which may at times have a territorial counterpart. The cultural features that signal such a boundary may change, and the cultural characteristics of the members as well as the group's organizational form may likewise be transformed, but the fact of the dichotomization between members and outsiders remains a permanent feature. As Nasong'o (2005:94) has observed, it is the fact of perpetuity of dichotomization, in Barth's view, that allows us to specify a national group's nature of continuity, and to investigate its changing cultural form and content. It is the context of the dichotomization of a national group into a strict sovereign border that fitted well into the political programs of the new independent Kenyan state.

Anxious to encourage a national sovereignty, or dichotomy to use Barth's words, the new Kenyan leaders were compelled to look inward and to rank as their first priority the political, economic and social developments of their own polities. The immediate concern, was to build viable national groups based on their traditions and customs. The more national consolidation received high priority, the less the attention paid to relations between communities that had strong cultural bonds. As Nugent and Asiwaju (1996) have pointed out, this reality arose out of the fact that:

> At the time of independence, African governments inherited citizens where there had once been colonial subjects. Formally at least, the new rulers imagined that the ensembles of citizens added up to nations- or at the very least nations in the making. But there was an inherent tension between the new ideology of 'nationalism', which assumed that people belonged to one nation or another, and the reality of ethnic bonds where communities merged into each other in spite of official lines of demarcation.

The history of independent Kenya is replete with examples on how the state used its power to construct a national community and curtail any attempts towards alternative thought systems. The Majimbo debate and the ideological rifts between the Kenya peoples Union (KPU) and KANU could serve as classic examples of such efforts in the 1960s. Equally important were the philosophical orientations behind *harambee* and *nyayo* social, economic and political policies in the Kenyatta and Moi eras respectively.

Conclusion

I want to conclude this paper with some scepticism. This scepticism is on whether we have tried to raise any issues touching on the debates around 'Kenyanness' as a concept or whether in fact there are any such debates anyway. As we have argued, if we consider 'Kenyanness' as an ethical and philosophical doctrine, then it relates to the broader context of Kenyan nationhood whose object is to aspire or inspire the Kenyan people into the love for their country, Kenya. This concept is informed by the assumption that Kenyans share a common identity as well as other attributes that include a common descent, language, culture, religion and so on. Yet, as we have observed, viewed in this light, 'Kenyanness' becomes a façade since it seeks to homogenize anything 'Kenyan'. Thus, far from eulogizing 'Kenyanness' as a concept, there is the need to appreciate the varied nature of the ethnic identities found in Kenya and their contribution to the national identity question. As is amply demonstrated by our historical experience, even as we have many points of similarity as Kenyans, there are critical points of deep and significant difference in either what we really are or we have become. These points of difference may be found at the level of ethnicity, gender, generation categorization and so on. In this sense therefore, we cannot speak with exactness about one experience or one identity without appreciating our points of difference that are subject to the continuous transformative process of history, culture and power. 'Kenyanness', as we argue, ought to recognize the two levels of similarity and difference as strong building blocks for our common nationhood.

Looking through the historical record from the different phases of Kenyan history however, the paper has demonstrated that part of the problem with 'Kenyanness' as a concept relates to the misrepresentation, and perhaps more critically, misreading of Kenyan history. More often than not our historical record has been influenced by the state whose agenda has been the reaffirmation of the nationalist project. Through state power, officially endorsed histories have tended to be stories of the *status quo* that favour the unique entities of the Kenyan nation as opposed to the manifest multiple realities that exist in the country. In this regard for instance the positive aspects of inter-ethnic relations are glossed over, conflated within the divisive forces of ethnicity and often projected as undermining the process of state formation and nation building. Our argument therefore is that it is meaningless, even anachronistic, to view 'Kenyanness' within this narrow perspective. Should we then burn all our history books? At least not for now. These same books have been critical repositories on whose pedestal this analysis and criticism has been based. If we can't burn them then the need to rewrite our history, becomes an urgent undertaking. This, as we hint in the paper, can only proceed once we answer critical questions regarding the centrality of state power in the process of knowledge production.

Notes

1 Most of the articles and commentaries by these leading columnists were published in the various editions of the *Daily Nation* and *The East African Standard* newspapers after June 2004.
2 See the lively debates generated around these themes on Mashada.com.
3 Waki Commission figures.

References

Anderson, B. (1983). *Imagined Communities: Reflections on the Origins and Spread of Nationalism.* London: Verso.
Aseka, E. (1989). 'Political Economy of Buluyia', PhD Thesis. Kenyatta University.
Barth, F. (1969). *Ethnic Groups and Boundaries: The Social Organisation of Culture Difference.* Boston: Little, Brown & Co.
Doornbos, M. (1991). 'Linking the Future to the Past: Ethnicity and Pluralism.' *Review of African Political Economy, Vol. 19* (52).
Ehret, C. (1998). *An African Classical Age.* Charlottesville: The University of Virginia Press.
Hall, S. (1994). 'Cultural identity and Diaspora', in P. Williams and L. Chrisman (eds), *Colonial Discourse and Postcolonial Theory.* New York: Columbia University Press.
Herbst, J. (2000). *States and Power in Africa: Comparative Lessons in Authority and Control.* Princeton: Princeton University Press.

Hobsbawn, E. & Ranger, T. O. (1983). *The Invention of Tradition.* Cambridge: Cambridge University Press.
Huntingford, G. (1944). *The Western Tribes of the Bantu Kavirondo.* Nairobi: Ndia Kuu Press.
Indangasi, H. (2003). 'The Kenyanness of Kenyan Literature'. *The Nairobi Journal of Literature No. 14* March.
Maddox, G., & Giblin, J. eds. (2005). *In Search of a Nation: Histories of Authority and Dissidence in Tanzania.* London: James Currey.
Mamdani, M. (1996). *Citizen and Subject: Contemporary Africa and the Legacy of Late Colonialism.* Oxford: James Currey.
Mudimbe, V. Y. (1988). *The Invention of Africa: Gnosis, Philosophy, and the Order of Knowledge.* Bloomington: Indiana University Press.
Muriuki, G. (1974). *A History of the Agĩkũyũ.* Nairobi: Oxford University Press.
Mustapha, R. (1992). *Identity Boundaries, Ethnicity and National Integration in Nigeria, Nov. 16–18.* Nairobi: CODESRIA Seminar.
Mwanzi, H. (1977). *A History of the Kipsigis.* Nairobi: East African Literature Bureau.
Nasong'o, S.W. (2005). *Contending Political Paradigms in Africa: Rationality and the Politics of Democratization in Kenya and Zambia.* New York and London: Routledge.
Nugent, P. & Asiwaju, A.I. eds. (1996). *African Boundaries: Barriers, Conduits and Opportunities.*

London: Frances Printer.

Nyairo, J. (2005). 'Zilizopendwa: Kayamba Afrika's Use of Cover Versions, Remix and Sampling in the (Re)membering of Kenya'. *Africa Studies*, 64, 1, July.

Ochieng, W. (1974). *An Outline History of Nyanza up to 1914*. Nairobi: East African Literature Bureau.

Odhiambo, E. (2002). 'Historicizing the Deep Past in Western Kenya'. In Ochieng W.R. (ed.) *Historical Studies and Social Change in Western Kenya: Essays in Momemory of Professor G.S. Were*. Nairobi: East African Educational Publishers.

Odhiambo, E., & Lonsdale, J. (2003). *Mau Mau and Nationhood: Arms, Authority and Narration*. Oxford: James Currey.

Ogot, B. (2002). 'A Historical Portrait of Western Kenya up to 1895' in W.R. Ochieng (ed.) *Historical Studies and Social Change in Western Kenya: Essays in Memory of Professor G.S. Were*. Nairobi: East African Educational Publishers.

Ogot, B. (2003). 'Mau Mau and Nationhood: The Untold Story', in E.S.A Odhiambo and J. Lonsdale (eds.) *Mau Mau and Nationhood: Arms, Authority and Narration*. Oxford: James Currey.

Ogot, B. (1967). *A History of the Luo*. Nairobi: East African Publishing House.

Ojo, O. (1985). 'International Actors' in J. C. Olatunde et al,(eds.) *African International Relations*. Lagos/London: Longman Group.

Okoth, G. (2002). 'International Relations Between Western Kenya and Eastern Uganda' in W. R. Ochieng (ed.) *Historical Studies and Social Change in Western Kenya: Essays in Memory of Professor G.S Were*. Nairobi: East African Educational Publishers.

Osogo, J. (1966). *A History of Baluyia*. Nairobi: Oxford University Press.

Ranger, T.O. (1983). 'The Invention of Tradition in Colonial Africa', In E. Hobsbawm and T.O Ranger (eds.) *The Invention of Tradition*. Cambridge: Cambridge University Press.

Said, W.E. (1994). *Culture and Imperialism*. London: Vantage Books.

Scott, J. (1998). *Seeing Like a State: How Certain Schemes to Improve Human Life Have Failed*. New Haven/London: Yale University Press.

Smith, A.D. (1986). *The Ethnic Origins of Nations*. Oxford: Blackwell Press.

Wagner, G. (1949). *The Bantu of North Kavirondo with Special Reference to the Vugusu and Logoli Vol.10*. London: Oxford University Press.

Werbner, R. (1998). *Memory and the Postcolony: African Anthropology and the Critique of Power*. London: Zed Books.

Were, G.S. (1972). 'Politics, Religion and Nationalism in Western Kenya, 1942–1962: Dini ya Musambwa Revisited', in B. A Ogot and J.A Kieran (eds.) *Zamani: A Survey of East African History*. Nairobi: East African Publishing House.

Were, G.S. (1967). *History of the Abaluyia of Western Kenya C. 1500–1930*. Nairobi: East African Publishing House.

Young, J. (1999). *The Exclusive Society: Social Exclusion, Crime and Difference in Late Modernity*. London: Sage Publications.

www.mashada.com

Iconic Representations of Identities in Kenyan Cultures

MBŨGUA WA-MŨNGAI

A callous question inevitably comes up whenever notable Kenyans associated with the independence struggle such as Paul Ngei, Bildad Kaggia, Achieng Oneko and Kisoi Munyao amongst others have died: "Why do we neglect our heroes?" The real reason that such people are neglected, that is by being left out of mainstream political discourse, is that the political class does not see any benefit to be derived from promoting such figures as national icons since the latter's stories and the values they represent do not dovetail with those of the ruling elite.

Introduction: From K'Osewe' to Rūrīng'ū Stadium[1]

How might stories of Kenyans' struggles with questions of identity be rendered? Is there any one modality of telling or showing that might be deemed to be more accurate and, consequently, be given precedence over competing others? Aware of the concept of pluralism—in theory and cultural practice—how do citizens determine what perspectives best tell their narratives of identity? These are key questions that will act as critical navigation points for this paper which interrogates icons—taken here as personalities invested with heightened symbolic worth—whose representational value is borne of the tension between consensus and contestation. The resultant dilemmas enable us to evaluate reasons as to why and how people choose particular icons over others to represent their identities and, even more critically, to ask what these choices tell us about peoples' views of themselves as well as others. This becomes a necessary undertaking especially within the context of the December 2007 General Election during which the idea of a civic identity ('what does it mean to be a Kenyan?') was repeatedly raised as a counterpoint to ethnic nationhood ('what is good for *my* people?').

Two spatially distant if somewhat related anecdotes might enable us to map some of the ground that might be covered in an examination of identity discourses purveyed through icons in Kenyan cultures. At a Hip hop conference held at Harvard University, Calestous Juma posed the following rhetorical teaser:

> We give the name gerontocracy to a government comprising of old men. We even have a name for a government run by thieves. But what do we call a government by the youth? There is no name for it simply because society has never conceptualised such a situation.[2]

Juma then invited participants to deliberate on the role that Africa's young people can play in the quest for social development through the creative arts, in line with the conference theme. The claim underpinning Juma's remarks, and one that will echo throughout this paper, is that the Kenyan society makes deliberate efforts to delegitimise any ideas that may suggest that the youth can legitimately hold power and wield it responsibly. Indeed, *Africa Report* alludes to this problem in the feature *'Kenya: No country for Young Men'* (2008). In Kenya, the exhortation that *'the youth are leaders of tomorrow'* is a popular mantra amongst older members of society. In the months leading to the December 2007 elections, under the *Vijana Tugutuke* (Youth Awareness) campaign, Institute for Education in Democracy (IED), a local NGO, had, in collaboration with *Reddyky-*

ulass—a trio of stand-up comedians—tried to mobilise the youth to register as voters with a view to leveraging their participation in Kenyan politics. Ironically, the youth who contested various legislative and civic seats under the Youth Agenda banner—including Reddykyulass's very own John Kīarie (a key member of the youth voter registration drive)—were all trounced at the polls by *wazee* (elders) for reasons that will be explored further below.

What is interesting and illustrative for our purposes from Juma's quote above is not so much the awareness that the youth in Africa have never had any real political control over their lives—youth exclusion from 'government' and thus 'power' seems to be a universal phenomenon anyway—but the fact that through its signifying systems, in our case onomastics/linguistics, society cleverly obfuscates important questions about the youth. Once this happens, elders are left to enjoy their stranglehold on power as *de facto* leaders; unchallenged by younger competitors. Stated differently, once the social category of youth is constructed as an invisible or irrelevant entity within political nomenclature, they are 'erased' out of existence. Systems of representation, whether these are set mechanics (numbers such as 3 and 13 in the Western mind) or creative ones (language and art), entail symbols that are wired within particular ideological and cultural frames that simultaneously exclude and include. In this regard, thinking about icons as a representation of identities within a social-cultural and political context, necessitates a consideration of templates and discourses that are used in the (de)construction of particular images. As such, a principal assumption undergirding the arguments in this paper is that individuals identify with icons who symbolise their aspirations. It is hoped that this discussion will demonstrate how iconicity as politicised discourse enables citizens to sunder dominant state-prescribed narratives of identities, allowing them instead to overwrite these impositions with counter-narratives based on a variety of icons. Thus iconic representations of identity are best read as a palimpsest.

The second anecdote is set in Kenya. On Tuesday 10th June 2008, news reports on TV showed Prime Minister Raila Odinga dining at K'Osewe with former Attorney General, Charles Njonjo, pop-turned-gospel musician, Joseph Kamarū and politician, Peter Kūgūrū. Amongst other things the lunch time tete-a-tete broached the subject of installing Raila as a Gīkūyū elder. This story is ironic in at least two senses yet, as I hope to show, it puts into sharp focus some of the strategies Kenyans use in negotiating the hazardous terrain of iconic identities. First, after the November 2005 constitutional referendum in which the Gīkūyū overwhelmingly voted with the government and lost to ODM, Charles

Njonjo was reported in the local press to have declared how ashamed he was to be associated with the Gĩkũyũ, apparently because the community had set itself apart from other Kenyans in voting as they had done. Such a claim seems odd coming from an individual who has distinguished himself, in public and in private, by his perpetual aspirations to English mannerisms even earning the epithet 'Duke of *Kabeteshire*' in local lore.[3] Ironically here he seems to be trying to cynically manipulate a core institution (eldership) of a people whose values he largely does not identify with in order to score a political point thus presenting his nominal Gĩkũyũ identity as something malleable to be bent to whatever cause he might wish. Njonjo's effort in getting Raila crowned a Gĩkũyũ elder would obviously have helped the latter to achieve something that the former does not believe in but which can nevertheless be milked for its political value. On his part, Kamarũ represents another level of irony in that he has hitherto expended considerable musical effort railing against 'enemies of the House of Mũmbi,' a euphemism for the Luo (see Wa Mũtonya, 2008); he has not stated any credible reason(s) for the turnaround.[4] That Njonjo and Kamarũ regardless of the contradictions inherent in what they stand for were keen on seeing Raila installed as a Gĩkũyũ elder enables us to see the immense value that politicians place on one of patriarchy's authoritative institutions.

The importance of eldership needs to be seen alongside the fact that for one to become a 'tribal' spokesman—and therefore to be a frontrunner in a particular community's pecking order—he has to be first installed as an elder.[5] This then becomes the basis upon which other crucial ideas and practices such as leadership, power, authority, success and social prestige are formulated. Thus a Kenyan tradition has emerged for politicians aspiring to national office to go round the country being installed as elders in various ethnic communities. Indeed the Meru *Njuri Ncheke*, the Luo *Ker* and the Miji Kenda's *Kaya* are some of the foremost councils of elders whose blessings are sought even by politicians from outside these communities. It is illustrative that ethnic groups that have hitherto not previously had much use for centralised councils of elders are now scrambling to form one, given the premium that current political practice places on the power of ethnic blocs as a negotiation strategy in national politics (Mburu, 2009). Whenever important decisions have had to be taken regarding communities considered key to the political survival of leading politicians, these elders' councils have been mobilised to negotiate with their equals from other ethnic groups such as was the case when the Kalenjin, Maasai, Turkana and Samburu (KAMATUSA) and Gĩkũyũ, Embu, Meru and Akamba (GEMA) elders were brought together by then President Moi to discuss peace after the politically-instigated Rift Valley clashes in 1997.

The state, understood here as a patriarchy keen on replicating itself, reproduces this leadership model through a combination of methods, but especially, through the images it conveys about itself. Overall, the moral of the eldership story is that icons can be bargained for, traded and discarded even as participants ignore particular contradictions; the implied message, not the denotational one, is what counts. At any rate, when eldership becomes one of the dominant narratives of the state, as is the case in Kenya, a concomitant demand is made of citizens to aspire to a particular, patriarchal identity. However, as subsequent discussions will show, one might make better sense of how citizens conceptualise their identities by disaggregating the state's totalising narrative of a Kenyan identity as we see in government spokesman Alfred Mutua's 2006 'Najivunia kuwa Mkenya' patriotism drive (see Wafula, this volume, and Wa-Mũngai 2007). Below I begin with a brief discussion of the theoretical possibilities for reading images as discourse before moving on to analyze specific icons. Methodologically, the paper will interrogate dominant icons at work during the periods represented by the reign of Kenya's three presidents; this is the elders' state. This will enable an examination of images that have predominated each decade up to the present. Such an effort will supply a basis for comparing the elders' state identity template to frames that emerge from alternative though not necessarily competing social-cultural spaces such as popular culture which seem bent on reproducing the idea of an eldership-based public life.

Towards a theorisation of iconicity
Walter Benjamin's thesis in his essay *"The work of art in the age of mechanical reproduction,"* (1968) raises useful possibilities for a discussion of iconic representations such as the one charted in the preceding discussion. He identifies three key aspects about works of art which need to be understood if one is to explain why particular images and not others appeal to and retain a firm grip on the human imagination over vast periods of time. These are: the aura of the work, the possibility for the work's ritual deployment and lastly the rootedness of the human mind within the realm of magic. The aura—understood as the uniqueness of an image especially when viewed teleologically—fades over time more so with constant reproduction. The thrall of the *original* quality of an image is what leads viewers to venerate it. This might explain why, for instance, Picasso's *Madonna*, or Micheangelo's *The Last Supper* attract profound feelings

of awe in viewers. The human mind finds a mystical appeal in phenomena that are distantly placed from it in both space and time and hence one might explain in this manner human appetite for science fiction. This appeal is rooted in fantasy which human beings indulge in to different degrees as a basis for imaginatively (re)ordering their everyday realities. In this manner, reproduction allows for a reconfiguration of the original image and this is the point where the insertion of 'new' (*fantastic*) meanings might take place. Human beings may reproduce art because of its ritualistic value, but then such renditions may only fulfill severely limited needs. Therefore, such veneration seems to be most necessary and potent to the functioning of the icon mainly in its early stages. Ultimately, Benjamin's work shows that the redemptive power of reproduced images is realised through investing art with a political rather than a ritual (i.e. cult value) function.

Basing this discussion on the theory of reproduced images outlined above, we might see how icons work as *floating signifiers*—objects dislocated from their initial contexts of use and whose meaning users continuously modify within new circumstances of usage. In these terms, the meaning of icons changes because, according to Benjamin, its "unique existence" and thus its historicity can be altered. Taken in this manner, icons are not mere reproductions; the agents who re/create them determine what stories these old images will re/tell. Similarly, and quite significantly, interpreters of images read them alongside and often outside their initial contexts of deployment as well as meaning. Icons are thus semiotically coded objects whose interpretation is based on contingent grounds. It is necessary to point out that even as these signs assume their own meaning, both global and local, discourses are actively brought to bear upon them. In other words, after Pred and Watts (1992), even when signs and narratives are sourced from a global context, their meaning is largely conditioned by local contexts. This point supplies a necessary basis for attempting a reading of the tensions that are often suggested by placing local icons against non-local images. In the Kenyan context the state has striven to elevate particular local icons over all others; local or otherwise. However, the reality is that communications media have a pervasive reach amongst the citizenry and this allows them to choose icons that they feel symbolise, meaningfully, their aspirations. In this sense, they might pick alternative narratives and icons regardless of whether attendant identities conform to those desired by the state. A study of iconicity in Kenyan political practice enables us to grapple with contending narratives of identity and by extension nationhood.

Patriarchs, populists and radicals: Political models

One of the key means through which the sorts of identity narratives referred to above exist might be found in modes of political induction. In thinking about the question of iconic identification in Kenyan political culture, one is immediately struck by the glaring absence of some globally recognisable icons such as those of the peaceful protest orientation like Mahatma Gandhi and Martin Luther King Junior. In a related sense, the 1960s anti-war 'peace now!' sign seems to never to have been known in Kenya. Instead, in different periods the names of Marcus Garvey, Che Guevara and Bob Marley have been invoked. In contemporary times, few icons on the political landscape have captured the public imagination more than 'the seven bearded sisters'[6] whose forte was a mixture of intellectual charm, charisma and radicalism. What might account for this phenomenon in which radical revolutionary icons are preferred over pacifists? It is not incidental, for example, that the Kenyan state has always disapproved when citizens, variously or collectively, have dabbled at leftist politics. From the 1965 assassination of Pio Gama Pinto, that of Josiah Mwangi Kariũki in 1974 to the early 1980s crackdown on (suspected) Marxist academics and later the persecution of '*Mwakenya*' activists, the lesson seems to be that the state has been consistently trying to railroad its subjects into a uniform mindset. This effort hasn't been based so much on political ideology *per se* than it has been driven by the need to preserve a gerontocratic state structure predominated by patriarchs wielding control over enormous wealth and, consequently, power. From early on, the post-colonial state strived to firmly define, through violence as well as persuasion, the position of (wealthy) elders in society. Taken in this sense the Kiswahili *mzee* (elder) thus shifts from being merely a salutary invocation of respect for those advanced in age and becomes a signifier of economic and political worth.

The iconicity of elders is rooted within the very foundations of the Kenyan state; the identities and poses assumed by the founding fathers have had a significant bearing on how successive generations of Kenyans have viewed themselves and others. Two different icons from the colonial period have singular semiotic worth given the potency of the ideas that they communicate about identity. The first is a 1954 portrait of a stretcher-ridden youthful Dedan Kĩmathi upon his capture, shackled and headed, ultimately, to the gallows.[7] Indeed the existence of another portrait depicting him as a sturdy upright youth was hardly known before its recent publication in Anderson's *Histories of the Hanged* (2005:278). The fact that this photograph had all along existed in official archives yet the Kenya government has never felt it necessary to release it during commemorations of the freedom struggle—even if for no other reason than historical accuracy—can only reinforce the perception that as a historical document it undermines the state's image of the Mau Mau icon that the establishment desired to project and hence its suppression. Incidentally, the state-commissioned commemorative bronze statue that stands on Nairobi's Kīmathi Street *depicts* a Kīmathi whose visage and demeanor suggests a man much older than the liberation war icon would have been. This might suggest that the state, being aware of the political resonance of the Kīmathi narrative, was making an attempt at 'sanitizing'—and thereby inscribing his body with meanings it could shape—by replacing the ruggedness and defiance of youth with the wizened looks of an elder, one supposedly worth of respect according to the parameters of patriarchy that the state stands for (see also Hirst 2007:6). This delegitimisation of youth *qua* youth may thus be seen as part of a political process aimed at ensuring that state power rests squarely upon the idea of eldership. As such, the conduct of everyday public affairs appears to be a struggle between *wazee* (elders) and *vijana* (youth) who have to be routinely whipped into toeing the line.

This is the sense in which might be viewed a second iconic portrait, a late 1950s photograph of the Kapenguria Six—Jomo Kenyatta, Paul Ngei, Bildad Kagia, Achieng Oneko, Kūng'ū wa Karūmba and Fred Kubai—which signifies on desired 'stately poses.' Kīmathi's prostrate position—indicative of humiliation and annihilation—contrasts with the upright posture of the six forward-looking, middle-aged-to-fairly-elderly men at Kapenguria. That Kenyatta had repudiated Mau Mau (and by extension Kīmathi's) violent approach to the twinned questions of land and freedom might in part explain why during his reign Kenyatta was hypersensitive to people like Pio Gama Pinto, Bildad Kagia, Jaramogi Oginga Odinga and Josiah Mwangi Kariūki who evinced a liberal mindset that the political establishment considered 'radical/destructive.' He preferred, instead, to cultivate political and business relationships with conservatives mainly from within his Gīkūyū in-group, particularly scions of colonial chiefs' families (the Koinange, Gathirimū, and Mūhūhū and Kībathi families are conspicuous in this regard). Indeed, during the annual Kenyatta Day commemorations, a video clip played on the public broadcaster KBC TV depicts the image of a subdued Kīmathi counterposed to that of a triumphant Kenyatta depicted literally receiving the flag of authority from the British governor powerfully reinforces the idea of a generational divide.[8] The implied 'lesson' seems to be that the rashness of young people inevitably leads to doom, a contention that is apparently borne out by the fact that Mau Mau cadres were mainly youthful men who, once they were killed or jailed by the colonial forces, left their families destitute. Consequently, the lesson holds, it shouldn't surprise that the Mau Mau and its leaders ended up 'vanquished' and 'humiliated.' As such, without the patience, born of the wisdom of older 'warriors' in Kenyatta's camp, Kenya's independence would not have been won. Within the framing of this narrative, the youth are depicted as being poor at making strategic decisions. Indeed, while not gainsaying that there exists a higher probability for younger people who are socially frustrated rushing to take up arms than that of older persons doing the same, it is nevertheless worth mentioning that whenever there have been uprisings in Africa, the tendency, too often has been to view them through the lens of 'youth' (see among others Straker 2007 and Momoh 2000). This might be illustrated in the Kenyan case by the prominence given to the term youth in media reports whenever the authority of the state has been called to question by groups like *Amachuma*, *Chinkororo*, *Jeshi La Mzee*, *Kamjesh*, *Mũngĩkĩ*, Sabaot Land Defence Force (SLDF), *Sungu-sungu* and *Taliban* amongst others. In effect, while there might be sound reasons for highlighting the youth component of such groups, unfortunately such emphasis not only occludes other important factors such as gender, regional inequalities in resource distribution and criminal motivation but, even more significantly, it ends up taking away the focus from the identities of the real beneficiaries of the patriarchal dividend—elders who sit at the core of state power.

In a related sense, the state reinforces its patriarchal ideology by means of the culture of presidential portraits that was introduced during Kenyatta's reign. The president's portrait is a potent symbol of power and ego of the office-holder. During Daniel Moi's reign (1978–2002), there were myriad stories about people being assaulted by chiefs for 'disrespecting' the president by merely displaying his portrait askew. By the time Kenyatta's official portrait was being taken, he was already a grey-haired elder and his unkempt beard had assumed a distinctive force of habit. There is none of the keen attention to grooming that one might expect to go into preparations for a formal portrait. Ironically, that seems to be the whole point of this photograph; elders are allowed certain excesses at the personal level because of the fact of their age, which everyone else is expected to *respect*. Kenyatta's casual pose might be read in many ways but his demeanor suggests an attitude of pride and contempt. This seems to be the case given the arrogance, for instance, with which he and his associates ran state affairs with little regard for the rule of law, thereby earning the epithet 'the Kiambu Mafia.'[9] Another of Kenyatta's widely circulated photographs—based on the statue that sits large at the KICC grounds in downtown Nairobi—which appears on old calendars, in themselves quite handy items of everyday circulation and regulation of desired meanings, he strikes the regal pose of a contented old man, wrapped up in a leopard skin with a flywhisk in hand, as he stares into the distance. The legend *Mūtongoria Njamba* (heroic leader) is inscribed beneath the portrait. The aura of the photograph suggests a fulfilled patriarch watching over his real estate. In a sense, Kenyatta's Kenya was exactly that; his personal property. It is little wonder then that towards the end of his reign the elderly members of the Kīambu Mafia were scrambling to inherit this estate in order to continue with the master-serf mode of governance established by Kenyatta (see Ochieng and Karimi, 1980). By the time Moi was succeeding Kenyatta in 1978 through official iconography, the state had already established the perception that Kenya was an old men's country.

If there is any difference between the Kenyatta and Moi portraits, it is merely at the point where Moi's looks give him the appearance of a youthful elder. Not incidentally he too features in another famous 1950s photograph visiting with the 'Kapenguria Six' and thereby establishing a claim to power even if for no other reason than by his being associated with those who are regarded in official history as heroes of Kenya's independence struggle. However, looks notwithstanding, the latter's conservatism was similar to, if not deeper, than that of his predecessor. This predilection was signaled early in Moi's reign by his rather cynical public declaration that his governance policy would *'fuata nyayo'*—follow in Kenyatta's footsteps. Overall, the patriotic pride that Moi's 'peace, love and unity' rallying call sought to evoke in citizens never quite caught on especially in the face of perceived wanton corruption and ethnicised governance. During the Moi years, possibilities for youth upward mobility diminished, a situation that coupled with the constriction of avenues for self-expression (see Atieno-Odhiambo 1987) saw Kenya's young people become increasingly disillusioned with the country's politicians. This disenchantment arose in part from the latter's role in sustaining Moi's venal and nepotistic state that never quite enabled the youth to access any tangible long term benefits beyond the hand-outs that were used to buy their support. Alongside age, ethnic membership to the general Kalenjin community was useful in accessing rewards from the state, but just as only few members of the Gīkūyū elite benefitted from Kenyatta on account of their ethnicity, so it was that even if they remained fiercely loyal to him the general mass of the Kalenjin community didn't reap any concrete spoils from Moi's presidency. Consequently, seeing themselves as a perennial underdog class, Kenyan youth began conceptualising their identities around ideas of militancy and hence the ascendancy in young people's minds of iconic revolutionary figures like Bob Marley, Malcolm X and Ernesto Che Guevara. While the political terrain during the period of one-party rule saw the emergence of youth groups allied to power brokers within the then ruling political party KANU (hence the KANU Youth Wing and later Youth For KANU '92) it also inspired many to oppose the central government which was perceived to be persecuting particular communities. Such opposition, in itself, partly conditioned by state repression, also began taking on a stridently violent character. Thus while the trigger for emergence of Mũngĩkĩ might be found in the early 1990s, state-authored anti-Gĩkũyũ violence (See Kagwanja 2003) this fact needs to be understood alongside citizens' broader discontent not just with Moi but with the post-independence Kenyan state.

It was almost inevitable that over time a generational cleavage was going to emerge amongst Kenyans who felt marginalised by the state and groups such as named above have become critical avenues for social identification and economic succor amongst the youth. These groups have also begun dabbling in politics. Nevertheless, it bears pointing out that not all of the militia groups currently in existence, whether urban or rural based, initially saw their purpose in political terms; some were content to simply play the role of politicians' goons (e.g. *Jeshi la Mzee*). However, socio-economic realities—marginalisation of the urban poor, weak government policy frameworks and dwindling economic opportunities in rural areas for instance—have forced them into an awareness of the political agenda that these often tightly-knit associations might serve. It is worth briefly mentioning that towards the end of his rule, Moi suddenly 'discovered' the immense profit to be milked from invoking the term 'youth' in the search for his successor. Consequently, he backed then 40-year old Uhuru Kenyatta's campaign against that of fellow elder Mwai Kibaki for the presidency. Given the ease with which he could manipulate the younger relatively politically inexperienced Kenyatta, over and above the fact that the younger man came from a wealthy ruling family, Moi was merely looking for a protégé who would remain beholden to the elders' class and thereby safeguard their interests.

In a fashion uncharacteristic of Kenya's rulers, when Kibaki ascended the throne in 2002 he declared that he had no wish to have his portrait placed on the Kenyan currency; indeed to signify this resolve for self-effacement the Central Bank issued new notes bearing his two predecessors' portraits instead. However even if in a minimal sense, Kibaki too seemed to have realised the power of currency-based portraiture and soon a commemorative 40-shilling coin bearing his portrait was produced. Be that as it may, there is little to be read in Kibaki's face that stares blandly outwards from the surface of the coin and as such a productive place to look would be his government's attitudes and policies towards the youth. As demonstrated by public discourse in Kenyan newspapers, FM radio and in private conversations amongst citizens, one of the most conspicuous aspects of Kibaki's approach to government, especially between 2003 and 2007, has been his preference for giving lucrative civil service jobs to old(er), post-retirement-age men. Indeed, the retirement age for civil servants was raised from fifty five to sixty years (Kumba and Ogosia, 2009). This led to accusations that he is anti-youth, a charge that is redolent with irony given that Kibaki came to power on the crest of a promise of, among other things, creation of employment opportunities for the youth. Kibaki's presidency might thus be seen as an extension of the Moi government's marginalisation of the youth, leading to the proliferation of youth militias (estimated at 25) brazenly laying all manner of claims at the government's doorstep: land, employment, loans and representation/participation in the political mainstream. Indeed, until the opening of the 9th Parliament when the president spoke of the need to formulate a youth policy for Kenya (*Daily Nation*, 2008) Kibaki had never seemed to appreciate the magnitude of the threat posed by hordes of unemployed youth to the security of the country's wealthy old men. However, given the nature of the experiences and narratives of wealth upon which he and leading members of his government have been weaned, it is a logical impossibility to expect that the president and other gerontocrats would willingly yield any significant resources to people whom elders contemptuously refer to as 'mere boys.' Overall, this is one of the stories that might suggest itself powerfully to unemployed youth looking at Kibaki's portrait. However it isn't clear whether the state has ever understood the hostility with which its subjects tend to view these icons of supposed national (elderly) pride.

A related question may be posed at this point: why is it that towering iconic figures like Kwame Nkrumah, Julius Nyerere and Nelson Mandela who are often invoked as exemplars of some of Africa's finest moral and intellectual ideals never really became rave icons in Kenya even as they were being adulated elsewhere? Though it sounds like an implausible claim, it might be that what they stood for never really resonated with Kenyans, or that perhaps these people's ideals were never (properly) understood. However, it may be asserted with greater conviction that had Kenyans overwhelmingly applauded these personalities cited above, such action would have radically upset the established order in Kenya where the state has at best fuzzy ideas about what constitutes social justice. Thus, for instance, Mandela visited Kenya in 1990, the state didn't facilitate his visit to Dedan Kīmathi's widow, Mūkami, despite the fact that in his speech at Kasarani sports stadium the anti-apartheid hero had expressed the wish to meet her; she and Mandela represent ideas of social justice that the state would rather not have brought to the fore.[10] In a related manner, a callous question inevitably comes up whenever notable Kenyans associated with the independence struggle such as Paul Ngei, Bildad Kaggia, Achieng Oneko and Kisoi Munyao amongst others have died: "Why do we neglect our heroes?" The real reason that such people are neglected, that is by being left out of mainstream political discourse, is that the political class does not see any benefit to be derived from promoting such figures as national icons since the latter's stories and the values they represent do not dovetail with those of the ruling elite. To the contrary, they remind those in power of their own failure on several counts—humanity, intellect and morality—in their dealings with the challenges that such persons might represent. In any event the four figures cited above do not conform to the image of *grand old men* that the state might have wished to see; instead their narratives negate this very ideal when these individuals come across as social failures (that is poor and of little or no social standing). Even where there have been women who have made significant social contributions—for instance professors Wangarī Maathai (environmentalist), Miriam Were (public health activist) and Elizabeth Ngūgī (HIV/AIDS worker)—the state hasn't been eager to let them iconified, since doing so would complicate the story of Kenyan masculinities in undesired ways that would decentre pre-eminent conceptions of the patriarchal state. By the same token, Kenyan men, especially, generally don't see women like Chelagat Mutai, Charity Ngilu and Martha Karua as icons precisely because their political careers—however outstanding they might be—are perceived as challenging male stranglehold on state power, a question to which we shall turn further below.

We might at this point ask what role Kenyan religious figures play in the various identity contests that have been taking place in Kenya. It is worth noting that these leaders have generally happily played along with the state's ideology and self-perception. Religious institutions, as vehicles for socialisation, have by their silence in the face of the state's excesses complicitly abetted such abuses; supporting the established order has obviously been deemed safer than allowing radicals within the church to chart and direct a new moral course. For instance, if one considers the role of mainstream churches (Presbyterian Church of East

Africa, Roman Catholic, Anglican Church of Kenya) during the days of acute state oppression, one notes largely complacency about the status quo. During Kenyatta's reign, the Gĩkũyũ political elite was prominently part of the P.C.E.A; logically it was going to be difficult for the clergy (and church elders) to oppose fellow elders. Similarly, Moi's membership in the African Inland Church largely saw the church's leading clerics ignore many of the excesses that happened under his watch. In a related sense since Kibaki ascended to power, the leadership of the Catholic Church has become inexplicably mellow about questions of governance. Thus, even where some clerics—notably Henry Okullu, Alexander Kipsang Muge, Caesar Maria Gatimu, Timothy Njoya and Raphael Ndingi—have, in challenging social-political and other injustices, convincingly stood on a higher moral ground than their colleagues, they have done so without much institutional support. Thus, as a beacon of moral leadership, the church seems to have fared poorly. This might explain why even revered religious icons like Mother Theresa, ironically known by many more for her humanitarian work than for her spirituality, attract little following outside orders of the Catholic Church. If the above discussion sounds like a harsh indictment of the church, it is precisely because the church has not sufficiently distinguished its interests from those of the potentate; a perception of the church as an extension of the patriarchal state is not just warranted but also neccessary.

Gender(ed) icons

In a related sense, the state has quite successfully created within the public imagination a specific notion of gender that conduces to the reproduction of elderly masculine power. This might be illustrated by an examination of the structure of public administration. Since independence, Kenya has only had two female Provincial Commissioners; these are the highest ranking government officials in a given province. As the president's chief representatives they wield enormous power over both administration officials under their charge as well as *wananchi*, the general population. In fact, there have been few female District Commissioners (DC) but quite a remarkable representation of female District Officers (DO), the latter being among the lower cadres of provincial administration. The irony is that women in public administration have held the position of Deputy Provincial Commissioner, meaning that their qualifications for public office are not in doubt, yet only two of them have risen to head a province in post-independence Kenya. Incidentally, where one might assume that amongst chiefs and their assistants (headmen) there might be found more female officials, the converse is true; there is only a sprinkling of female government officials at the grassroots level, a question to which we revert shortly. While the overtly chauvinistic masculine character of colonialism would not have allowed the employment of female officers in the civil service, it is necessary to ask what might account for the persistence of the latter state of affairs in post-colonial Kenyan government practice? Indeed, when President Kibaki directed that women should get 30% of all new employment vacancies in the civil service (Office of Public communications, 2006), he was consciously speaking to an ethos inherited from colonialism but buttressed by the popular wisdom that women's 'proper' place is the private, domestic sphere. It can be argued that the paucity of senior female public administrators has to do with a generally upheld conception of public space, of which state's governance institutions might be taken as the ultimate example, as one exclusively for male occupation. *Given the predominance of the state's authority in public life, its gender practices have over time become both a model, and possibly an explanation, for citizens' own behavior and thinking with regard to gender.*

Two dominant ideas—age and wealth—undergird practices of power in Kenya and they might shed light on the nature of public space. There is always at play "multiple ways—some new, others merely invented—through which social and political relationships are structured by age" (Ogola: 2006:569), something that takes on even greater significance given that (old) men are firmly at the helm of *all* critical social, political and economic institutions in Kenya. Where a man might lack seniority in terms of age, he can negotiate this hurdle simply by accumulating wealth and thereby ascending to leadership. Indeed, in its denotative sense, the Kiswahili title *mzee* (elder) is gender-neutral but in Kenya, it signifies more than age; the ability to take care of others' financial needs is often a greater yardstick by which men are assessed. Thus, where popular opinion expects wielders of authority to be wealthy men, it would seem odd for the government to appoint women as chiefs or headmen to be its public face amongst a population that understands leadership as a male institution. Indeed, the colonial designation headman, which is still widely used instead of the more neutral 'assistant chief,' seems to have been deliberately crafted to allude to the idea of male authority. The same is true for the appointment of the senior-most provincial administrators; it can be assumed that the paucity of female PCs has to do with the fact that as a patriarchy based structure, the state, at the helm of which is an elderly man, cannot reconcile itself to being represented by women at senior levels. Political parties, which are key to shaping the patriarchy of the state, have played critical roles in shunting women out of significant public leadership positions. This point is perhaps best illustrated by Charity Ngilu's failed attempt at capturing the presidency on a Social Democratic Party (SDP) ticket in 1997. Both the secretary general and chairman of her party worked to undermine her campaign claiming that she didn't hold an academic degree which they said was a requirement by the party constitution. The irony is that even Wangari Maathai lost in her presidential bid the same year despite her holding high academic titles. In reference to both contenders, citizens often stated in ordinary conversations that they wouldn't vote for them because 'they are women.'

The pattern of gendered public space is replicated in other key institutions most notably the church. In mainstream churches, women do not feature prominently within the senior hierarchy of leadership; where women have emerged to lead non-mainstream churches—the case of Wairimu Nelson and more recently that of Margaret Wanjiru, Member of Parliament for Starehe, are illustrative—their leadership is often called to question through innuendo about their morality. Though there could obviously be other reasons to account for the under-representation of women at the top tier of these religious structures, it can be asserted that this situation has something to do with customary understanding of leadership as a male role. Overall, the success of these Evangelical female church leaders can be seen as a direct challenge to the patriarchal structures of mainstream churches. Hence, the passion with which men fight back to see that they don't become icons in Kenyan public life; the *Kamangũ vs Wanjirũ* case in which the former sued the preacher, Margaret, for having abandoned her marriage to him, might be read in this light (see wa-Mũngai 2007 b:354–355).

Popular culture icons: Alternative states

At this point, it is necessary to consider the place of popular culture icons in the expression of ideas of identity in Kenya. One of the key ways in which gendered tropes of the Kenyan state have been brought into active circulation within the social imaginary is through popular culture. Few can argue against the idea that in recent times the thick flows of popular culture (the electronic and print media especially) have been the single most instrumental resource with which Kenyans have tried to constitute alternative ideas of themselves outside state regulation and surveillance. This might explain the uneasy relationship that has historically existed in Kenya between the state and agents of popular culture such as magazines and private broadcast stations. Through mainly the "building blocks" (Appadurai 1997) found in the music, films and folklore that Kenyans consume via these media, citizens can imagine their lives in ways other than those the politicians might desire. *It therefore becomes profoundly ironic that ideas of masculinity that are enacted in popular spaces tend to be overly patriarchal.* This might be seen in newspaper writing such as *Whispers*, a long-running Sunday series. In this family narrative that is in fact a thinly-veiled rendition of Kenyan history, "the [main] character Whispers, who personifies the *old male face of power*, is portrayed as the ultimate patriarch: *an image worn by the state but almost routinely reproduced by subject populations*" (Ogola *ibid*: 574. Emphasis added). Being a representation of some of the ways in which masculinity plays out in everyday Kenyan life, *Whispers* takes on added valence in the sense that the bar, of which the eponymous hero Whispers is a perpetual denizen, is in many ways the series' setting and inspiration. Indeed, the bar is one of the prominent social spaces for the enactment not just of the 'old male face of power' but also its conflicted iterations as younger men—some basking in the glamour of newly acquired riches and seeing themselves as 'better' than their seniors—directly challenge the authority of older men. However, though their props and idiom might appear new (car model, fashion labels, expensive cologne, drinks, jewelry and watches) the younger men's masculinity grammar seems to be based, still, on the old order: it seeks, understands and thrives upon control over and display of symbols of wealth. The practices that obtain in these popular spaces of leisure, thus, supply a crucial reinforcement of the state's gender ideology. Given the heavily-gendered structure of the nation then, other structures of political and economic organisation become more so; post-colonial Nairobi for instance has assumed an aggressive character especially in the face of the various crises of masculinity facing its male residents (see Granqvist, 2006). If we accept the preceding claims, then it might be seen that at one level popular culture generally tends to valorize both masculinity and age-based concepts of leadership because there already exists other larger legitimising discourses of the state as well as in local customs.

However, it bears pointing out that at a symbolic level when new worlds are opened up through popular culture the new icons are formulated to contest pre-existing ones, especially those prescribed by the state. This eclectic assembly—ranging from Hip Hop artiste Snoop Dogg to controversial pop stars like Michael Jackson, from basketball stars to wrestlers, from fallen heroes like Mike Tyson, Notorious B.I.G and Tupac Shakur to talk show hosts Tyra Banks and Oprah Winfrey—may or may not represent normative mainstream values but the fact that the youth, especially, find their stories inspiring is reason enough to make us pay attention to their function in society. The simplistic 'explanation' usually is that these images exemplify a rapid decay of Kenyan society under the unrelenting onslaught of Western decadence (see particularly Shorter and Onyancha, 1997). At the very least, this somewhat patronising position is an attempt at denying and thereby delegitimising the idea of cultural plurality or that Kenyans/Africans are capable of thinking for themselves through questions of value. At any rate Fabian's (1998) and Barber's (1997) work have shown that the persistence of popular culture in Africa involves deliberate deployment. This, therefore, requires us to seek useful ways of thinking about the appropriation of icons from what Hannerz (1996) has called a "global ecumene." For instance, the use of symbols—whether these are images or tangible objects such *Nike* shoes in the West Indies (Halstead 2002)—to imagine oneself differently can in this case be seen as fulfilling a social need: they enable an interrogation of ideas of citizenship and identity. Iconicity also has a cathartic function; a good many despondent citizens find emotional salve for their aches merely by vicariously sharing in the dream life of their idols. This might explain the preponderance of an iconography culture on *Matatu* (in itself both a marketplace of ideological commerce and a metaphor for social survival and transcendence) as well as other popular social spaces such as bars and restaurants. The icon's identity here becomes the viewer's mental state.

As such, having realised that the state is indeed 'no country for young people', and aware that whatever models of social success available are not realistic given especially the various economic constraints erected in their paths, citizens, especially the youth, have actively sought to imagine themselves within alternative identities. These appropriations of popular culture icons become an act of social critique. A growing corpus of recent studies (see Samper, 2002; Gīthiora, 2002; wa-Mūngai, 2004c; Gīthīnji, 2006; Ogechi, 2007) shows that some Kenyan youth are increasingly becoming conscious of the ethnicisation of the state and society and have been devising ways of countering such polarisation through *Sheng*, a linguistic code that is often put to functional and symbolic uses in their everyday lives. They realise that reaching out to others across ethnic groupings is a more viable model of social survival than reaching inwards to 'my people.' On the other hand, the folly of conducting national politics within an identity framework informed by the my people syndrome has recently been seen when in the fractious events before and after the December 2007 elections Kenya antagonists conceptualised Kenya according to the "*K41/K1*" matrix.

According to the clearly erroneous popular 'wisdom' upon which this categorisation is based, Kenya is deemed to have forty two 'tribes'; inter-ethnic Kenyans are not classified. Thus, in a myriad devious schemes that predominated the run-up to the 2007 elections and during its violent aftermath, a prominent appeal that was widely circulated via email advocated for Kenya's forty one "tribes"(*K41*) to unite against, isolate and annihilate the Gĩkũyũ (*K1*). It is the same thinking that is involved in not-too-subtle on-going efforts aimed at demonising particularly the whole of the Gĩkũyũ community as seen when Makali (2009) blithely states: "Let us call a spade a spade. *This country is facing a serious Kikuyu problem.* We must confront it head-on if Kenya is to be a peaceful, stable and democratic country." (Emphasis added). Whatever the nature of the confrontation might lead to is not difficult to figure out within the context of the early 2008 violence. It also helps to further erase whatever residual ideas about their Kenyan identity that citizens might still be clinging to. This sort of identity politics, particularly when it is perpetuated by 'respectable' ethnic-minded members of elite society, is precisely the kind of politics that most youth attempt to transcend by seeking inspiration in mostly Western popular culture icons. If anything, it demonstrates that some *wananchi*, ordinary Kenyans, yearn for a cosmopolitan view of the world that transcends the narrowness of politicians and other apologists for ethnicity. It is for this reason too, one might surmise, that Kenyan youth find few if any icons and ideals amongst an elite that is perceived to be so narrowly focused on furthering ethnic agenda that social good counts for nothing. Whatever the case, popular culture's icons allow citizens to think beyond the stifling grip of the state and to build alliances, real or symbolic, with others wherever they might be found.

Post-script: Surviving Serena
Around 4.00 PM on 28th February 2008, at the front steps of Harambee House, Mwai Kibaki and Raila Odinga, chaperoned by among others former UN Secretary General Kofi Annan and Tanzanian president Jakaya Kikwete, signed what has come to be called The National Reconciliation Accord. In various states of anxiety patrons at Rabi, a bar in Nairobi's Ngara area, watched the live transmission of the event on Citizen Television.

"We have a deal," Annan stated.

To this an evidently inebriated man stated loudly:

> I am totally ashamed to be called a Kenyan. Look at those two men. If I were in their shoes, I would be totally ashamed. Do they stand for anything that I believe in? Did they have to wait

for three months of bloodshed and misery in the country before they could sign that piece of paper? Has anything changed on the ground to convince them of the need to ask their followers to pursue peace? But of course, they think their positions are more important than the lives of Kenyans!

The man tottered out of the bar as he continued churning more gems of 'bar-room wisdom.' What was striking, regardless of the nature of his comments, was the passions with which he read a photo session through which he invoked other profound meanings of identity. The episode also enables us to see how the media and other spaces of popular habitation play a crucial role in fomenting discourse amongst Kenyans. The everyday life of most Kenyans is replete with interesting narratives, the telling of which is often provoked by the occurrence of what might seem to be banalities. TV images, by the very proliferation, might be taken in this way but for the perceptive individual, like the drunk, they mask deeper tales.

This paper set out to examine ideas of identity as purveyed through icons and to analyse how these work to create desired forms and practices of identity amongst the citizenry. I have attempted to weigh the patriarchal identity of the state against other contestatory identities. Ultimately, what emerges is that within the context of a discourse on identity, the state and its subjects often operate at variance because a definition of what it means to be Kenyan is conditioned by and anchored within specific material cultural realities which not everyone understands or relates to in the same way. On this count, if there is any lesson to be learnt from the December 2007 General Election and related fiascos, it is that Kenya has many fault lines most of which society has always been aware of but which it seems to have blithely ignored all along. Whatever other fractures there might be, the identity question is centrally placed amongst them. In other words, until an acceptable idea of what makes for a Kenyan identity or identities has been clearly figured out it is possible to carry on with the delusion that Kenyans have shared aspirations, or indeed that there is a people called 'Kenyans.' It is also clear that the question of identity, and the possibilities for its manipulation to suit particular political agendas, is one about which citizens need to address with extreme caution. Such vigilance is particularly urgent given the increasingly strident push by various communities to have elders' councils speak 'for the people.' When such councils are allied to individuals rather than autochthonic cultural institutions, then it is apparent that their agenda, and the identities they prescribe for their members, can only be narrowly driven.

In this regard, one of the interesting products of the Serena parley is the proposal to create a law on ethnic relations and consequently a commission to oversee the implementation of such regulation. Whatever the shape such legislation might eventually take, it will be interesting to see how the state is going to deal with traditional structures and institutions such as 'tribal' spokesmen, traditional councils of elders, ethnic welfare associations amongst others which might be useful for the state's own survival but which are inimical to the realisation of a meaningful civic identity that might be called 'Kenyan'—there is something in our present case that suggests that these two are necessarily exclusionary. Thus, within the current ideology of eldership, it is clear what that little dinner at K'Osewe cited at the beginning of this paper was all about; political succession within the framework of the eldership model. Beyond GEMA politicians' flippant defensive rhetoric that Raila's proposed Gĩkũyũ eldership was intended to act as a building block for pan-ethnic unity and thereby national cohesion, it is necessary to seriously attend to erstwhile folkloric stereotypes and suspicions that exist amongst the Luo and Gĩkũyũ (and other communities as well) which might detract from the presumed iconic value of Raila as a Gĩkũyũ elder. However, Kenyans might choose to go about devising, revising and deploying iconic identities it bears remembering that such a process always intersects with other narratives. For icons to have significance especially at the collective level, the totality of meanings embedded in the various discourses need to be plausible. If Serena is going to bequeath Kenya a useful legacy, then some serious re-engineering around the problem of identity/identities needs to be done urgently. In the absence of such an effort, the Harambee House photograph loses its signification value—a yearned-for-re-birth of Kenya—and becomes merely one more icon depicting old men setting the basis for yet another stage that perpetuates an elders' state.

Notes

1 An eatery on Nairobi's Kimathi Street officially called Ranalo Foods but popularly known as K'Osewe, after its proprietor. Rūrīng'ū Stadium in Nyeri is the site for what had been proposed to be the installation of Raila Odinga as a Gĩkũyũ elder on 20th July 2008. The event didn't take place.

2 African Hip Hop conference held at the Kennedy School of Government, Harvard University, 13th–15th March 2008.

3 Kabete is the name of the constituency that Njonjo formally represented in parliament. For Njonjo English values and mannerisms cut deep into his family which might be explained by the fact that his wife is English (see Muindi and Wanja, 2009). Be that as it may, popular opinion amongst ordinary Gĩkũyũ folk holds that he has been 'married by the English,' a severe indictment that negates any claims he might want to make on behalf of the Gĩkũyũ. Matters are complicated by the fact that his father Chief Josiah Njonjo was a loyal servant of English colonialism.

4 For an extended discussion of identity politics in Kamarũ's recent popular music see Wa Mũngai (2008) and Wa Mũtonya (2007). In an August 2008 interview with the author, Kamarũ stated that whereas he was not privy to the initial proposition to have Raila installed as a Gĩkũyũ elder, he nevertheless was of the view that the politics of the process aside the real benefit was to be found in what the symbolism of the gesture portended for "the unity of Kenyans." "If the Luo begin getting circumcised, what reason will the Gĩkũyũ have for not voting for a Luo president?" He posed. Incidentally three months later Raila and the Luo political elite got busy advising Luo men to undergo circumcision 'for medical reasons.'

5 The word 'tribe'—to refer to a group of families related to each other by blood and a common ancestry—is inappropriate as a description of the ethnic entities in Kenya. The reality is that people who speak the same language or dialects of it are not necessarily related. Formulated within colonial experience tribe is an administrative term devised for purposes of policing rather than as a reference to objective sociological formations, a situation that unfortunately was reinforced by colonial anthropology. In the present work, 'ethnicity' is the preferred term (see also Kakai, this volume).

6 The "Seven bearded sisters" was then Attorney General Charles Njonjo's epithet for seven radical back bench MPs who were often assumed to be ideologically leftist. Comprising Abuya Abuya, Chelagat Mutai, George Anyona, James Orengo, Jean Marie Seroney, Koigi wa Wamwere and Lawrence Sifuna, the bearded sisters distinguished themselves in parliament as a watchdog over the government during the era of one-party dictatorship in the 1970s. Of these, James Orengo, now an establishment politician, is the only one remaining in parliament as MP for Ugenya and Minister for Lands.

7 The photo depicting a prostate Kimathi is the most-widely circulated one; few people were aware of the existence of one showing a sturdy upright youth before its publication in Anderson's *Histories of the Hanged* (2005). The fact that this photo existed in official archives yet the Kenya government never felt the need to release it can only reinforce the perception that as a historical document, it undermines the official image of the Mau Mau icon that the establishment desired to project and hence its limited circulation. Kimathi was hanged on February 18, 1957.

8 There have been calls especially by civil society groups to rename Kenyatta Day—celebrated on 20th October every year—Heroes Day (see *Daily Nation*, 2009). The state hasn't been keen to this attempt to correct history, apparently given the ways in which the new name might be used to remove the focus of the narrative of the freedom struggle from Kenyatta as an individual and bring it to bear upon the collective struggle by Kenyans to liberate themselves.

9 For instance, in Kenyatta's then larger Gatundu Location, sources narrate the terror that his bodyguards and other highly-placed state functionaries would pistol-whip locals for such 'offences' as overtaking these officials while driving on the dusty roads. However, it was the more wanton corruption especially associated with the coffee smuggling through Chepkube in the 1970s that saw the Kiambu group gain notoriety as a band of vicious 'businessmen.'

10 Mūkami lives in a dilapidated colonial era house in Njabini, South Kinangop. When the Kibaki government came to power in 2003, and within then-ongoing government sponsored 'discussions' of who should be regarded as a Kenyan hero, the state undertook to put up a 'decent' house for her. By the time of writing this paper construction had not been completed. To be fair, regardless of its worth, Kibaki's administration has accorded Mūkami some 'recognition' by inviting her to national celebrations—something that neither Kenyatta nor Moi would have even remotely countenanced—and asking her to 'monitor' the erection of the 2006 state-commissioned Kīmathi monument.

References

Africa Report. (2008). 'Kenya: No country for Young Men', No. 11, June–July.

Appadurai, A. (1997). *Modernity at Large*. Minneapolis: University of Minnesota Press.

Atieno-Odhiambo, E.S. (1987). 'Democracy and the Ideology of Order in Kenya.' In M.G Sharzberg (ed.) *The Political Economy of Kenya*. New York: Praeger.

Barber, K. ed. (1997). *Introduction: Readings in African Popular Culture*. London: James Currey.

Benjamin, W. (1936[1968]). *The Work of Art in the Age of Mechanical Reproduction. Illuminations*. H. Zohn (Trans). New York: Schocken Books.

Daily Nation. (2008). Kibaki spells out coalition plans, March 7, p. 14.

Daily Nation. (2009). Make it Heroes' Day, October 20, p. 12.

Fabian, J. (1998). *Moments of Freedom: Anthropology and Popular Culture*. Charlotsville and London: University Press of Virginia.

Githinji, P. (2006). *Sheng and Variation: The Construction and Negotiation of Multiple Identities*. Ph.D. diss. Michigan State University.

Githiora, C. (2002). Sheng: Peer Language, Swahili dialect or emerging Creole? *Journal of African Cultural Studies 15(2)*, pp. 159–181.

Granqvist, R.J. (2006). Peter Pan in Nairobi: Masculinity's postcolonial city. *Nordic Journal of African Studies 15(3)*, pp. 380–392.

Halstead, N. (2002). Branding Perfection. Foreign as Self; Self as Foreign-Foreign. *Journal of Material Culture 7(3)*, pp. 273–293.

Hannerz, U. (1996). *Transnational Connections*. London: Routledge.

Kagwanja, P. (2003). 'Facing Mount Kenya or Facing Mecca? The Mungiki, Ethnic Violence and the Politics of the Moi Succession in Kenya, 1987–2002'. *African Affairs, 102*, pp. 25–49.

Karimi, J., & Ochieng, P. (1980). *The Kenyatta Succession*. Nairobi: TransAfrica.

Kumba, K., & Ogosia, S. (2009). Youths cry foul as civil servants' retirement age raised. *Daily Nation*, March 28, pp. 4–5.

Makali, D. (2009). The Kikuyu problem we must address. *The Star*, October 26, p. 14.

Mburu, S. (2009). Plot to form Kikuyu council flop as rifts emerge over Luo-Meru elders' meeting. *Saturday Nation*, Special Report, October 10, pp. 10–11.

Momoh, A. (2000). 'Yoruba Culture and Area Boys in Lagos.' In Attahiru Jega (ed.) *Identity Transformation and Identity Politics under Structural Adjustment in Nigeria*. Nordic Africa Institute.

Muindi, B., & Wanja, J. (2009). Njonjo's daughter weds at a private ceremony. *Sunday Nation*, October 11, p. 2.

Ogechi, N. (2007). 'Building Bridges through Trichotomous Youth Identities in Kenya; Evidence from Code-Choice.' In Kimani Njogu and G. Oluoch-Olunya (eds.) *Cultural Production and Social Change in Kenya: Building Bridges*. Nairobi: Twaweza Communications.

Ogola, G. (2006). The idiom of age in a popular Kenyan newspaper serial. *Africa, 76(4)*, 569–589.

Pred, A., & Watts, M. (1992). *Reworking Modernity: Capitalisms and Symbolic Discontent*. New Brunswick, NJ: Rutgers University Press.

Samper, D. (2002). *Talking Sheng: The Role of Hybrid Language in the Construction of Identity and Youth Culture in Nairobi, Kenya. Ph.D. diss.* University of Pennsylvania.

Shorter, J., & Onyancha, E. (1997). *Secularism in Africa. A Case Study: Nairobi City*. Nairobi: St. Paulines Publications Africa.

Straker, J. (2007). Youth, Globalization and Millenial Reflection in a Guinean Forest Town. *Journal of Modern African Studies, 45(2)*, pp. 299–313.

Wa-Mũngai, M. (2007a). "'Ismarwa!' It's Ours!": Popular Music and Identity Politics in Kenyan Youth Culture. Kimani Njogu and G. Oluoch-Olunya (eds.) *Cultural Production and Social Change in Kenya: Building Bridges*. Nairobi: Twaweza Communications.

Wa-Mũngai, M. (2008). "Made in Riverwood:" (Dis)Locating Identities and power through Kenyan Pop Music". *Journal of African Cultural Studies, 20(1)*, pp. 57–70, June 2008.

Wa-Mũngai, M. (2004c). *Identity Politics in Nairobi Matatu Folklore. PhD Dissertation*. Hebrew University of Jerusalem.

Wa-Mũngai, M. (2007b). Tusker Project Fame: Ethnic States, Popular Flows. *Journal of East African Studies, Vol. 1 No. 3*, pp. 338–358.

Wa Mũtonya, M. (2007). 'Joseph Kamaru: Contending nations of Kenya's politics through music.' In *Cultural Production and Social Change in Kenya: Building Bridges* (pp. 27–45). Nairobi: Twaweza Communications.

Gerontocracy and Generational Competition in Kenya Today: An Observation

TOM ODHIAMBO

All of us stand as critics, the question that should exercise our minds is: *what is to be done* in a situation where a significant part of the population is increasingly restive and prone to violence? It is easy to assume that we know *why* the country is experiencing the problem of youth restlessness but it is still necessary to interrogate further the much that we know of the *why* just as we seek the *what to do*.

People are born at different times. Age differences are a factor of nature. It is an inevitable reality of human existence. Yet looking at the phenomenon of aging a number of questions beg: how come that societies experience intergenerational crises? Why do elders and 'the youth' conflict? Do we even need to really talk about conflict, crises and competition between generations given that it is probably inevitable that the young and the old will differ in their perception of social reality anyway? In everyday life such contestation over issues and resources is normal. However, a crisis point is reached when there is seemingly endless competition between the two social groups over practically every facet of life. Evidence from many parts of the world suggests that the youth are almost always losers in such competition. Why is this so? There are many reasons to explain why young men and women appear to be generally marginalized in the society. Generally, competition for political power and economic opportunities/resources ranges generations against each other.

In this essay I will briefly comment on these two subjects of politics and economics. But I pay more attention to the political element because in a developing society such as Kenya, politics principally determines the distribution of economic resources and an individual or a group's political alliance may and indeed does influence access to economic opportunities including employment, financial credit, trade licenses or the success of a commercial venture. In fact the most touted 'explanation' in Kenya today for the violence that followed the declaration of the presidential election results on 30th December 2007 is the perceived political and economic favouring of some regions and groups in the distribution of economic wealth and political power. I preface the comments on politics, power and generational competition in postcolonial Kenya with a note on why *age* remains such a potent construct in socio-cultural and political relations in Africa. Consequently I argue that intergenerational differences should be taken as a serious analytical and discoursal category in the study of contemporary African societies.

I also attempt a reading of how gerontocracy—rule by the old—has produced what appears, on the surface, as a general competition over political power and economic opportunities in Kenya but is actually a state of generational differentiation characterized by gate-keeping and isolationism. I suggest that an analysis of this subject of intergenerational competition in postcolonial Kenya can be approached from three inter-related processes of translation, interpretation and transition all of which reflect the primacy of language in (re-)solving the crises in Kenya today. By briefly drawing on the literary text—and comparing it to the political sphere—I argue that it is important to effectively perform the tasks of translation, interpretation and transition if we are to successfully negotiate and ameliorate the relationship between generations in contemporary Kenya.

Assuming that Kenya is a text—the constitution of Kenya is probably the most significant text that highlights the problem of translation, interpretation and transition in this country—and all of us stand as critics, the question that should exercise our minds is: *what is to be done* in a situation where a significant part of the population is increasingly restive and prone to violence? It is easy to assume that we know *why* the country is experiencing the problem of youth restlessness but it is still necessary to interrogate further the much that we know of the *why* just as we seek the *what to do*. However, I wish to borrow Jon Abbink's caveat that 'the dilemma is how to write about youth in Africa without falling back on the bleak picture of crisis, crime and violence that the available statistics and research reports seem to confirm time and again' (2005:2). I also wish to note that these are provisional comments given the fluid nature of the subject that we are discussing.

'Old is gold' and wisdom

All over Africa, and much of the world, age is revered. Old people are respected for obvious reasons. They are parents and grandparents; they are experienced in certain matters; they know things that those younger than them do not know much about; but probably most importantly they are respected out of the awareness that at one time or another, all *younger people will grow old*. It is this realization that fate has predetermined our date with age that naturally demands respect for old age among most people in most societies.

However in Africa age still holds much awe for many in many communities for other reasons. Probably the most important among them is the existence of the institution of patriarchy. The paterfamilias, irrespective of his age, is a key cog in the wheel of patriarchy that still controls all facets of social, cultural, political, spiritual and economic lives in many of communities, what we otherwise refer to as ethnic groups or more popularly as 'tribes'. The paterfamilias decides what it costs to marry his daughter (and the value of other daughters in the community), when it is circumcision or planting time, which son gets what piece of land or family wealth and so on. In other words, the paterfamilias and the institution of patriarchy, in which he plays an instrumental role, essentially determines 'what power means in its local context' to borrow Patrick Chabal and Jean-Pascal Daloz's (2006) analytical formulation. It is the 'local context'—

the community, the family, the kin-based network, the church or even the nation which has institutionalized the notion, especially in Africa, that old age is an automatic qualification to leadership and authority (see also Mbugua in this volume).

The reverence that old age draws in Africa is also partly attributed to residuals of indigenous cultural practices such as the age-set system that ensured some form of power relations and transfer between different sets in the community. I say 'residual' practices in the sense that it is nearly impossible, in contemporary Kenya, to find a community that would claim to still wholly adhere to some specific form of cultural practice—such as initiation rites—that binds the entire youth of that community to a communal philosophy. Migration and resettlement of people from different communities in other places has actually destabilized the homogeneity of the 'tribe' or the ethnic community, at least in the sense that anthropologists would have described it in the past.

Another obvious reason that accounts for the elevation of age above any other qualification in the struggle to access resources and opportunities in Kenya today is the direct effect of the creation of socio-economic and political hierarchies by the colonial system. As Terrence Ranger (1983) puts it, it is partly an 'invented tradition.' He has argued that:

> "European invented traditions offered Africans a series of clearly defined points of entry into the colonial world, though in almost all cases it was entry into the subordinate part of a man/master relationship. They began by socializing Africans into acceptance of one or other readily available European neo-traditional modes of conduct—the historical literature is full of Africans proud of having mastered the business of being a member of a regiment or having learnt how to be an effective practitioner or the ritual of nineteenth-century Anglicanism" (227).

What Ranger describes above explains the common 'requirements' such as a specific qualification, age and experience to which the young in general are subjected before they can be employed or attain some social privilege. Consider the requirement that for one to run for the presidency in Kenya, they have to be 35 years of age or older. What exactly is the magic formula that this age represents? At another level it is nearly impossible to attain professorship in Kenyan universities if one is below a certain age—irrespective of the person's academic qualifications and intellectual achievements such as publication record, peer respect and research output. In other words, the gate-keeping that we see in Kenya today is partly attributable to the colonial system that naturalized hierarchies which demanded that Africans had to not only 'be experienced' in certain things before they could be employed, which was a code word for being 'old', but also perpetuate the culture of keeping out the young. That is how we came to have the unfortunate cliché 'the youth are leaders of tomorrow.'[1]

It seems, therefore that unless Africa is able to transcend the socio-cultural hierarchies that place the youth at the bottom of the social scale, we are stuck with the reality of inter-generational competition and conflict.

On the postcolonial power transitions and the age question

Some of the papers in this volume revolve around the postcolonial power equation in Kenya. It is not necessary to rehash the arguments but I think it is worth reflecting again on how power in Kenya has dramatized the inter-generational dynamics. I will briefly look at how postcolonial Kenya transited from a colonial piece of territory into an estate of the new gentry led by Jomo Kenyatta. Mbũgua wa-Mũngai (this volume) asserts a critical assessment of Jomo Kenyatta's portrait reveals a patriarch looking (more appropriately lording) over his estate—the land of Kenya. Indeed the production of landed gentry, according to Terrence Ranger, was one of the objectives of the colonial project (1992). The colonists, especially in the British protectorates, sought to reproduce the socio-economic and political structures of their mother country in which men owned land and 'lorded over' such 'territories.' When Africans took over the new nation-state, they generally reproduced these colonial constructs and imposed traditions.[2] The major shortcoming of the generocratic models of socio-economic differentiations that the postcolonial leadership reproduced was the marginalization of the majority of the African population. As such the most disadvantaged among the socially marginalized groups were the youth. This situation explains why Meja Mwangi's novel *Kill Me Quick* to which we shall return later, is so prophetic of the fate of many young people in Kenya.

But how was the idea of old age and political power institutionalized in those celebratory years of the 1960s? In fact one can argue that the incarceration of Kenyatta and other independence struggle leaders and their subsequent release as national heroes could have been a neatly packaged scheme to 'produce' old and experienced politicians. The years spent in detention were deemed, by the colonizers, the leaders themselves and even the citizenry, to have panel-beaten them into 'wiser' elders and leaders. But going back a little would reveal that Kenyatta had already been involved in inventing himself as a modern intellectual-cum-politician who nevertheless was steeped in his community's wisdom. His book *Facing Mount Kenya* (1938) projected him as a believer in his community's cultural and religious philosophies. By reproducing what he deemed to be a homogeneous Agĩkũyũ traditions and customs, Kenyatta claimed himself an elder in and of the community. It needs remembering that among the Agĩkũyũ Kenyatta was not necessarily the pre-eminent anti-colonial struggle leader. But he carefully cultivated an image of a community elder who not only knew its ways of life but one who was also capable of transmitting knowledge to both future generations—by appropriating modern technologies of archiving—and the larger world. Therefore Kenyatta naturally metamorphosed into a national elder—consider that during Kenyatta's lifetime, the title *Mzee* (elder) was generally reserved for him.

Many of Kenyatta's peers in the anti-colonial struggle such as Paul Ngei, Oginga Odinga and Daniel Toroitich arap Moi were not loath to claim themselves as regional leaders thereby claiming that their power and leadership were authored by their respective communities' philosophies on leadership. These philosophies, as I have pointed out above, were based on the notion of age hierarchy. Therefore, even for those who were young in this group of independence-era leadership, their authority was circumscribed by a gerontocracy within the 'local context'—a gerontocracy that passed off as a 'Council of Elders.' This is relevant if we consider that in the immediate postcolonial era only two prominent, and relatively young politicians, were elected to parliament within constituencies where elders from their ethnic communities had little say; Tom Mboya and Mwai Kibaki in Nairobi. However Mwai Kibaki could not resist the pull of local affirmation and relocated to his native Othaya, in Nyeri, where he has been Member of Parliament for close to half a century.

The tradition of seeking political office in one's own backyard although now characterized by scholars as evidence of the ethnicization of the nation-state is really an old one that has been with us since the pre-independence days. It has just become more sophisticated as aspiring political leaders in the country, across the generational divide, reinforce it by reverting to 'refashioned traditions', to rephrase Ranger, such as 'making one a tribal elder,' 'building a house at home'—as a mark of belonging and affirming one's local identity, 'marrying from within one's community'—as a means of accessing clan votes, among other practices. Indeed the cumulative effect of all these practices is to confirm the potency of gerontocracy and its hold on the national political psyche. One either pays allegiance to the old or one is doomed to fail in seeking political power, as well as social status, economic opportunity or even just a livelihood.

Consequently, Kenyan youth have generally been forced to acquiesce or ally themselves with the old politicians or to other institutions controlled by gerontocrats. The political arena, probably because of its publicness, provides the best site for the analysis of the complicity[3] between generations that otherwise may camouflage powerful subterranean oppositional forces at play. Briefly, in Kenya, KANU ruled the country for a long time by using its infamous KANU Youth Wing to terrorize dissenters; KANU won the elections in 1992 thanks largely to the Youth for KANU '92. On the other hand, Mũngĩkĩ (generally associated with the youth despite membership bridging generations) has claimed in the recent past to have facilitated some politicians' success at the polls. Several gangs operate across the country, and are said to be affiliated to particular political figures, even though credible evidence of these relationships is scant[4]. Most Kenyans remember the cohabitation of the popular music duo of 'Gidi Gidi and Maji Maji' and their popular song *'I am unbwogable'* that forcefully retailed the NARC dream to Kenyans from different social, cultural, ethnic and generational backgrounds. There was also the *'Vijana Tugutuke'* campaign that ostensibly was meant to educate the youth on how to be politically responsible (or 'politically correct'?). These are just a few instances of the old order successfully manipulating the youth in postcolonial Kenya to assist *wazee* hold onto power.

Kill me quick: subsisting in a state of permanent despair

In 1973 Meja Mwangi's novel *Kill Me Quick* was published by Heinemann Educational Publishers. The book continues to be reprinted by East African Educational Publishers. It is probably less known compared to Mwangi's other books such as *Going Down River Road* and *Carcass for Hounds*. Yet this novel is one of the most prophetic texts by a Kenyan author on the fate of the youth in the country. Consider the following points about *Kill Me Quick*.

First, the novel was published 10 years after attainment of independence. Second, it is the first novel in Kenya to emphatically dramatize the experiences of the youth caught between the aspirations of anticolonial struggle to free Africans from poverty, disease and ignorance and the realities of postcolonial capitalism. Third, Meja Mwangi is still not rated as worth serious enquiry in our universities' departments of literary studies ostensibly because his books have not seriously tackled the question of anticolonial struggles and nationalism; could this form of censorship be indicative of denial by Kenyan scholars (and the political class) of the marginalization of Kenyan youth from the early postcolonial period? Or is it instead suggestive of the intellectual gate-keeping at the university? Fourth, 35 years later, the fate of the protagonists of the novel probably still best captures the destiny of many Kenyan youth. Other writers, especially John Kiriamiti (*My Life in Crime*; *Son of Fate*; *Sinister Trophy*), have followed in the footsteps of Mwangi by offering compelling diagnoses of the realities faced by Kenyan youth.

How does *Kill Me Quick* help us understand the subject of gerontocracy and intergenerational competition in Kenya? Was Mwangi presaging the current state of our society when he wrote *Kill Me Quick*? Is it implausible to speculate that the Mejas and Mainas of *Kill Me Quick* metamorphosed into the Mũngĩkĩ, Taliban, Baghdad Boys, Kamjesh, Chinkororo and the recently emergent Siafu,[5] (safari ants)?

I suggest that *Kill Me Quick* probably manages to offer one of the earliest critiques of the relationship between society (the state and its leadership) and its youth. To this extent, Mwangi attempts to translate the contrasting realities of rural subsistence existence which defined (and still defines) the lives of the majority of Kenyans, especially young men and women, into the language of urban life characterized by individualism and capitalism. Translation is defined here not merely as the "expression of the sense (of a word, sentence, speech, book etc) in another language" but also as "move or change, especially from one person, place, or condition to another".[6] The life of deprivation that Meja and Maina lead on the margins of the socio-economic mainstream of postcolonial Kenya is attributable to a new economic language that the two are incapable of translating and interpreting. Consequently they cannot transit their state of peripheral existence to access any form of privilege. The (new) language of 'NO VACANCY. HAKUNA KAZI' prevalent in the text is a cipher for exclusion.

Although Maina has an impressive school leaving certificate, like so many unemployed graduates in Kenya of today, structural deficiencies limit his chances of joining the new socio-economic class. Meja, Maina and their friends are not prepared for the world of capitalistic accumulation that defines postcolonial Kenya. They lack the requisite attributes needed to integrate them into the new socio-economic order. To paraphrase Mahmood Mamdani, Meja and Maina have become postcolonial subjects rather than citizens, where they are mere onlookers rather than actors. This analysis of Meja and Maina's subjectivity does not deny the two characters their agency; rather, it simply seeks to underline that their agency is mute. The muteness derives from the ordering of the nation-state in which privilege and access to resources and opportunity are circumscribed by membership to specific group(s).

The group that Mamdani characterizes as citizens, because they have full membership of the nation-state by virtue of their wealth, political power and other networks of influence, determines who does and who does not belong to it. Control of state power apparatus such as the police creates an impenetrable buffer between the two groups. Consider that it is the police who are the most dangerous 'enemies' of Meja and Maina. The subterranean antipathy between the two groups is played out in the war between the police and the likes of Maina. To guard against being involved in this war, which Maina acknowledges he has no chance of winning, he has a 'secret rule': *if ever a policeman in uniform who seems to have a vacant place on his chest walks up to you and says, "hello", turn right round and run as fast as you can and hope he does not catch you*' (72). Although they may be victims of the gate-keeping by the old, wealthy and powerful in the society, policemen are quite effective and willing gate-minders. They actively participate in the self-serving closure of meaning that is necessary for the society to transit between a socio-economic and political order that serves the interests of the old and wealthy and one that is inclusive.

The 'last' word

These provisional comments could have chosen to use any other category, such as religion, culture or economics, rather than the political to reflect on gerontocracy and intergenerational competition in Kenya. I chose politics because it occupies a significant portion of our daily discourse. Politics colonizes the pages of our daily newspapers from the front page to the back page. Churches have become political playgrounds. FM Radio talk shows thrive on politics. What we have in Kenya is a culture that has privileged politics to the exclusion of other quite important subjects. Therefore, it is probably correct to place our discussion within the field of politics.

The vision presented by Mwangi in *Kill Me Quick* is that of a youth that is in search of the language with which to unlock the new reality of postcolonial Kenya. In fact, as Meja ponders his and Maina's case whilst in prison, he seems lost for words to explain his predicament:

'I don't know,' he said. 'But Maina was no murderer. I can swear that. I have known him for years. I knew him when we were at school, when we were eating from bins...' .... 'More than anything else, Maina had always wanted to remain clean,' he went on. 'He would rather eat from the dustbins than steal. I knew him well. He would not just kill people. It is not like him to hurt anyone. I don't even understand how we came to be among criminals. I honestly don't know. We never even thought of it when we were together. It is so ... so ...' he shook his head painfully and the tears overflowed. He did not dry them. 'Why did this have to happen to him? They say it is fate but is it really? Is it?' (149).

The sense of loss, impotence and the exasperation evident in Meja's words and the author's description of his character clearly demonstrate the inability of the individual to translate and interpret these (new) realities? And in the absence of such interpretative capacity, the characters have no chance of transiting to a better state. That is why Maina has a date with the hangman and Meja remains in prison. But this is the situation that Meja Mwangi projects in the 1970s. How about the 21st century Kenya?

The prognosis is clearly different. The youth remain at the centre of national debate. They have been accused of participating in pre- and post-election violence. Thousands of them, like Meja, Maina and their comrades, are in prison. They fared poorly at the national polls where very few of them managed to compete for office; even fewer were elected. Now the gerontocrats—and the few middle-aged co-opted politicians—in power discuss the fate of hundreds of young men (and women) languishing in Kenyan jails for various crimes apparently committed during the electioneering period. The debates over amnesty camouflage the reality that many of these young people acted at the behest of old(er) politicians who are now unwilling to negotiate for their release. But as Meja wonders in the quotation above, are these youths merely fated to be in prison?

If there is a lesson to be learnt from the events of the post-December 2007 general elections in Kenya, then it is that gate-keeping, exclusionism and protectionism will not keep the youth at bay for ever. Gerontocrats should have noticed that old age—and claims to eldership—did not guarantee one immunity from attack by young people during the violence. There were reports of old people forced by youths to vote for particular candidates; government representatives such as Chiefs and District Officers—generally revered as nominal elders in some cases—were hounded from their offices, which were then burned or demolished. Gangs of young men blockaded and manned roads, extracting fees from road users (imitating the rent-seeking traits of the geron-tocrats). So-called 'tribal militia' were mostly composed of young men, and not merely of uneducated idlers, as it has commonly been assumed. What do these instances of 'youth power' portend for gerontocrats and social order in general in Kenya?

I do not wish to sound alarmist, but I think it is right to argue that events may overtake the elders, unless they not only provide the young with the language with which to translate and interpret correctly the current hierarchies of inter-generational relations but also engender the necessary conditions for transition from one socio-cultural (and political) order that still relies on some residuals of outdated traditional claims to power to a more modern one that respects the individual's abilities and potential to lead. It is vital that the older generation realises that it is erroneous to continue to assume that the youth will have to wait for some day to grow old enough before they can access political power. Evidence from places such as Sierra Leone, Liberia and Côte d'Ivoire suggest that the 'waiting' can transform otherwise potentially productive energies into destructive infernos. The elders have to make available the idiom that would enable the youth transit from mere observers of 'power' to useful participants in it.

That idiom resides in the moral authority and wisdom that old age is generally associated with. In other words, our gerontocrats have to claim their rightful place and responsibility as dispensers of wisdom and moderators of power games instead of hanging onto power till they die in office. One of the features of inter-generational power relations in many African societies in the past was transfer of power from one age-set to another one. Part of the power Mũngĩkĩ leadership holds over its followers is founded on the promise to accelerate the intergenerational transition power among the Agĩkũyũ people. In fact many coups in postcolonial Africa have been justified by the claim that the old generation wanted to hoard power.

Some African scholars such as George Ayittey (1998) have suggested that one remedy to Africa's problems is to revert to 'traditional institutions' in which power was vested in 'clan elders, gray-haired men who have won inherited status in their communities as scholars, clerics and business leaders' (312). Probably what a society such as Kenya needs is some middle path in the distribution of political and economic power between generations. It may be in the interest of the youths to understand what motives inform the older generations' hold onto power. It would help to allay the fears (real or imagined) of the gerontocrats that their removal from power will severely diminish their status. However, it is difficult to argue with the ominous analysis—found in most commentaries in Kenyan media—that an uprising led by the youth may destroy the society if the older generation does not plan how to properly manage intergenerational transitions.

Notes

1 Mshai S. Mwangola (2007) opens her insightful critique of the question of the 'youth and democratization in Kenya' with an analysis of how this cliché, beloved of Kenyan politicians, has been used in the past to lock out the youth from politics. Mwangola adopts a historical methodology that lays bare how structural differentiation that has limited the participation in politics by Kenyan youth is an outcome of postcolonial power dynamics which have generally favoured the old.

2 The new 'lords' and landed gentry is one of the obnoxious pseudo-cultures of the postcolonial African elite that Ngugi roundly criticizes in *Matigari*.

3 I use the category 'complicity' here as it is used by Sanders (2002) who argues that the term could be deployed in a situation such as the apartheid South Africa in both its pejorative and positive sense. He argues, 'At another level, in order to resist, victims need[ed] to be aware of and overcome an intimacy of psychic colonization that led them to collaborate with the oppressor.' (x) What needs to be problematized in the case of Kenyan youth and their involvement with the older generation (of politicians) is whether that relationship is conscious and an attempt to penetrate the fold of power or a case of individuals in search of self advancement.

4 Even Peter Mwangi Kagwanja's essay 'Clash of generations? Youth identity, violence and the politics of transition in Kenya, 1997–2002' does not specifically identify any serious political figure associated with Mũngĩkĩ, the most prominent and controversial youth group in Kenya today. The association of the group with Uhuru Kenyatta, and many other politicians from Central Kenya and the Gĩkũyũ community in general, remains fairly speculative.

5 See *Sunday Nation* 22 June 2008 'Police sound alarm over another city terror gang.' p.6. This gang apparently operates in Nairobi's Eastlands running extortion rackets.

6 *The concise oxford dictionary of current English* (1990).

References

Abbink J. (2005). Being young in Africa: the politics of despair and renewal. In Jon Abbink and Ineke van Kessel (eds.) *Vanguards or vandals: youth, politics and conflict in Africa*. Leiden: Brill.

Ayittey G.B.N. (1998). *Africa in chaos*. New York: St. Martins Griffin.

Chabal P and Jean-Pascal Daloz (eds.) (2006). *Culture troubles: politics and the interpretation of meaning*. London: Hurst and Company.

Comaroff J and John Comaroff. (2005). Reflections on Youth: from the Past to the Postcolony. In Alcinda Honwana and Filip De Bock (eds.) *Makers and breakers: children and youth in postcolonial Africa*. Oxford: James Currey.

Kagwanja, P M. (2005). 'Clash of generations? Youth identity, violence and the politics of transition in Kenya, 1997–2002.' In Jon Abbink and Ineke van Kessel (eds.) *Vanguards or vandals: youth, politics and conflict in Africa*. Leiden: Brill.

Mwangi M. (1973). *Kill me quick*. London: Heinemann Educational Books.

Mwangola, M S. (2007). 'Leaders of tomorrow? The youth and democratization in Kenya.' In Godwin R Murunga and Shadrack W Nasong'o (eds.) *Kenya: the struggle for democracy*. London: Zed Books.

Ranger, T. (1983 [1992]). 'The invention of tradition in colonial Africa.' Eric Hobsbawm and Terrence Ranger (eds.). *The Invention of tradition*. Cambridge: Cambridge University Press.

Sanders M. (2002). *Complicities: the intellectual and apartheid*. Pietermaritzburg: University of Natal Press.

Culture

Socialization and Violence: Ideas and Practices in Kenya

RUTH WANGECI NDŨNG'Ũ

Analysis of dominant discourse shows the voices that are heard and the voices that are silenced, whose knowledge or world view is privileged and whose is marginalized.
—van Dijk, 1996.

Language is rarely neutral and it always shapes our perception of life.
—Shakila, 2001.

Crime breeds in the gap between aspirations and possibilities.
—Netter, 1974.

It is human nature to react with disbelief and disappointment when things go wrong. It is also human nature to look outside ourselves for someone or something to blame (Fairclough, 2003). This according to Cramm (2006) is the culture of finger pointing that appears and reappears when we do not accept responsibility when things go wrong. It is attributed to the observation that success has many fathers and failure is an orphan (Cramm, 2006). This finger-pointing culture was amply demonstrated in the Kenyans' reaction to the failure that was evident in the violence emanating from the contested presidential results of the December 2007 general elections.

> What has really upset Edward Mudiba is how almost everybody finds it so easy to blame Electoral Commission Samuel Kivuitu for the poll debacle and the resultant violence. Says Edward: 'Humans are endowed with free will unlike animals. We can choose how to respond to any stimulus. Will the man who rapes his neighbour's wife or kills her husband and burns property stand before God on judgement day and say, 'I killed, raped and stole because Kivuitu made me do so?" (*Saturday Nation,* January 12, 2008)

Kenyans were subjected to violence on a massive, unprecedented scale and an uncertain future. Many pertinent questions regarding this mayhem have preoccupied Kenyans since then: Who perpetrated this violence? Who directed or encouraged the killings, looting and burning? Who will bear the responsibility of these abuses? Fundamental to all these questions is the one on the root cause or source of this widespread violence and related social fractures. In every crisis of such magnitude a culture of finger pointing emerges. The argument in this article is that we have been socialized into violence through multifaceted ideas and practices; politics, economics and culture all have something to do with this socialization.

The events of the first six weeks of the year 2008 emphasized the fact that Kenya is a very fragile and politically unstable entity. Kenya may be a state or a country but certainly it is not a nation. Before a country can achieve the status of a nation, a plethora of fundamental issues need to be in place (Young, 1999). The fundamental issues touch on politics, the economy and the culture of the individuals who make up the nation.

In January and February of 2008, if any Kenyan had been told that there would be calm and free movement by mid 2008, they would have called the speaker a dreamer. Ironically, anyone who followed the events prior to the general elections knew that there was trouble brewing. For instance there were the subtle warnings at the place of work '*Wainaina mi nitakuwa boss.*' [Wainaina I will be the boss.][1] What no one knew was the magnitude and the extent to which the violence would go. In retrospect, however, Kenyans should have been prepared for the worst for we have been socialized for violence, of an extent similar to what we experienced. Divisive and inciting information was transmitted before, during and after the general elections through the news media, the short message services (sms) on mobile phones, emails, blogs and internet papers.

The lingual-cultural factor in violence

We address the pertinent questions related to the massive violence from a critical discourse perspective that takes into account the linguistic and sociological constructs of human interaction (Fairclough, 1995). The critical discourse perspective provides a framework for a pragmatic and pro-active way of dealing with a violent situation through addressing lingual-cultural ideas and practices that brew and serve violence. Human beings cannot claim their humanity in exclusion of the language that carries their culture because there is a very strong symbiotic relation between culture and language (Fairclough, 2003). So through a lingual-cultural experience we can imbue violence. The lingual-cultural factor can be the agent that promotes peace or violence. If a violent culture is institutionalized through linguistic choices in a group, community or nation the individuals, groups, communities and nations may be obligated to enforce it and thus promote misunderstanding, intolerance and lack of appreciation of diversity.

In embracing this understanding and approach to the lingual-cultural factor one is able to deal with the multifaceted challenges facing Kenya including how to deal with the aftermath of the violence such as the one Kenya experienced after the general elections.

Defining lingual-cultural violence

Violence is whatever inflicts harm, damages or violates. It can be subtle or aggressive. Violence has for centuries been a common place feature of social life with its causes embedded in the socio-cultural, historical and economic contexts of societies (Kurtz, 1999). Violence can take varied forms: physical, economic, political, ethnic, religious, or linguistic (Cohen and Machalek, 1994). Linguistic violence is embedded in the language: the thoughts or ideology and the expressions of a community or group of people long before it is physically manifested.

All human beings are implicated in the generation of violent conflicts. Conflict is a product of social interaction and violent conflict is fuelled by the institutionalization of difference (Fisman and Miguel, 2008). We are implicated by acts of commission or omission. Social conflict at both micro and macro levels involves exclusion and inclusion (Coulmas, 2005). Violent conflict at any level for example, in homes, in schools, at the national level, or at the international level involves a process where parties 'dig in' to their positions and construct the 'other' as the enemy. The 'we' and 'they' is equivalent to 'the good' and 'the bad', respectively as indicated by the 'young voice' heard in the extract presented here below:

> "As soon as the results started being announced we knew we were winning. There was no doubt about it. My mother is from one of the tribes that had a presidential candidate but my father is a member of the other tribe that had a presidential candidate. As soon as Kibaki was declared the winner, actually half an hour after the ECK chairman announced the results we heard loud knocks on our door. A rowdy mob broke down our door and begun beating us up! They even beat my 6 year-old brother who had nothing to do with anything. They asked us to leave and never come back to the area, burning our house which we had lived in since I was born. They never even asked who we supported, they just assumed that because of my father's tribe we were pro the candidate from that tribe. I am so bitter and angry. If I could, I would run away from this country," Faith, 15 yrs old from Eldoret (*Saturday Nation*, January 12, 2008).

A critical discourse develops norms which normalizes formations between 'we' and 'they'. Norms develop through what people talk about others and how they talk about them. The normative discourse supports the cause of one and denigrates that of the other. It produces divisive relationships that threaten safety and survival in the long term (Fairclough, 2005). In Kenya, for instance, the legitimization of war and violent conflict in our homes, schools, and work places is in most cases situated in discursive practices based on exclusion identities and a hierarchical construct that favours some voices and marginalizes others.Ideologies are linked to language since language use is the most common form of social behaviour, where we rely most on common sense assumptions. Language rests on common sense assumptions which can be ideologically shaped by relations of power (van Dijk, 2008). Power exists in various modalities: concrete and the unmistakable modality of physical force. Language contributes to the domination of some people by others on the basis of race, sexual orientation, gender, ethnicity, class or religion.

How lingual-cultural factors promote violence
Ideas, through language, may be used negatively to demean differences among social groups and to inflict violence among them. Language usage that hurts is termed offensive. Language that harms is termed oppressive. Language that hurts and harms has a continuum that includes subtle, abusive and grievous (van Dijk, 2008). The factors discussed in this section are evident in the Kenyan context and they may have contributed to violence in the society. Most of the examples are drawn from January and February, 2008, the period immediately after the general elections in which Kenyans experienced unprecedented scales of violence.

Subtle forms
Subtle forms include jokes and choice of languages. Jokes include issues about power and domination. At other times the linguistic violence of jokes contributes to prejudicial attitudes that subsequently can be directed at the 'enemy' later on. Some questions and answers could be altered to make fun of an ethnic, racial or religious group. A child during playtime may ask, 'How do they eat fish'? The answer could be 'They throw the head away' or 'How do they eat *ugali*?' The answer would be 'With just the soup or one piece of fish'. Such humour when intended to make members of a community seem stupid contributes to the acceptance of violence later in life against these types of persons.

Abusive forms
These are conspicuous in ethnic, racist, sexist, heterosexist and classist discourse (Fairclough, 2003). Abusive forms rely on offensive discourse and seek to hurt those they are directed at. Both the practitioner and the victim are aware of the degrading intent of these forms of communication such as when a man calls a lesbian a 'dyke'; the intention is to hurt. These abusive forms also feature in war discourse. For instance in Kenya, considering of an ethnic group proud, arrogant, unproductive or incapable of fighting back are forms of aggression used in war discourse. Soldiers exhibiting fear are called 'sissies' and girls'. A case in point the Harry Thuku Massacre in Nairobi on 16th March, 1922 when women led by Nyanjiru provoked men to violence by using language that questioned their manhood.

> You take my dress and give me your trousers. You men are cowards. What are you waiting for? Our leader is in there. Let's get him. (Thuku, 1970; Brownhill and Turners, 2004).

Many speakers and those who hear such heterosexual language and sexist language may not think it is oppressive, but it is. Even those who employ these terms and the targets may not think it is oppressive at times.

Grievous forms

These are found in warist discourse, nuclear discourse, totalitarian language and genocidal language. Nazi's used 'special treatment' in place of 'execution'. In Bosnia, ethnic cleansing referred to genocide. In Kenya, Rift Valley, 'appropriating our land' and 'ethnic cleansing' referred to killing and displacing of people who were not considered natives of the region. These grievous forms attempt to silence or eliminate a social group. Warist discourse is the most intractable practice of linguistic violence. In its multifarious and nefarious manifestations, it leads to killings of large numbers of people by organized groups like states, sub national political organizations, religious, racial and ethnic groups (Fairclough, 1995).

The language of war be it subtle, abusive or grievous involves the use of euphemisms for war which involves manipulation to deceive. It may be intentional or not. It involves corrupting language to make cruelty, inhumanity of war and horror to seem justifiable. The language of war hinders civilians from recognizing that people are being mutilated, tortured and forcibly removed from their dwellings, wounded and killed. At times, high levels of abstractions are used to prevent citizens from challenging military policies. This involves use of acronyms and euphemisms, for example, 'the Army's operations'.

The use of propaganda is intentional linguistic misrepresentation. Propaganda and brainwashing seek to manipulate the minds and behaviour of the citizens. The adversary is presented as an evil enemy and the practitioner as an embodiment of good. There is use of euphemisms, question begging terms, vagueness and outright falsity such as catchy headlines (van Dijk, 2008). In violent situations there is imposition of warist discourse as legitimate by coercing the citizenry to tow the line and stifling the voices of dissent. The discourse becomes the language of negative peace which can also support injustice. Negative peace is the lull between wars. There is a false kind of peace where there are unspoken prejudices in which case detection and eradication is difficult.

The settings of hurtful and harmful language

Interpersonal and social conflicts emerge in institutional and social settings such as home, school, work place, community or region where discourses of violence which usually feature a 'good guy' and a 'bad guy' are developed. Discourse is the way we speak about things such as conflict. It is a powerful way of determining our realities as 'truths' which is the meaning we give to things. Dominant discourses are culturally bound and dictate how we view the world. For instance, there are statements or 'truths' embedded in the implicit and explicit rules of various governments, societies, families and schools which form part of our discourse. Analysis of dominant discourse shows the voices that are heard and the voices that are silenced, whose knowledge or world view is privileged and whose is marginalized (van Dijk, 1996).

Militant language in theological settings can encourage violence in both subtle and blatant ways; the former being the most dangerous. Christian songs may embody combative metaphors. Some religions may also exhibit these phenomena in their theology and when this mixes with fundamentalism, it promotes violence. Kenya has witnessed gospels songs that are re-worded during national elections for example, *Yote Yawezekana Bila Moi* (All is possible without Moi); *Anatosha Kibaki* (Kibaki is adequate) *Wakenya Msilale, Bado Mapambano* (Kenyans do not tire the battle is still on). Sermons from the pulpits have also been used to create the image of the 'other' as the devils incarnate. Prophesies have also been used to focus on achieving of particular goals such as Alice Lakwena's prophecy (Behrend, 1999) and Prof Owour's prophecy (Owour, 2008). Violence that is presented in religious contexts and philosophies is volatile since the divine aspect is considered unquestionable.

Music promotes violence since it arouses emotions. It has a brainwashing power especially when it is repetitive. Violent images and emotions are reinforced by music. Music that involves a violent input of language is reinforced by constant repetition of strong negative emotions. The music may depict a sense of achievement for cruel actions or pride in evil which inspires violence in the listeners.

The media propagates violence in varied ways (Fairclough, 1995). These could be visual reminders, audio reminders, oral reminders, discussion of gory details, sublimal reminders through broadcasts, talk shows or visits to places associated with violence. For instance, in the violence following the general elections of 2007 in Kenya news captions such as *Poll Violence* were presented in caps, red and centred.

Language is instrumental in constructing a particular view of conflict and thereby has political implications. The media for example fan emotions of war by taking up war phrases and using them tactlessly such as 'declare war on terror' 'war on poverty' wage war on high fuel prices (Daily Nation, 23rd September, 2008) yet the targets are vulnerable people often in poor countries. The media also use emotive phrases that legitimize war and create panic responses. For example, collateral damage in international media means killing of people.

There is also the use of war language in schools in reference to expulsion and suspension when it comes to the administration of discipline. Such language fails to look into the cause of conflict and gives rise to increased opposition. Students in schools are also 'othered' by peers through name calling and verbal abuse if they do not comply with the dominant ways of being masculine or feminine. All the above illustrations are grounded in the way language is used to achieve certain goals.

In interpersonal relations, like domestic violence, abused women have been objectified and dehumanized through verbal abuse by being called abnormal, stupid etcetera which sets the stage for physical violence since the victims come to believe they are actually stupid and even blame themselves for the violence at times (Figuera-McDonough, 1984).

Language is rarely neutral and it always shapes our perception of life (Shakila, 2001). Language is power and those who exercise control over the language of war and peace have much influence on how we perceive war and peace and what behaviour we accept. For example, the debate on amnesty for the youth involved in the political clashes in 2008 left many questions begging. Amnesty means one is guilty and they are getting official pardon yet the Kenyan leaders were saying that the youth were not guilty (Daily Nation, May 22nd, 2008).

War has an institutional character and so has discourse about war and peace so that acts of violence committed by soldiers working as a social group may be legitimized while the same act by someone else is criminalized. Language is one of the most conservative social institutions (Fairclough, 2005). It shapes our perception and behaviour and influences our thoughts and actions. Practices are shaped by the linguistic perspective of an individual's thought. Hence, language gives a structure to consciousness which guides action for instance, if the person from community X is an animal then there is no problem killing him. For if the person is an outsider, it is not wrong to send them back to where they came from. If one's language view is negative, then they may exploit the differences that exist between people to fan the fires of violence. Language has the power to transform social relations for better or for worse.

There are linguistic units which vary fairly systematically according to the social variables such as the users' class, religion, ethnic group, race, gender or religion (Shakila, 2001). Language reflects the relationship between societies. The choices of people's words depend on their worldview so that language does have an influence on people's cultures. People may have positive or negative worldviews which in turn dictate their choice of words.

Language plays an important role in relation to war and peace. Language, which is rarely neutral, shapes perception and behaviour. Language can be used to demean differences and inflict violence or to affirm diversity and achieve recognition. The language of war usually functions to mask the reality of the violence that is occurring. Official discourse about war makes extensive use of euphemisms and misrepresentation. By imposing itself as legitimate, it co-opts efforts by critics of war. The language of peace, like the condition of peace, can be negative or positive. A language of negative peace perpetuates injustice by only establishing a verbal declaration of an end to war and hostilities. A language of positive peace fosters open and inclusive communication that affirms diversity.

The negative power of ideas and practices

As language is used in a negative way, rules for human behaviour change and behaviour which is normally taboo or unacceptable becomes legitimate such as killing, rape, burning of property, looting and torture. There is a close relationship between violence and resources that is reflected in the lingual-cultural practices of any group (Fairclough, 1995).

Deprivation and the gaze upward mentality
Crime breeds where there is a gap: Merton's (1968) strain theory argues that crime breeds in the gap especially due to imbalance or dysfunction between culturally induced aspirations for economic success and structurally distributed possibilities of achievement. Though the theory is embedded in economic success it could be seen to apply across a broader spectrum. Those who feel they are not going to benefit economically, socially, theologically or politically could be considered the lower classes. These lower classes result to the least legitimate opportunities for achievement and advancement. "It is the combination of cultural emphasis and social structure that produce intense pressure for deviation" (Merton, 1968:199). "The lower classes are the most vulnerable to this

pressure, or strain, and will maintain their unfulfilled aspirations in spite of frustration or failure". When regulation is inadequate, a variety of social problems occur, including crime. For instance, the demonstrations in January and February, 2008 in Kenya could be viewed in terms of the gap perceived by the refusal of different groups to acknowledge the presidential win of the two leading contestants for the seat. This lack of acknowledgment led to a perceived gap in leadership.

Structural strain refers generally to the process by which inadequate regulation at the societal level filters down to how the individual perceives his/her needs; for example, the 'we are marginalized' concept. Individual strain, in contrast, refers to the frictions and pains experienced by the individual as each looks for ways to meet his needs (the motivational mechanism that causes crime). For example, an individual who considers himself marginalized could adapt an 'I have a right to live in this house' attitude as was evidenced in the forceful occupation of houses in the low income settlements in parts of Nairobi after the contested December, 2007 election results.

According to Merton (1938:26–29), the concept of anomie refers to the disjunction between "cultural goals (material, wealth and power) and institutional means to achieve them". Merton's basic premise in this theory is that deviance occurs due to the gap between the goals of culture and the means of achieving them in modern societies. The 'gaze upward' mentality results in frustration emanating from denied equality in the market place in comparison with those of equal merit and application (Young 1999:9). The importance of this concept is that it leaves behind simplistic notions relating to discontentment and collective violence. The perception of deprivation engenders a feeling of resentment and hostility that stimulates impulses that are ultimately expressed as crimes (Fisman and Miguel, 2008). Relative deprivation has two effects: it alerts parties to conflict to the existence of incompatible interests and the frustration and indignation associated with relative deprivation are a source of energy that increases the likelihood and vigour of any reaction. If those who are victimized feel offended, the energy takes the form of anger, which is particularly likely to produce violence (Rubin *et al* 1994). This was evident in Kenya in the destruction and looting that characterised demonstrations in January and February, 2008.

Deprivation as such does not lead to discontent, but discontent occurs when comparisons are made between comparable groups, which suggest that unnecessary injustices are occurring (Lea and Young 1996:135). Thus, if people living in a particular area feel that the distribution of wealth is natural, it will be accepted and individuals will conform to normality. However, if very poor people live next to wealthy people, then competition arises. Lea and Young (1996) further indicate that in contemporary industrial societies, social groups that have high degree of economic and political marginalization, but a low sense of relative deprivation, tend to be first-generation immigrants. They include individuals migrating from one place to another as a result of seeking a better living standards or even employment.

Marmor (1978:13) suggests that violence is highest among deprived groups when their circumstances are actually improving. When a group or an individual considers that better living conditions are in fact possible, they become less tolerant of circumstances that they had previously regarded as insignificant, when they were still in a state of hopelessness. Frustration arises due to the limited period during which goal achievement decreases, followed by a long-term increase that generates expectations. It is the discrepancy between goal achievement and expectations that in fact becomes unbearable, so that it leads to an outbreak of violence.

Clearly, discontent and frustration are at the core of the problem. Aspirations of realizing socially valued goals have become limitless in Kenya: everyone wants to drive a good car, to own a nice house, and above all to amass wealth, and yet the society is unable to make plentiful what it values most. The result is anomie, as defined by Merton: "a situation in which an individual resorts to illegitimate means to acquire what is socially valued when legitimate channels are blocked" (Merton 1938:103). Illegitimate means are selected as alternatives in an economic system in which the gap between rich and poor continues to widen. Statistics show that Kenya's poorest 20% of the population live on $238 per person annually in real terms, whilst the richest 20% live on $4,347 (United Nations Human Development Report, 1998). This means that there is wide economic stratification in Kenya. According to Harer and Steffensmeier (1992), the unequal distribution of wealth in a community because of unemployment is an important factor in generating high crime rates.

Goals and the approved means of obtaining them
In using this concept of anomie, Merton argues that all social structures have two common characteristics. Firstly, they establish goals, which are to be aspirations to all individuals within the society, and secondly, they establish the

approved means to obtain these goals. Every society has norms that govern conduct, although they differ in the degree to which folkways and institutional controls are effectively integrated with the goals, which stand high in the hierarchy of cultural values. Society is regarded as being made up of culture and social structure. Culture consists of systems of values and norms that establish behaviour patterns that are socially acceptable to be adopted in order to achieve goals (Merton 1968:186–7).

Adaptation to the cultural goals
Merton classified the major possible responses in terms of whether a person would accept or reject cultural goals (the approved norms), and whether he or she would accept or reject the means of achieving them. He distinguishes between the various means of adaptation, which include *conformity, innovation, retreatism / withdrawal* and *rebellion*. Rebellion and innovation seem to have the most criminogenic significance. Behaviourally, Figueira-McDonough (1984) has shown that innovators tend to be more involved in property offences, ritualists more in deviance, retreatists more involved in drug use, and rebels represented in all crime categories.

Conformity arises when all members of society accept both the means and the social goals, and if it is recognized that for any stability in a given social formation, there has to be consensus among its members over a given period. People do their best with the means available to them, and remain committed to the belief that they will eventually reach society's goals—regardless of whether they ever achieve them or not. Merton calls this response the path of *conformity*, for example, the Kenyan use of the vote in December, 2007 to determine who would be the next president.

Innovation in terms of this model involves social situations where goals are accepted and means are rejected. In *innovation*, since the socially approved means are blocked, people innovate or use unlawful methods to achieve success; for instance, partitioning the country along ethnic lines through the vote or making the Rift Valley a one ethnic group space through violence. The use of mass action to achieve a desired goal would also fall into this category of reactions. This could explain why there exist high crime rates in the lower socio-economic groups of a community. This view is supported by Scull (1990) who notes that all these responses are less common than conformity, but differences between the goals and the means increase as one moves towards the bottom of the social hierarchy, and that one should expect to find deviance inversely related to social status.

Ritualism arises when cultural goals are rejected, but the means of achieving them are accepted. Behaviour in this state is expressed both ritualistically and neurotically (Fisman and Miguel, 2008). This behaviour is linked to the bureaucratic tendencies in most contemporary formal organizations; for instance, putting in place mechanisms that safeguard the interests of a group such as *jeshis* (militia groups), oaths or trainings (Kagari and Thomas, 2006).

Retreatism occurs when both cultural goals and institutional means of achieving them are rejected. Merton argues that this includes psychological cases such as psycho-neurotics, alcoholics and habitual drug addicts. Members of society who fall into this category are characterized by having learned the cultural goals, but lacking the legal means to realize them. Ultimately, they withdraw from reality, becoming psychological escapists in most cases; for instance, the debate on whether the Kenyan people will vote again. Will they go out in such large numbers ever again? Mediation or peace talks would also fall into this category of adaptation as would the debate on whether the perpetrators of political violence should be tried at the local courts or at The Hague. Retreatism leads to apathy as people seem not to care one way or the other what happens because they have lost hope in the systems and mechanisms that are meant to protect them.

Rebellion involves social situations where both goals and means are not only rejected but also substituted. This activity is relevant for revolutionary changes in a given social structure. It is possible to classify this category as part of radical-militant ideologies. Militant extremists and fundamentalists in the world today fit into this mode of adaptation. Thus *Rebellion* is another method of adaptation that has particular significance for crime causation. It means changing the existing goals and norms, and replacing these with alternatives. This happens when existing structural facilities are regarded as obstacles in the pursuit of achieving goals. The obstruction of individual needs leads to frustration and aggressive behaviour, which can account for violent crimes. Netter (1974) recognized the same view, viz. that "crime breeds in the gap between aspirations and possibilities"; for example, making the government in place yield to specific demands through mass action.

Reflections and Suggestions

The whole dynamic of being Kenyan, bearing a sense of identity and purpose as Kenyan is sadly lacking in the fabric and sensibility of people. It is lacking in the lingual-culture of Kenyans too. To this end there is a historical experience—the colonial government thrived on a policy of divide and rule. Their basic interest was economic in nature and therefore exploited and oppressed the indigenous folk through cheap labour and raw materials to feed their motherland. They pacified their souls in this degrading pursuit by dehumanizing and inferiorising the indigenous people. The lack could be addressed by use of language of positive peace, a change of social goals and developing a sense of accountability.

Use of the language of positive peace involves facilitating the move from a lull in the occurrence of violence to its negation. It involves the creation of critical vernaculars, a language of empowerment that is inclusive of and understood by the vast majority of citizens. It involves removal of adjectives that convey biases in form of race, ethnic group, gender, sexual orientation, cultural and educational exchanges, trade agreements/travel exchanges etcetera. The language of peace is democratic rather than authoritarian, receptive rather than aggressive and meditative rather than calculative. It also seeks to build lasting peace and justice. It gives hope and empowers. The language of positive peace provides a communicative means to overcome linguistic violence and linguistic alienation. It is pacific in that it provides an alternative to the language of war and even to the language of negative peace.

There is need to change social goals, especially those that indicate what is important. There is need too to re-evaluate the established means of achieving the goals. On the economic front, we shall be able to decide by consensus on the system of economic governance we wish to adopt. We need to thoroughly examine our current regime with all its residual incapacitations such as the widening gap between the have-s and the have-nots. We should also address the very explosive land issue and the situation of diminishing arable land against an ever expanding demand for it.

On the political front, we shall have to make the political arena adhere more vigorously and vigilantly to the principles of transparency and accountability. The political class will have to be more accountable as other institutions too come under scrutiny—judiciary, executive, media etc. These are sensitive institutions that have far reaching consequences in the lives of Kenyans and must be accountable to the people of Kenya. These measures would not offer an instant solution to the violence in Kenya. However, they would minimize the culture of finger pointing and focus on provision of tangible solutions to violence.

Notes
1 Wanderi, Wainaina (October, 2008) *Personal interview.*

References

Behrand, H. (1999). *Alice Lakwena and The Holy Spirits: War in Northern Uganda, 1986-97.* Oxford: James Currey.

Brownhill, L. S. & Turner, T. E. (2004). 'Feminism in Mau Mau Resurgence.' *Journal of African Studies 39, 1/2,* 95-117.

Cohen, L. & Machalek. (1994). 'The Normalcy of Crime: From Durkheim to Evolutionary Ecology.' *Rationality and Society 6,* 268-308.

Coulmas, F. (2005). *Socio-Linguistics: The Study of Speakers' Choices.* London: Cambridge.

Cramm, S. H. (2006). The Folly of Finger Pointing. *CIO. 19,18:1.*

Fairclough, N. (1989). *Language and Power.* London: Longman.

Fairclough, N. (1995). *Critical Discourse Analysis.* Boston: Adison Wesley.

Fairclough, N. (1995). *Media Discourse.* London: Edward Arnold.

Fairclough, N. (2003). Political Correctness: The Politics of Culture and Language. *Discourse and Society 14,* 17-28.

Fairclough, N. (2005). *Discourse in Organization Studies: The Case for Critical Realism.* Sage Publications Inc.

Figuera-McDonough, J. (1984). Feminism and Delinquency: In Search of an Elusive Link. *The British Journal of Criminology 24:4.*

Fisman, R. & Miguel, E. (2008). *Economic Gangsters: Corruption, Violence and Poverty of Nations.* Oxford: Princeton University Press.

Kagari, M. & Thomas, S. (2006). *The Police, The People, The Politics: Police Accountability in Kenya.* Commonwealth Human Rights Initiative.

Kurtz, L. (1999). The Language of War and Peace 2. San Diego: Academic Press.

Lea, J. & Young, J. (1993). *What is to be Done About Law and Order?* London: Pluto Press.

Lea, J. & Young, J. (1996). 'Relative Deprivation' In Muncie, J. Maclaughlin, E.and Langan, M. (eds.) *Criminoloty Perspectives.* London: Sage Publications.

Merton, R. K. (1938). Social Structure and Anomie. *American Sociological Review 5,* 672-682.

Merton, R. K. (1968). *Social Theory and Social Structure.* New York: Free Press.

Netter, K. (1974). *Explaining Crime.* New York: McGraw Hill.

Owuor, D. (2008, July 28). *Top Scientist Turned Prophet.* Retrieved from http://www.asakpa.com.

Saturday Nation. (2008, January 12, p.13).

Scull, A. (1989). *Social Order/Mental Disorder.* London: Routledge.

Shakila, M. (2001). Re-reading the Media: A Stylistic Analysis of Malaysian Media Coverage of Anwar and the Reformasi Movement In *Asia Pacific Media Educator II.*

UNDP. (1998). *United Nations Development Report 5:3.*

Van, D. (1996). Discourse Power and Access in Caldas-Coulthard and Coulthard, Malcom (eds.) In *Texts and Practice: Readings in Critical Discourse Analysis* (pp. 84-104). London: Routledge.

Van, D. (2008). *Discourse and Power.* Palgrave: Macmillan.

Young, J. (1999). *The Exclusive Society: Social Exclusion, Crime and Difference in Late Modernity.* London: Sage Publications.

Gendered Identities: Women and Power(lessness) in Kenya

SOPHIE MACHARIA

(African) women need to claim an "identity politics" that foregrounds their ability to fluctuate between the margin and the centre, wherever those margins and centres might be, but will also enable them to move beyond constructed and constituting margins and centres, creating their own margins and centres along the way... Since different women can create new spaces and social locations for themselves within the dominant culture, marginality (be it represented as racial, sexual, historical or cultural difference) will therefore be the point of intersection for identity politics, the location where identity politics finds full expression. By creating these new spaces and location, women take the margins to the centre and vice versa. This constant shifting subsequently subverts dominant political, economic, cultural conceptions of gender, both at the centre and at the margins.

—Nfah-Abbenyi: 1997:32.

This epigraph captures some of the dynamics of identity, gender and power which contribute significantly to the debate of Kenya's political economy. It immediately reveals the challenge of fixed definitions by introducing the subject of one's ability to blur the boundaries between margin and centre to their own advantage. The essay is premised on the capacity of those occupying spaces in the margins (in the case of this paper by their gender) to 'de-stabilize' dominant categories of definition and thereby fixed relations of gender and power hierarchies. Instead they 'dis-organize' these categories and thus create simultaneous margins where sexual difference will be in fluid, shifting locations. The essay subsequently prioritizes the discussion of women as the marginalized in terms of economic and political identities within a contextualized Kenyan post-colonial space. Examples will be drawn from actual practices within the Kenyan national context as well as from literature.

Exploring the subject of identities within the Kenyan socio-political context requires a perception of the ambiguities of gender and power as experienced within defined cultural and political spaces. Understanding the social relations of gender requires that it explicitly recognizes its systematic roots in the historicity of social structure. For instance within popular culture comprised of the media, the political and the social spaces the subject has presumed an oppositional hierarchy between the categories "women" and "men" and created binary view of the "women as victims" "men-as-the-problem". Definition of "gender" often assumes automatically a relation of inequality between men and women. Indeed gender is equated to oppositional and unequal power relations. However this simplistic reading of victim/oppressor in the collusion of men in the subordination of women fails to capture women's agency in exploiting available opportunities to empower themselves. Popular discourses have continued to position women as victims of neglect and repression, or where they succeed as unfeminine go-getters. It is the duty of the artist and intellectual to interrogate these images by re-examining the social, cultural economic and political borders that create those positions, but more significantly, by highlighting women's attempts to take up agency.

While acknowledging this popularized dichotomy, often by direct beneficiaries,[1] I choose to engage instead through a process of theoretical, historical and literary analysis of questions on Kenyan women. In effect I hope to raise, not provide answers to, several questions, which if satisfactorily pursued would not only revise our notions of gender and identity representations, but also inspire a re-thinking of power and its relations between margins and the centre.

Must every struggle for power be understood around the issue of identity? Because the subject of power in Kenya is predominantly male, is inclusion of women necessarily an act of desired change? How does the current socio-political situation invite new consciousness in the relationship between men and women? Do the facts of historisized categories of men and women provide a motive for collective action in challenging male political domination? If women are largely perceived as passive followers of (male) nation builders how do women respond to and shape nationalist consciousness? What role do women play in the dissemination of power? How is the youth engaging in the discourse of patriarchy?

Theorizing women's issues

I anchor this paper within a multiple complimentary theoretical frameworks primarily because any one single framework may not comprehensively subject the discussion to a thorough analysis of the diversity and complexity, the fluidity and subjectivity of gender, power and identity. I remain aware that such an attempt to bring different gender and identity theoreticians who speak at different times, in different locales, for different audiences, and who in effect engage with subjectivity and conviction may in itself create further complexities both of meaning and application. Indeed, the conflicting theories of gender constructs and identities circulate in an ever changing field of inquiry, yet the very title of the paper calls for further problematization of the terms, their understood and sometimes subjective meanings and applications within a fluid terrain that Kenya's socio-political canvas is and has more acutely become in the recent months. I will later look into literature, a site that offers an interesting space upon which to explore questions of power, identity and sexuality. Literature here will be defined as the fictional world, in which stories of men and women, in their attempt to build relations among themselves, within ever-changing socio-cultural, political and economic terrains, are told. The world of narration helps us reflect on our selves, enjoy life's journey of those characters penned[2] by craftsmen and women over time, space and boundaries. David Lodge sums the function of literature and criticism even better: "to enable us to enjoy life, or better, to endure it" (Lodge 555.)

The definition of 'woman' assumed in this paper is largely informed by Judith Butler, the theorist of power, gender, sexuality and identity. In her influential book *Gender Trouble*, (1990), Butler argues that feminism has erred in asserting that women are a monolithic group that shares common interests, a view she says introduces a binary view of gender relations. Butler states that there is no seamless category of women and any implied unity is fictive, often produced and restrained by the very structures of power through which emancipation is sought. She argues that instead, a person should have the possibility of choosing their own individual identity and gender then should be seen as a fluid variable which shifts and changes in different contexts. If gender is according to Butler "a performance" and therefore, it is what you *do* at particular times, rather than a universal *who you are* it is possible to add that biological difference between men and women accounts for the smaller part of the actual difference. In other words, Butler invokes subjectivity and agency. The "doing" in this "performativity" assumes some measure of agency. The concept "who you are" again invokes passivity, an identification by "others". Only therefore through agency can the subject assume self-identification.

The subject of identities is both fluid and complex and this has been acknowledged by gender and identity theorists. In a widely discussed text on identity, *Questions of Cultural Identity,* (1996), Stuart Hall and Paul du Gay raise more questions than they provide answers to the complexities of identity. One of the questions that captivates my thinking and which the authors pointedly raise, is "Who needs "Identity"? In this essay, Hall asserts that the concept of identity is a paradox and suggests that identity is not an essentialist but a "strategic and a positional one" (3). For him identities are: "never unified... [but they are] increasingly fragmented and fractured; never singular but multiply constructed across different, often intersecting and antagonistic discourses, practices and positions... they are subject to radical historicization, and are constantly in the process of change and transformation" (4).

Although identities invoke an origin in a historical past, for instance when/where were you born, identity here is understood as a process of "becoming rather than being" for indeed there is no finality in identity apart from possibly in death[3]. For both Butler and Hall, identification belongs to the imaginary realm and can therefore be contested. This means that identity as closure should be interrogated.

The idea of contesting identities because they are not fixed is also discussed by Margaret Hall (1990) in her detailed study of women and identity. Like Butler and Hall above, she correctly states that there is no single definition of the term identity and further highlights the centrality of the question of agency. Identification for Hall is a process; never complete, always in process. In other words, identification is never a totality; never a proper fit. Whereas identities may claim some level of 'cultural belongingness' my claim here is that identity is never singular but multiply constructed across different, often intersecting and sometimes antagonistic discourses. Identities are never unified, and can be increasingly fragmented. What emerges is an understanding of the concept captured in her conclusion: "Identity defines our uniqueness and at the same time pulls us into social integration" (Hall, *ibid*, 167). All these definitions point to one factor: the multiplicity, and fluidity of identities, depending on the context in which the definition is required. What becomes directly significant here is the fact that there is no single definition if identity that can claim absolutism and therefore any 'fixed' category could only become a site of closure, of summarization and totalization. Instead, any attempt at defining should attempt to harness multiple significations. That way, the category woman is not "fixed" or "paralyzed in positions of subordination" (Butler 16) but instead expands the possibility of enhanced agency.

Ifi Amadiume (1987) challenges Western understanding of gender as women's subordination by men. In her famous text, *Male Daughters Female Husbands* she frees the title husband from power, masculinity and men and affords women "male" attributes such as strength, courage and fortitude. For her, sexuality alone does not exercise power because femininity and masculinity are socially constructed and practiced in society, and because these structures are historically mutable, so too are the categories of men and women, who are constantly being produced by changing social formations. She argues that in indigenous African societies, before the advent of colonial rule, women's political positions varied extensively across Africa's multiple ethnic groups. In her study of the Igbo society of Eastern Nigeria, for example, she finds that women exercised extensive authority. During the colonial period, however, European administrators imposed a legal and cultural apparatus that undermined women's traditional bases of power; women became politically and economically subordinated and marginalized. This marginality was not reversed by postcolonial independent governments even where women had been active participants in nationalist and liberation movements.

The theorists examined above all suggest, in their own ways, that any attempt to "fix" and "freeze" gender identities is a means to deny agency. Agency is a means to self re-definition and enables one to challenge power relations that exist between the margins and the centre. The interrogation of gender identities within a fractured political economy such as Kenya has recently been necessarily demands that all players, both men and women, participate in all the reflections that aim at the healing of the social, political, economic and cultural fractures.

Problematizing power: *Maendeleo ya Wanawake*[4] and beyond

Feminist analysis claims that it is gender difference that is used to justify male appropriation of power, time, property and even leisure. If we take the definition of power as the control by one person, group or nation on the behaviour and conditions of life of another, then the subject of gender differentiation is significant. Only when one is identified as inferior can the other exercise power and control. There are of course various modes of power; power exercised by force, compulsion, influence propaganda, charisma, bureaucracy and so on. Power has also been embodied in political parties, groups of people and even gangs[5] in contemporary Kenya. African power and leadership is agreeably not intrinsic and therefore this power must come from somewhere else. Most former colonies negotiated, demanded and some engaged in armed struggle for independence. Such power, therefore, comes from the people; both men and women. Kenyan women have historically engaged in the process of political struggle and have continued to pursue their interest to date[6]. Power is central to the production of social identities and therefore being powerless assumes that one has no agency in the construction of their identities. However, on examination of post colonial Kenya history demonstrates a deliberate sidelining of women from political power a reflection of the nature of colonial power which was traditionally male with a negligible sprinkling of women used as support for male power. This modern form of governance was not based on African cultures which traditionally accommodated women within structures of leadership. Modern government moulded itself according to colonial government that was based on Western culture and practices that perceived women as helpers and never central to the running of leadership and governance. In Kenya, this situation was easy to copy because most of the people poised to take over political leadership had been exposed to Western culture through education, travel, and even trade. Political leadership then assumed a male face, and has continued to do so.

Consequently women have over the years been pushed to situations of political powerlessness, to the margins, because, again, active political participation requires economic independence and a sound economic base yet few women have achieved this. Although women's journey towards visibility started long before independence, post independent Kenya hardly created spaces for them to express themselves. The historical journey of women's attempts to claim political and economic agency in post independent Kenya is seen in this essay as a case of attempting to shift their participation from the margins to its situation in the centre. It is imperative to take cognisance of what has been achieved.

Women's organisations in Kenya have increased and today women are organizing locally and nationally on an unprecedented scale. Women are challenging laws and constitutions that do not uphold their interest. In recent years, there has been an increase in women's political participation at national level government, legislative and party structures that have traditionally marginalized them. What circumstances have aided women in these pursuits? The international women's movement, especially the UN women's conference, has provided a platform for women's mobilization, networking and a platform to address issues that cut across borders, class and race. This paper appreciates that Kenya is a land of diversity based on culture, language, and a rich socio-economic fabric at the same time as it recognizes that notable changes have occurred and have influenced the participation of women in their environment. For instance, shortly after independence, Maendeleo ya Wanawake was formed but it was largely confined to the improvement of childcare, promoting handicrafts businesses, literacy and farming techniques, (Wipper 1975:100). From this humble beginning Maendeleo grew to offer women spaces for economic participation through marketing of their crafts both nationally and internationally. The organization gave women a chance to network with others nationally and internationally through forums that prioritized gender equality and direct women's participation in education, economy and politics. Maendeleo participated in most international meetings and made the women's voice audible there. Some of the leaders also got exposed to international politics and became active at higher levels of government operations. The few well-known women politicians in Kenya trace their political roots in Maendeleo[7]. On the ground however ordinary rural and urban poor woman could hardly participate in the leadership affairs of Maendeleo and therefore to a large extent they did not feel represented within this organization.

The autonomy of this body however was compromised under the one-party rule of the KANU government, and by the 1980s it had emerged as a movement with political potential, but it was covertly driven by powerful male political operators. It emerged as a political wing of KANU, and it mobilized women's participation only if this was in the interests of the political regime of the day. Women with contrary political inclinations, like the rest of the population, had no space for expressing such views. It is for this reason that only those that toed the line were rewarded with political favours. The leaders of the movement at the time were charged with the duty of empowering women through mobilization and political participation. During the single party era Maendeleo ya Wanawake assumed a political base that had not been seen before and the then president Moi demanded that it be an annex of Kanu; hence assuming a new identity, *Kanu Maendeleo ya Wanawake*. Because it was a government outfit which received funding from the exchequer its leadership could neither challenge the status quo nor push for women's advancement. In other words, women had power but they were powerless to challenge institutions of government that made them so. During that era each locality had a Maendeleo ya Wanawake representative, and it soon became a powerful resource in the single party era to mobilize political support largely because of the national mapping it enjoyed. Wheareas it claimed to represent the interests of all women, especially those in rural areas, it "often served as a mechanism for generating votes and support for the country's single party, getting women to attend party rallies and meetings, and sing, dance and cook for visiting dignitaries" (Tripp 2003:236). It would therefore be correct to observe that an important function of this group was to contain women's political activity within these designated organizations and largely make women's functions apolitical. As a result, whereas women were seemingly involved in government, they were in reality politically marginalized since they were largely absent from central government operations. Their moments of greatest visibility was when they attended the KANU government public rallies.

The expansion of educational opportunities since independence saw a large pool of educated women who had the capacity to head national organizations. At the same time, a considerable number of women joined the formal economy and formed groups that were largely economic. This saw the rise of independent women's groups and therefore the need for national women's groups slowly diminished. Again with the opening up of political spaces with the advent of multi party democracy there emerged opportunities for women's social, economic and political participation. Women formed economic groups and associations which gave them space to operate independently. Donor funding agencies also found it easier to deal with such smaller associations. Indeed women have a strong presence in NGO's owing to their long experience in creating and sustaining associations such as church-related, income generating, self-help groups, welfare associations, 'merry-go-rounds' and community based organisations. Other categories such as the professionally based women's groups emerged e.g. Kenya Women Medical Association and Association of Media Women in Kenya. There were also regional ones with branches all over Kenya such as Forum for Africa Women Educationists (FAWE) while others were international such as Federation of Women Lawyers-Kenya (FIDA) and Young Women's Christian Association (YWCA). All were concerned with advancing women's social, economic and political status. A group such as Women Parliamentarians, were later formed as a caucus for parliamentary debates. Subsequently women have pushed their agenda more vigorously, through donor aided programmes than they have through government. The groups have developed the ability to drum up political support around various issues. Around the 1990s and early 2000s for instance in Kenya, donors placed great emphasis on funding NGO activities because they argued that being smaller units it would be easier to demand accountability from them than it would be to demand the same from the state.

Soon owing to the politics of the day, donor agencies shifted from solely funding economic activities such as health and education and included in their work advocacy especially of women's rights and the promotion of women's political leadership and participation. These donor agencies supported NGOs that championed the legal and social rights of women and even funded parliamentary bills that supported among others, the larger representation of women through affirmative action. They also supported legislation regarding marriage, inheritance and the fight against domestic violence and even sponsored regional networkings around these issues. Beyond regional operations international pressure such as that from the 1995 UN Beijing Conference on Women influenced women's movement in mobilizing and demanding accountability from government. Subsequently women's organizations in Kenya developed the capacity to mount campaigns to build political support especially for women in political leadership. In 1997 for instance many women groups rallied their support for the presidential female candidate Charity Ngilu. Women who occupied high offices in women's organizations enjoyed great public visibility and it is little wonder therefore that many of them then moved on to vie for parliamentary seats[8]. The autonomy of these organizations began to challenge state patronage and other social ills such as corruption and injustice but even more significant is the platform it gave women to forge alliances across ethnic, religious, racial and the rural/urban divides. Within these organizations women selected their own leaders, and created their own agendas which grew with time from welfare to political participation. The associations made women's awareness broad and provided the tools to challenge legal structures that disempowered them politically.

With enlarged spaces of socio-political expression, media coverage on women's issues increased, and subsequently they began featuring prominently in spaces of public discourse. At the same time a sizeable number of female journalists rose to positions of decision making and this ensured that women's issues were mainstreamed within the media industry. As a result women became more visible not merely as cover girls, but as instruments of policy and socio-political change. Then there are the churches, especially the Evangelical largely privately-owned/founded ones, whose leaders have the power to mobilize their constituents both spiritually and politically.[9] With these developments, women organizations have slowly shifted from domestic agendas to emphasizing political participation as seen in Kabira and Nzioki's (1993) statement that "women have to go where power and resources are by being powerful and resourceful themselves" (73).

Narrating socio-political experiences

How does literature respond to the issue of identities and power in Kenya? Ngũgĩ wa Thiong'o has grappled with the subject since he began his literary career in the 1960s and has attracted a lot of literary attention. His female characters such as Muthoni who defies circumcision in *The River Between*, Mumbi the idealized mother of the young nation in *A Grain of Wheat*, Wanja the complex character in *Petals of Blood* who is immersed in the economic gluttony of post-independent Kenya and Waringa the spirited fighter against corruption and economic mismanagement in *Matigari* are agents of change in their society. In the urban novel, identity becomes even more problematic after the link between rural and urban life is complicated by economic insecurities in the city. Writers such as Meja Mwangi represent and critique the peripheral socio-economic situations that most females are pushed to. Grace Ogot, Rebeka Njau, Muthoni Likimani and Margaret Ogola are some of the first and second generation writers who interrogate women's agency and have significantly contributed to the overall subject of women and agency in Kenyan literature[10]. Third generation writers Binyavanga Wainaina, Yvonne Awuor and other youthful and often non-conventional voices that find agency through *"Kwani?"*, a journal that engages the cross-section of urban/rural, popular/orthodox, tradition/globalization realities, have continued to inform the debate of identity within the larger space of the Kenyan political canvas. They continue to invoke the subject of mobility from the margins to the centre.

Leaving writers aside we will interrogate briefly a story that was constructed within the shifting subject positions of Kenyan politics. Hopefully it illustrates how women's agency negotiates multiple identities as a survival strategy. During the height of the election euphoria in December 2007 a female relative born and raised in central Kenya and married by a man whose family lives in Western Province, went "home" with her family for Christmas. Given the various prevailing accounts of ethnic animosity I naturally got anxious for her and inquired often about her security. Initially she was gripped by anxiety but one day she told me that she had decided to overcome it by reassuring her relatives that it was to their advantage if she died there, for it would save them the cost of transporting her body from Nairobi, where she works, and since all her in-laws lived in Western Kenya anyway, they too would not need to spend any money on travel. This story is not isolated in the environment before and after the 2007 elections and many families whose members have diverse identities suffered great anxieties. Many grouped together to form support networks in the face of possible disintegration. Even without the multiple ethnicity and diversities, women necessarily suffer political instability on account of gender; my relative suffered because she is a woman and a Kikuyu then in the 'wrong' place. Women are traditionally socialized to assume the role of ensuring family stability and when society disintegrates, it is the family that disintegrates first leaving women desolate. In the eyes of women, the males who get involved in political violence are first and foremost husbands, sons, sons-in-law, uncles, cousins and brothers. Violence for women assumes a great personal and family challenge because while they do not commonly participate in its execution they carry the weight of the tragedy through loss of their male relatives. The identity of women during and after the 2007 election period acquired an additional identity. Women wondered "What ethnicity am I identified with by others, irrespective of what identity I claim for myself, and what does this mean, for both myself and my family, and perhaps my business, residence and occupation?" These issues continue to occupy the public spaces of debate.

There are four reasons why I isolate this story from the myriad of others that were being told around the country about the post-election period. First, it deals with the multiple identities that women assume within specific socio-cultural realities. Second, it deals with the politics of "home" and belonging that is further complicated by the notion of "otherness" through gender, ethnicity and political hostility. Third, it deals with the agility of the story teller to deconstruct margins and the centre, by gliding from the position of the narrator with agency to tell her story, to that of a character constructed by a writer yet who must live within the socio-politics of the day. Finally the character that has been "othered" in this political crisis primarily on account of ethnicity refuses to occupy the margins of otherness, and assumes the centre position by claiming her identity through the location of "home". While on the one hand the implied death of the character at the hands of her people at "home" may indicate total powerlessness, it also suggests the power of the character to shift herself to the centre of belongingness through marriage. It is therefore correct to observe that the character accepts death as a fact of life, and further empowers herself in shifting its cause paradoxically to those traditionally and culturally responsible in preserving the female subject in their capacity as producers, reproducers and nurturers. A sense of satire is drawn when the character agilely participates in her own funeral by fictively cutting down the costs by dying at "home". In other words, the narrator empowers herself by narrating the story of own socio-political power(lessness) constructed through identity situation. By telling their own stories, women shift their situations away from victimhood to claiming agency. The narrator positions herself within the events, looks into the identity politics and power and seizes the opportunity to tell her story.

Conclusion

The point of the whole discussion has been to argue that we must think of identities in the context of process. Any attempt to discuss identity as "being", forecloses the possibility of growth, change, and dynamism. Socio-cultural relationships develop through history, through the accumulation and re-telling of stories that about ourselves and about others. Some of these stories may reflect fear, anxiety or ignorance. Some may develop into stereotypes or mythologies that obscure and deny the reality of others, consequently inhibiting social, cultural and political interaction, experience, tolerance and transformation. This inevitably destroys cultural, social and political dynamism and ultimately destroys society. This paper has been an attempt to re-open the hearths of our socio-cultural and intellectual engagement, about the events we experience, for we are sometimes in the margins and other times in the centre of these events and therefore we must continue to engage with the realities of our multiple identities.

Notes

1 The debate relating to women and men as constantly in struggle with each other has been popularized through the media and the political spheres. Several NGOs, most collaborating under gender research, have raised this competing relationship that often leaves the woman as victim.

2 This paper acknowledges the various genres of literature, from the oral narratives of our foremothers, to the song and dance of our tradition, past and present, to the quilts of our sisters across the oceans, and to "our mothers' gardens" both nurturing and resplendent with artistry, colour and scent.

3 The state of death does not always bring closure, for history has a way of moulding new identities of the dead through memory and attributes. Through folklore and oral tradition for instance, the dead can be brought to life with a capacity to engage with the living through the spirit world. Further yet, the immortalization of the dead through images such as currency notes, iconic images, naming of innate objects, religious statues, even embalming for periodic viewing by the public are some means that are deployed to remember and re-imagine the dead.

4 Directly translated from Kiswahili this phrase means the advancement of women. This 'advancement' is assumed to be at all levels including education.

5 In the post-December 2007 violence, a proliferation of both urban and rural groups 'defending' various interests such as land, property, regions and so on emerged. Most of them operated as gangs without formal structures but executed extreme force and even death to those who stood in their way.

6 Tabitha Kanogo's *Negotiating African Womanhood in Colonial Kenya* in which she discusses the women's political participation from colonial period to the present.

7 Examples are Beth Mugo, Charity Ngilu and Zippora Kittony.

8 Most female politicians confess that they started their political careers from their activities as community mobilizers within their respective often rural communities through the Civil Society sector.

9 One such example is Jesus Alive Ministry's JIAM) Margaret Wanjiru who popularized her church and in effect created national visibility for herself through televangelism; she is now Member of Parliament and Assistant Minister for Housing. Most recently—in October 2009—she has garnered even greater visibility by welcoming into her church Maina Njenga, head of the banned Mungiki gang, after the state withdrew murder charges against him.

10 Tom Odhiambo, Sophie Macharia and Rodger Kurtz for instance, interrogate Margaret Ogola's theme of women's agency, Grace Ogot's redefinition of identities, Marjorie Macgoye's women's empowerment respectively.

References

Amadiume, I. (1987). *Male Daughters Female Husbands: Gender and Sex in an African Society.* London: Zed Books.

Berman, B. & John, L. (1992). *Unhappy Valley: Conflict in Kenya and Africa.* London: James Currey.

Bhavnani, Kum-Kum & Pheonix, A. (1994). *Shifting Identities Shifting Racism: A Feminism & Psychology Reader.* New Delhi: Sage Publications Ltd.

Butler, J. (1990). *Gender Trouble: Feminism and the Subversion of Identity.* New York: Routledge.

Chukukere, G. (1995). *Gender Voices and Choices: Redefining Women in Contemporary African Fiction.* Enugu: Fourth Dimension Publications.

Cornwall, A. ed. (2005). *Readings in Gender in Africa.* Oxford: James Currey.

Davies, C. B. & Graves, A.D. eds. (1986). *Ngambika: Studies of Women in African Literature.* Trenton New Jersey: Africa World Press Inc.

Delgado, C. F. (1997). "Mother Tongues and Childless Women: The Construction of 'Kenyan' 'womanhood'" In Nnaemeka, Obioma. ed. *The Politics of (M)Othering: Womanhood, Identity and Resistance in African Literature.* London and New York: Routledge.

Hall, M. (1990). *Women and Identity: Values in a Changing World.* New York: Hemisphere Publishing Corp.

Hall, S. &. Paul du Gay. eds. (1996). *Questions of Cultural Identity.* London: Sage Publications.

Hay, M. J. & Stichter, S. eds. (1984). *African Women South of the Sahara.* Essex: Longman.

Jones, E. D. et.al. (1987). *Women in African Literature Today No. 15.* Trenton NJ: Africa World Press.

Kabira, W. &. Nzioka, A. (1993). *Celebrating Women's Resistance.* Nairobi: Africa Women's Perspectives.

Kibera, V. (1991). "Adopted Motherlands: The Novels of Marjorie Macgoye and Bessie Head" In Nasta, Susheila. (ed.) *Motherlands: Black Women's Writing from Africa, the Caribbean and South Asia.* London: Women's Press.

Kurtz, R. (1998). *Urban Obsessions, Urban Fears: The Postcolonial Kenyan Novel.* Trenton: Africa World Press.

Lonsdale, J. & Berman, B. (1992). *Unhappy Valley: Conflict in Kenya and Africa Book One.* Nairobi: Heinemann.

Maharaj, Z. (Spring, 1995). "A Social Theory of Gender: Connell's 'Gender and Power'". *Feminist Review, No. 49, Feminist Politics: Colonial/Postcolonial Worlds,* pp. 50–65.

Mohanty, C. &. (1991). *Third World Women and the Politics of Feminism.* Indianapolis: Indiana University Press.

Mudimbe, V. (1988). *The Invention of Africa.* Bloomington: Indiana University Press.

Nasta, S. ed. (1991). *Motherlands: Black Women's Writing from Africa, the Caribbean and South Asia.* London: Women's Press.

Nelson, N. (2002). "Representations of Men and Women, City and Town in Kenyan Novels of the 1970s and 1980s" In Newell, Stephanie. ed. *Readings in Africa Popular Fiction.* Indiana: James Currey.

Nfah-Abbenyi, J. (1997). *Gender in African Women's Writing: Identity, Sexuality and Difference.* Bloomington: Indiana University Press.

Nnaemeka, O. ed. (1997). *The Politics of (M)Othering: Womanhood, Identity and Resistance in African Literature.* London: Routledge.

O'Barr, J. & Firmin-Sellers, K. (1984). "African Women in Politics" In Hay, Margaret J. and Stichter Sharon. eds. *African Women South of the Sahara.* Essex: Longman.

O'Barr, J. (1987). "Feminist Issues in the Fiction of Kenya's Women Writers" In Jones et.al. *Women in African Literature Today No.15.* London: Africa World Press.

Sharp, G. (1973). *The Politics of Nonviolent Action.* Boston: Porter Sargent.

Stratton, F. (1994). *Contemporary African Literature and their Politics of Gender.* London: Routledge.

Tripp, M. A. (2003). "Women in Movement: Transformations in African Political Landscapes" In Cornwall Andrea. (ed.) (2005) *Readings in Gender in Africa.* Oxford: James Currey.

Walker, A. (1983). *In Search of our Mother's Gardens.* New York: Women's Press.

Werbner, R. &. Ranger, T. eds. (1996). *Postcolonial Identities in Africa.* London: Zed Books Ltd.

Freedom

Cross-media Ownership and the Monopolizing of Public Spaces in Kenya

FREDERICK K. IRAKI[1]

Yet, television, and other media, tends to destroy the very public space of dialogue they open up, through relentless trivializing, and personalizing of political issues. Moreover, the growth of giant multinational media corporations means that unelected business tycoons can hold enormous power.

—Giddens, 1999.

Kenyan media: A brief history
Media in colonial Kenya

Ochieng (1992) asserts that the oldest newspaper in Kenya, *The African standard*, sprung up in 1902 as a monthly paper in Mombasa[2] under the ownership of an Asian named A.M. Jeevanjee[3]. W.H. Tiller, the paper editor, took an anti-colonialism stand against the establishment, as a result of which the owner, Jeevanjee, too humiliated, decided to sell it to Anderson and Mayer. The two businessmen renamed it *The East African Standard*. After that then the paper was to propagate white settler interests in East Africa.

Other less significant newspapers linked to *The East African Standard* included *Baraza* (1939), *Mombasa Times, The Tanganyika Standard* (1930) established in the 1930s (Mbuthia, 1995). Mbuthia further argues that even the East African Broadcasting Corporation established in 1927 was an extension of British colonial interests. On their part Asians started a series of ill-fated newspapers such as *Samachar* (1902), *The Kenya Daily Mail* (1926 *The Colonial Times, Daily Chronicle* (edited by the late Pio Gama Pinto), *Tribune,* and *The Observer* (Mbuthia, 1995).

African politicians created a few publications but in view of British hostility, coupled with lack of editorial training, these were short-lived. They included Jomo Kenyatta's *Mũigwithania* (The arbiter), 1928–1934, Henry Mũoria's, *Mũmenyereri* (The Caretaker), 1945, *Ramogi* and *Nyanza Times* edited by Achieng' Oneko and Jaramogi Oginga Odinga[4]. The African newspapers aimed at providing a voice to African political grievances.

The pressing concerns of the oppressed Kenyans were muted and therefore insignificant in the colonial newspapers. Put differently, there was only one point of view in the media, i.e. the colonial master's standpoint since the African media had imploded. This absence of a variety of voices presumably undermined the concept of democracy. However, in the late 1950s and early 1960s, the African media scene bounced back, this time with more staying power.

According to Ochieng (1992) Charles Hayes established the *Taifa*, a weekly Swahili paper, in 1958. Two years later, Michael Curtis acting at the behest of Prince Karim Aga Khan, created the East African Newspapers Limited and purchased *Taifa* from Hayes. The *Sunday Nation* and shortly after the *Daily Nation* were launched the same year)[5]. Ideologically, the Nation Group publications marked a departure from the settler newspapers as they sought to provide a voice to the silenced Africans. They thus represented the voice against colonial oppression and subjugation. In other words, they were the Kenyan

African voice. Indeed on 12 December 1963, these papers screamed loudly in their headlines about Kenya's ultimate independence. Here the link between the media and politics became more and more apparent. Further, it can be noted that the monopoly enjoyed by the settler publications was neutered by the entry of the East African Newspapers (Nation Series of newspapers) Limited. Henceforth, the Kenyan people could read about other opinions other than colonial propaganda.

In 1964, Hilary Ng'weno, a Kenyan African, became the first African editor-in-chief of the Nation papers. In contrast, *The East African Standard* only appointed its first African editor, Mr. Henry Gathigira, in 1975. Oblivious of Kenya's political independence, the paper had "continued in its great white way" (Barton 1969; Ainslie 1966; Mwaura 1980; cited in Mbuthia (1995)).

Media in Independent Kenya
Since 1963, the most visible, influential and stable newspapers were *The Standard, Taifa Leo* and the *Daily Nation*. The Kenyatta government (1963–1978) had no newspaper to inform, educate or entertain its people, but rather it had the sole monopoly of airwaves via its two main mouthpieces: Voice of Kenya (VOK) radio and television. These two media had nation-wide coverage, hence their great potency in shaping public opinion across the land. Although, a television set was the privilege of the well-heeled for many years, the radio was more accessible to the low-income groups. In fact, in some instances, a single transistor radio could be listened to by more than ten people. This means that the radio was the more powerful of the two instruments in shaping the opinions of Kenyans around issues, especially their government.

It can be further argued that in view of the high levels of illiteracy among citizens before and after the Kenyatta years, most Kenyans depended on information from the radio. This meant that since VOK was a government appendage, most people only heard the government side of the story, be it facts or sheer propaganda.

It is worth noting the presence of other important publications such as *The Weekly Review* established in 1975 by Hilary Ng'weno. Ng'weno also founded the *Nairobi Times*, a paper that was subsequently sold to the ruling party, the Kenya African National Union (KANU) in 1983 (Ochieng 1992).

Media, multipartism, globalization, liberalization & cross-media ownership
The fall of the Berlin Wall and the implosion of the Soviet Union in 1989 ushered

in a new wave of changes across the globe. In Kenya, the clamour for political pluralism gained a new momentum amidst unmitigated hostility from the Moi Regime (1978–2002). Ultimately, Section 2A was removed from the Kenyan Constitution in 1991 paving the way for multiparty politics.[6]

The new political dispensation ushered in some changes in the media topography. The Kenya Media Trust established the Kenya Television Network in 1990. Soon after, the Nation Media Group (NMG) established Nation Television (NTV). NMG further added an FM station, Easy FM. Later, Royal Media Services introduced Citizen Radio and Television, and a host of vernacular radio stations. The ten years between 1992 and 2002 saw a proliferation of vernacular FM stations providing all sorts of opinions on issues of the day. Other papers that sprung up during and after the "Second Liberation" include *The People Daily, The Leader*[7], *The Nairobi Star* (now *The Star*), etc.

The proliferation of media outlets appears like a prima facie case for the blossoming of democracy. It is assumed that the presence of many media outlets translates into plurality of voices and therefore fairness (democracy) in a country. This position is problematic in the light of two critical issues, namely the role of the media in practical terms and media ownership i.e. who owns the media and what is their agenda?

Critique of the role of the media

Mwita (2009:20) observes that in the literature on media as an agent of democracy, the media is expected to play a watchdog role on behalf of the public by pointing out the wrongs of the government and showing the way forward. In this view, the media keep "the rest on the straight and narrow path, serving the public interest, defending the common good at all times."

However, another view, this time Marxist, perceives the media as an integral part of the system whose role is to protect the interests of the rich (politicians, merchants and the landed class) against the wishes of the poor.

Mwita further provides another view from Herman and Chomsky that is not dissimilar from the Marxist viewpoint. In their book, *Manufacturing Consent: The Political Economy of the Mass Media*, the authors claim that the mass media are "effective and powerful ideological institutions that carry out a system-supportive *propaganda* function..." (Our emphasis).

What role do the media play in Kenya? Can media be an agent of democracy, or are they merely a tool for protecting the interests of the rich/the government? Nyamnjoh (2005:1) notes that "The media [...] can in principle, facilitate popular empowerment as a societal project". He further argues that for the media to achieve its watchdog role, the liberal democracy model has to be domesticated to reflect African realities and sensitivities (Nyamnjoh 2005:27).

In Kenya, it can be argued that media play both roles—watchdog and agent of the bourgeoisie—at various times. Ochieng (1992) demonstrates out how media have been at the forefront exposing scandals and other ills that need to be addressed by the government. However, he also provides instances where media act at the behest of powerful politicians or media owners to distort the truth. This means that it is important that we understand who owns/controls the media as a necessary first step to understanding how the media operate in Kenya.

Cross-media ownership. An attempt at definition.
A document entitled CROSS-MEDIA OWNERSHIP[8] issued by the Radio Authority to restrict controlling interests in both newspapers and radio services in the United Kingdom takes for granted that the concept is self-explanatory and therefore offers no definition of the expression. However, the authority finds it appropriate to define the term *newspaper*. Among the restrictions, we read in Part IV schedule 2 part 3:

> National newspaper groups with 20% or more of the national newspaper market are prohibited from holding a licence to provide a national or local radio service.

In an article entitled *Cross-media Ownership*, Asim Kumar Mitra[9] argues that:

> If any branch of media holds a stake in other media e.g. broadcast or television, it will be in a position to control the opinions of a large section of people which will ultimately injure the very root of pluralism in democracy.

According to CBC news of 15 January 2008, the Canadian broadcast regulator, CRTC, has broached "new regulations to restrict cross-media ownership as a way of ensuring a diversity of editorial voices in the same market." It further states that "in future, a person or entity will be permitted to control only two of the three types of media outlets—radio, TV, or newspapers."

David Flint in an article entitled *A dangerous dinosaur*[10] observes that "the purpose of cross media rules is to make media barons choose between being a 'Prince of Print' or 'Queen of the Screen'." From these citations of the Radio Authority in the UK, Asim, CRTC and Flint it can be safely surmised that the concept of cross-media ownership brings to the fore notions of *control, monopoly, regulation, plurality or diversity of voices, and democracy* in the arena of the media. Control and monopoly appear to be antithetical to plurality or diversity of voices and therefore detrimental to the concept of democracy. For the purposes of this article, cross-media ownership is a situation where a media house or a person owns more than one media outlet. We now turn to Kenya to analyze how cross-media ownership plays out.

Cross-media ownership in Kenya

In the introduction we traced the history of the media in Kenya and placed the genesis of political and media pluralism in the late 1980s. The floodgates of political pluralism opened the way for the media houses to venture into new media outlets. Let us examine the main media houses that have spread their wings to other media investments (radio, TV, etc.)[11].

The Nation Media Group (NMG)

The Nation Media Group (hereinafter as NMG) owns *Taifa Leo, Daily Nation, Sunday Nation, The Daily Metro, The East African* in the newspapers category. The first two are dailies while the other two are weeklies. The *Daily Nation* is arguably the most read newspaper in Kenya. *The East African* and the *Sunday Nation* are not as old as the first two. The former is read in the East African region as the name suggests. It is also noteworthy that NMG has its papers available on the Internet.

In the early 1990s, NMG acquired a television station, NTV, with coverage limited to the City of Nairobi. Currently it is available in all the major towns in Kenya. The station, like all the rest, presents news in Kiswahili and English, educational and entertainment programmes. With FM stations cropping up of large numbers in the 2000s, NMG secured radio on FM wavelength and thus the birth of *EasyFM* that provides abbreviated news, commentaries and mainly music entertainment.

His Highness the Aga Khan, the Ismailia spiritual head, is the major shareholder of NMG[12]. Politically, NMG enjoys relative objectivity and it is not associated with any of the current political camps, Orange Democratic Movement (ODM) and Party of National Unity (PNU). In terms of circulation, the *Daily Nation* has had a lead as compared to her competition.[13]

Indeed, a recent survey by Steadman Group (2008) indicates that the Nation has 23% of the newspaper daily readership market. The next serious contender, *The East African Standard*, has 10%. *Taifa Leo* and *Business Daily* (offshoots of NMG) have 6% and 1 % respectively. Quite clearly NMG has the lion's share in the newspaper category. It can thus be argued that the NMG—when the radio and Television outlets are added—has a monopoly on information flow. This means that most Kenyans only hear the opinion or voice of one media owner, the NMG. If democracy, as we contend above entails the concept of "plurality of divergent voices", then NMG poses a serious threat to the entire process. Let us now look at the Standard Group of papers, NMG's rival for the Kenyan market.

The East African Standard (EAS)
The *East African Standard* (EAS) does not enjoy an assemblage of newspapers like the NMG. It is the only newspaper in the Standard Group. Although its ancestor, *The African Standard,* as we have shown in the introduction is the oldest paper in Kenya, the readership at 10% remains small though not insignificant.

The ownership of the EAS is shrouded in mystery. In an article entitled *Will the real owner stand up?* in Expression Today (ET)[14], Otsieno Namwaya chronicles the vicissitudes of *The Kenya Times* newspaper which are eventually linked to the ownership of EAS and the Kenya Television Network (KTN). Away from company names such as Kenya Times Media Trust (KTMT), the ownership of Standard Group Limited brings to the fore names such as Daniel Arap Moi (second Kenyan president) and his lieutenants, Gideon Moi and Joshua Kullei (Mwita 2009).

The Standard Group was the first to launch a private television network, KTN, in 1990. The mystery surrounding the ownership of these media could be attributed to the fact that Daniel Arap Moi, a major shareholder in the KTMT, was the supremo of KANU (ruling political party) and president of the Republic of Kenya until 2002.

Although the paper demonstrates relative editorial autonomy, it cannot be said that it can ignore the interests of its owners.

The Royal Media Services
Royal Media Services has Citizen Radio and Citizen Television. The radio division is best-known for introducing myriad FM band radio stations for vernacular broadcasts (news, commentaries and entertainment). These include *Mulembe FM* (Luhyia), *Radio Ramogi* (Luo), *Inooro* (Gĩkũyũ), just to mention a few; in total RMS owns 13 such vernacular radio stations.

The television station started with a bang poaching the best journalists (news presenters, anchors, etc) from across NTV and KTN thus clearing the field for its own ferocious entry. *The Leader* newspaper was also added to this impressive collection of media outlets. However, after the 2007 general elections, the paper folded up. Apparently, it had already served its purpose of supporting the Kibaki re-election. Royal Media Services is owned by Mr. S.K. Macharia whose political sympathies lie with the Kibaki administration.

Kiss FM, Classic FM, Radio Jambo, East FM and The Star

Kiss FM, undoubtedly one of the most popular stations with the youth, sprung up around the same period of liberalizing the airwaves in Kenya. The station has had a number of clashes with the political class with some ending up in litigation[15]. *Classic FM* supplements *Kiss FM*. *The Star* (previously known as *The Nairobi Star*) is a recent newspaper with a national coverage but its readership is relatively small at 1% (Steadman Group 2008). The radio stations and the paper belong to Radio Africa and the personalities behind it are the Kittony family, Patrick Quarcoo and William Pike (Mwita 2009:75). Politically, the outlets are relatively neutral, occasionally lashing out at the government of the day.

Kenya Broadcasting Corporation (KBC)[16]

The Kenya Broadcasting Corporation, a state entity, had a monopoly of radio and television services until the advent of political pluralism in the early 1990s. It owns and runs the KBC radio and KBC *Channel 1* both that enjoy nation-wide coverage.

In the 1983, the ruling party KANU under Moi introduced a daily newspaper, *The Kenya Times,* to counter what it perceived as political subversion from the *Daily Nation* and the *Standard* newspapers. The paper became the political mouthpiece of the government making obvious the claim that newspapers are often tools for propaganda[17]. The newspaper's readership waned considerably as the Moi regime set its eyes on acquiring *The Standard*. Once this was done it was no longer necessary to channel the government voice via the obvious government newspaper; *The Standard* newspaper provided the Moi clique with a private organ to voice its political agenda.

KBC also boasts of a number of vernacular radio stations on AM frequencies. These have been there for more than 30 years. But it also has FM radio, *coro FM* broadcasting in the Gĩkũyũ language.

Currently, none of the political parties in the grand coalition owns a newspaper for any of the political parties forming the Grand Coalition. The *Kenya Times* ceased to be the government paper after Mwai Kibaki won the presidency on a Narc[18] ticket in 2002. Politically, KBC supports the government of the day although the editors enjoy relative autonomy in collecting and disseminating news. We now turn briefly to discuss the more elusive notion of monopoly in the context of the media.

Monopoly in the media and in the political economy

The *Oxford Advanced Learners Dictionary* defines monopoly as 1) sole right to supply or trade in some commodity or service and 2) sole possession or control of something. Within the context of our discussion, monopoly seems to apply as follows.

First, the colonial government employed *The East African Standard* and *Baraza* to rationalize its colonial occupation of Kenya. The papers thus had a monopoly of information, mainly government propaganda. At the onset of independence, Voice of Kenya (VoK) continued to be the sole provider of television and radio services, a monopolistic tendency that was only arrested in the 1990s. Politically this position afforded unfair advantage to the government in relaying information to the people. In a society with relatively low literacy levels in the period after independence, television and radio were by far more influential in shaping opinions than newspapers.

In the arena of print media, the dominant role (read quasi-monopolistic) of *The Nation* deserves special mention. Coming in as the voice of Africans (read Kenyans), *The Nation* enjoyed a place of pride among Kenyan readers. In independent Kenya, the newspaper came to be identified with revealing the excesses of the Kenyatta government and subsequent regimes. This adversarial role appears to be the prototypical raison d'être of the American press. In *Government and the media*, Ithiel de Sola Pool[19] observes that most journalists' books on government defend the following theory:

1. The media are the people's tribune against government oppression.
2. Media and government are adversaries.
3. A journalist should, therefore, publish whatever he can learn, however damaging to the government.

The Nation and *The Standard* seemed to echo this very same theory. The two newspapers kept the government in check despite the latter's monopoly of television and radio outlets. They had begun to define the Fourth Estate and its privileges and responsibilities, chief among which is serving as a custodian of public interests.

Macharia Munene in *The Media, Ethics and National Interests*[20] notes that:

> As a custodian, it [journalism] tends to refer to itself as the Fourth Estate, meaning that it is part of the elite power structure in any given place. It is not a constitutionally established branch of government as are the executive, the legislature, and the judiciary but it wields a lot of power and sometimes more power than the official branches and so it subsequently arrogated to itself that title.

The rationale of the Moi government in establishing *The Kenya Times* and later insinuating itself in the ownership of *The Standard* newspaper and KTN station becomes clearer now. The government was facing the unwieldy onslaught of the media and decided to counteract it using its own version of journalism that would negate the assertion alluded to by Ithiel above.

In terms of monopoly, none of the three newspapers could claim to be the *sole* source of news. However, at one time the government decided that all state contracts would only be advertised in *The Kenya Times*. This announcement was meant to attract more readers for the government newspaper. Indeed, there was an upsurge of readership as most business people had to buy a copy of the newspaper in search of government jobs and contracts[21]. However, the upsurge in readership did little to dent the sales figures of *The Nation* and *The Standard* (Ochieng 1992:151). The point to make here is that three newspapers were in open competition to shape the opinions of Kenyans. However it should not be forgotten that *The Nation* was by far the most popular newspaper, thereby enjoying a quasi-monopoly (Ochieng, *ibid*).

Political pluralism, media explosion and control

With the advent of political pluralism where there is a diversity of political thoughts and formations, Kenya has witnessed an explosion of media outlets. The palette of electronic media today includes KBC, NTV, KTN, BBC, CNN, Sky news, DSTV, Aljazeera and Citizen just to mention a few but the newspaper domain has grown modestly to include *The People Daily* and *The Star*. The main newspapers remain DN, EAS, *Taifa Leo* and *The East African*[22]. It seems as though competition on the political plane is replicated at the media level. But competition can be either fair or unfair. In the case of Kenya the various media houses, including the government, are locked in a fierce competition whose rules are yet to be defined clearly to avert unfairness and promote equity and democracy.

Cross-Media ownership and democracy

We will not split hairs with a definition of democracy but it will suffice for our purposes here to say that it is a system of government by the majority of the people through their elected representatives. Defined as such democracy creates room for equity or fairness, equal representation, plurality of opinions and a sense of justice (more difficult to define).

In the discussion above, we described the media as the custodian of public interest. In this perspective then the media becomes an essential ingredient of democracy as it champions the interests of the people. Nonetheless, it can be argued that when and if cross-media ownership becomes a monopoly then the diversity of points of view, the very glue of democracy, is substituted by a singularity of thought. This bias could undermine democracy.

Writing on the notion of bias Ithiel De Sola Pool (1976) argues that a journalist is inexorably faced with the dilemma of describing an event since *describing* means *selecting* some things and leaving others. Unfortunately, social research shows that selection is value-laden. Faced with this descriptive dilemma, one begins to appreciate the value of having a diversity of sources of information since the values of one newspaper may not necessarily reflect those of rival newspapers or electronic media outlets.

In the Kenyan scenario, the culprits for cross-media ownership would comprise the Kenya Broadcasting Corporation (KBC), Nation Media Group (NMG), The Standard Group, Royal Media Services, and to a less degree Radio Africa and Capital FM. But the relevant question here is the impact of the cross-ownership on democracy. Clearly none of the entities mentioned here can be said to be the sole source of information, be it for educational or entertainment purposes. Kenyans can access news from a variety of sources including foreign news via the Internet.

The internet has become a fertile ground for gathering and disseminating information. Through blogs, Facebook emails and Twitter. Kenyans can source and comment on topical political, economic as well as social issues. For instance, during the 2002 and 2007 General elections, most Kenyans learnt of the results through mobile phones, not the conventional media. The internet blogs and emails allow Kenyans to read and comment on issues that conventional media houses prefer to ignore.

It is important to mention the alternative press in Kenya that is looked down upon by the established media houses. Although publications of the alternative press category (disparagingly referred to as 'gutter press' or 'rags') may not have the financial stability of the big papers, they invariably come up with stories that are later confirmed by the bigger papers. These papers despite, their editorial inadequacies—poor training and vested interests—are alive and kicking in Kenya.

The Constitution of Kenya provides unequivocally for freedom of expression. This freedom, although threatened for a long time by monolithic KANU politics before 1992 through detentions and torture, guarantees Kenyans the right to express themselves without fear. This right is more evident in the light of numerous media outlets present in the country. Press freedom seems to naturally arise from the freedom of expression. But can both freedoms also jeopardize democracy? We answer in the affirmative since freedom without responsibility is a recipe for anarchy. The question for us is whether there is any need to curb cross-media ownership in Kenya.

Curbing cross-media ownership

Asim Kumar Mitra (*op.cit*) argues in the same article that in 2006 India was contemplating introducing the Broadcast Regulation Bill to "control so many unwanted developments which have negated the basic motto of journalism i.e. free flow of news among the citizen (*sic*)". He provides examples of monopoly of news claiming that in the US, two TV channels (NBC and CBS) are owned by "corporations involved in arms manufacture and nuclear power (General Electric and Westinghouse)." Further, Times-Warner and CNN merged in the late 1990s to create a media monopoly, while Rupert Murdoch remains the largest owner of television stations in the US. Such monopolistic tendencies provide one source of news and invariably one point of view and mainly the standpoint, moral or political, of the media owner.

Flint (op.cit) argued that for the Australian context there was no need for extra cross media rules but rather "laws to encourage diversity and pluralism, which encourage new entrants." He further argues that "governments are the last people (sic) who should determine who owns what in the media." The last remark is interesting since it underscores the lack of trust in government among citizens of Australia. The observation rings very true of Kenyans.
Konrad von Finckenstein, chair of CRTC in Canada while commenting on the need to curb cross-media ownership opined that "It is an approach that will preserve the plurality of editorial voices and the diversity of programming available to Canadians [...] while allowing for a strong and competitive industry."[23]

In Kenya, unlike the UK where the Audit Bureau of Circulations (ABC) provides accurate statistics on "share of voices" among the media outlets, it is challenging to gauge the reach of any one particular newspaper[24], radio or television in terms of percentages. In fact, the restrictions enacted by the Radio Authority in the UK are very clear on the manner in which to avoid monopolistic behaviour among media companies. For instance, part 10(i) of the guidelines reads as follows:

> Local newspaper groups with 50% or more of the local newspaper market within the coverage area of a local radio service may not own that service, if that service is the only local radio service (on either waveband) in that area.

This rule, it appears, averts monopoly of news by a big paper that may want to own the only radio service available in the same area. This creates room for what Flint and Konrad are referring to in terms of *diversity, plurality of voices* and allowing for a strong competitive industry. It affirms Assim's greatest fear of having a monolithic source of news.

From the foregoing, it seems desirable that Kenya should also enact similar rules to those in the Radio Authority in the UK to promote the values described above that underpin a democratic dispensation. This calls for more accurate determination of market shares in terms of voices rather than arbitrary percentages. It is necessary to carry out detailed surveys to determine the share of voices for each of the media players in Kenya as a preliminary study of cross-media ownership and its implications on monopoly and democracy in Kenya. The argument here does not in any way suggest that cross-media ownership is a bad thing *per se*; rather unbridled cross-ownership could undermine democracy by negating pluralism of voices and equity via unfair competition between media outlets.

Media regulation
Due to the adversarial role of the press in Kenya *vis-à-vis* the government of the day, the latter has always sought ways and means of taming the former. But the questions we pose here are: (1) Does the media in Kenya need regulation? (2) Who should regulate the media, the government or the press council?

The question of whether or not the media should be regulated seems rhetorical to some extent. In a functional democracy, it is inconceivable that any constitutive body operating ostensibly in the interest of the public should be allowed to conduct its business without any form of check or restraint from the same public it purports to serve. The separation of powers (executive, legislative and judiciary) serves a critical role in quality assurance providing a sure way of checking the excesses of each of the arms of government. The media, if we grant them the title of the Fourth Estate, comes in naturally as the other "arm of government" that checks the other three in the interest of the public. In this case is it desirable that the other branches of government should also be involved in checking the excesses of the media?

First, it is clear that according to the Kenyan Constitution no-one is above the law. Therefore, media have to operate within the province of the Kenyan legal framework. Instances of defamation, slander, larceny (in the name of securing secretive documents) are well-known cases of the Kenyan jurisprudence where media are called to account for their deeds before the law.

Second, media operate within the purview of the freedom of expression when they assert the so-called press freedom. The media thus become a platform for the public to air their views about virtually anything under the sun provided that their actions are not inconsistent with other provisions of the Constitution (see defamation for example). In other words, freedom cannot be unconditional. John C. Merill (1974) is opposed to this view. He asserts that press freedom is autonomous and should not be linked to responsibility. One cannot help wondering what would happen in society if all freedoms guaranteed in the Bill of Rights had no limitations or implications of responsibility. The very essence of a right would be significantly eroded and ultimately rendered nonsensical.

Third, and this is contestable, there are instances where the media are seen to serve the interests, not of the Kenyan public, but of foreign agencies (read governments). While commenting on press coverage of the post-electoral violence after the December 2007 General Election in Kenya, Wanjohi Kabukuru records in his article *Kenya: spare us the agony and bias* the obvious negative bias by the Western media, namely *The Economist*, BBC and CNN. The writer further notes that:

> "..the Kenyan media, which openly took sides during the December elections, has been engaged in its own soul-searching, trying to find out where it went wrong".[25]

Indeed, the ethnicisation of the December 2007 election and attendant conflict seemed to have been effected by foreign media houses working in cahoots with Kenyan journalists. The conflict was more on age-old political, economic and social injustices rather than "tribalism" as reported in the media.

Macharia-Munene (*op. cit*) is even more blunt about media and national interests. He asserts:

> [...] the Kenyan media are unable to look after Kenyan's (sic) national interests because they have what amounts to a *master-client* relationship with foreign media or "missionaries". That

relationship is one in which Kenyan media tend to be recipients and conveyor belts of foreign values and interests in the name of news and programs but they are not supposed to project Kenyan values and interests in the home countries of the "missionaries".

Werner A. Meier in *Media Ownership—Does it matter?*[26] argues that while playing a "powerful democratising" role, the media can also contradict the same role. He quotes Giddens (1999) who observes that:

> Yet, television, and other media, tends to destroy the very public space of dialogue they open up, through relentless trivializing, and personalizing of political issues. Moreover, the growth of giant multinational media corporations means that unelected business tycoons can hold enormous power.

Clearly, Werner echoes the concern expressed above on cross-media ownership and monopoly where a small group controls what the people see, read and hear. In the case of Kenya, The Aga Khan, S.K. Macharia, Quarcoo and Arap Moi's clique, or KBC for that matter, could single-handedly or in a duopoly provide Kenyans with a single perspective, thereby stifling any other voices. Clearly, such a scenario threatens public interest and therefore undermines democracy.

If the arguments above are valid in Kenya, then it is natural that the media should be held in check by one mechanism or another to safeguard the interests of the public and enhance democracy. While the first two instances above can be dealt with by the laws of Kenya, the last set of arguments are harder to apprehend within the law. Cross-media ownership can be addressed using laws governing competition in business but other issues like pushing a foreign agenda, focusing on trivia or "majoring on minors and minoring on majors" where important issues are trivialized and flimsy ones afforded prominence in news is a much trickier enterprise.

The question of who should regulate the media has been a subject of much controversy in Kenya. When the government hinted at the idea the media and the public became extremely suspicious of the authorities. The prevailing ethos was that the government was bent on curtailing the freedom of expression for the public and *ipso facto* it was keen on "muzzling the press". According to this logic then nobody trusted the government's motives. Nevertheless, as the tempers cooled off, the public (and some journalists too) saw the sense of having responsible press freedom. The issue was not suppression or muzzling of the press but ensuring responsible behaviour by journalists over and above legal matters. The question became more an ethical rather than legal one. But the government has little say on ethical matters hence the need for an independent body to address them when they arise.

The Media Council, a press body in Kenya, has tried its level best to uphold responsible, ethical and value journalism in Kenya. But its mandate and scope does not seem to go beyond reprimanding. To many Kenyans, the Media Council is impotent in the face of awesome corporate media interests, chief among which is control and manipulation of Kenyan minds. In India and Canada, the Press Council fares no better as it has little more than *advisory* power to media conglomerates that wield immense economic and therefore political power.

It is apparent that a Media Council may be a good idea but it needs sharp teeth to be able to check wayward journalists and media houses. For instance, it would have been extremely helpful if the Media Council had tried to publicly warn media houses that were fanning the embers of ethnic bigotry in the run-up to the December 2007 General Election and after in Kenya. Its deafening silence as the Kenyan public was fed with unchecked stories and impressionistic images underscores its limited efficacy and therefore legitimacy in a complex media scenario. It might not be purely speculative that the Council itself was a victim of the same manipulation by the media.

The Media Council in Kenya should assert itself on all ethical matters touching on the content, quality and format of information channelled to the public by the media. Of particular concern are the numerous polls conducted by media houses. These do not in the main follow established rules of conducting a poll and therefore they remain impressionistic and erroneous. Some polls especially those conducted by Steadman & Associates (now Synovate) do respect sound research parameters[27]. The Media Council should protect the public from poll fraudsters and promote well-grounded scientific research methods in carrying out opinion polls.

Conclusion

The media scene in Kenya has undergone significant mutations following the expansion of democratic space in the early 1990s. The advent of political pluralism in 1992 signalled a new era of political freedom in Kenya. The corollary of the opening up of political arenas was the liberalization of the media. The latter has lead to rapid expansion of media investments to form giant firms like NMG, Standard Group, Royal Media Services and Radio Africa among others. The media companies have also ventured into television, cyber newspapers, and FM radio hence the need to address the issue of crossmedia ownership.

We have argued here that to the extent that media companies operate within the confines of the laws of the land, there might be no cause for alarm. These laws should be examined to determine whether they can cater for unfair competition or exclusion of other parties keen on joining the media domain.

However if the media are perceived as a democratising phenomenon, opening up more and more spaces for public dialogue and engagement, then it might be salutary to put measures in place to curb cross-media ownership that may lead to monopoly of information. The latter move would torpedo the entire democratic process by having one or two media conglomerates determining what the people should hear, read, see and not see, hear, read.

Finally the ethical question of who should watch over the media could be resolved by reconfiguring the current Media Council with a view to equipping it with sufficient authority to rein in irresponsible journalism. As it stands today, it is more ornamental than effective and therefore media houses will have no effective or responsible regulation.

Notes

1 I am indebted to Adelaide, my research assistant, for the excellent background work for this paper.
2 Mombasa was then the headquarters of the British East African Protectorate.
3 Some academics argue that *Habari za Mwezi* is the oldest newspaper, published in the 18th century in Lamu (personal communication from Dr. Alfred Mutua, journalist and Spokesman of the Kenyan government).
4 The doyen of opposition politics and father to Raila Odinga, Kenya's current Prime Minister under the Grand Coalition government with Mwai Kibaki.
5 Currently, they belong to the Nation Media Group (NMG).
6 The section had been inserted into the Constitution by the Moi regime in 1982 to create a *de jure* one-party state.
7 The paper is no longer in circulation. It is common in Kenya to have sporadic papers that support a political candidate before elections but then fold up soon after. *The Leader* was clearly a pro-Kibaki publication before and during the 2007 General Elections.
8 See www.ofcom.org.uk.
9 http://www.organiser.org\dynamic.
10 See www.presscouncil.org.au\pcsite\apcnews\aug95\dinosaur.
11 *The People Daily* has been less impressive than its weekly predecessor, *The People*. It has no other outlets and is owned by Kenneth Matiba, Moi's arch-rival in the 1992 General Election.
12 He owns 51% of the shares.
13 In 1992, the Nation, The Standard and The Kenya Times had circulation figures of 200,000, 50,000 and 40,000 (Ochieng 1992).
14 *Expression Today* of August-September 2009.
15 The main presenter, Caroline Mutoko, locked horns with Hon. Martha Karua, then Justice Minister, who sued the radio station for defamation. The matter was settled out of court.
16 Previously known as Voice of Kenya (VoK).
17 Under one party rule, the party was the government and the government was the party. Therefore *The Kenya Times* could be described as both a party and government paper. The paper had been bought from Hilary Ng'weno when it operated as *The Nairobi Times*.
18 National Rainbow Coalition (NARC) formed from the radical elements of KANU, Labour Democratic Party, Social Democratic Party of Kaluki Ngilu and the conservative Democratic Party of Kibaki. Kibaki trounced Uhuru Kenyatta of KANU.
19 In The *American Political Science Review*, Vol. 70, No. 4 (Dec. 1976), pp. 1234–1241.
20 *In Journal of Language, Technology & Entrepreneurship*, inaugural issue, pp. 151–164.
21 The government is normally the biggest source of lucrative contracts.
22 A case can be made for duopoly since NMG and EAS dominate the media scene; KBC being considered an organ of government propaganda.
23 http://www.democraticunderground.com/discuss. The article is entitled 'CRTC imposes cross-media ownership restrictions, Tuesday January 2008.
24 The Report by the Kenya Media Sector Analysis (2008) provides very solid information on newspaper readership but it does not provide percentages for radio and television stations.
25 See June 2008 issue of *NewAfrican* entitled *Exposed: Western Media bias against Africa*.
26 Cited in http://lirne.net\resources\netknowledge\meier.pdf.
27 The accuracy of their findings, it seems, depends on one's political inclination. When they favour ODM, PNU fans dismiss them as fabricated and vice-versa.

References

Ainslie, R. (1966). *The Press in Africa: Communications, Past and Present*. London: Trinity Press.
Barton, F. (1979). *The Press of Africa: Persecution and Perseverance*. London: MacMillan.
Ithiel, D. S. (1976). Government and Media in *The American Political Science Review, Vol. 70, No. 4*, pp. 1234–1241.
Mbuthia, J. (1995). *Coverage of Science in the Kenyan Daily Press*. Unpublished MA Dissertation. University of Wales.
Merril, C. (1974). *The Imperative of Freedom: A Philosophy of Journalistic Autonomy*. NY: Hastings House.
Mwaura, P. (1980). *Communications Policies in Kenya*. UNESCO series on policies. UNESCO.
Mwita, C. (2009). *Citizen Power: A Different Kind of Politics, A Different Kind of Journalism*. Nairobi: Global Africa Corporation Ltd.
Nyamnjoh, F. (2005). *Africa's Media: Democracy & the Politics of Belonging*. London: Zed Books Ltd.
Ochieng, P. (1992). *I Accuse the Press*. Nairobi: Initiatives Publishers.
The Kenya Media Sector Analysis, 2008.

The Politics of Media Culture and Media Culture Politics

KARAMBU RINGERA

Culture is about relationality—the relationships among individuals within groups, between groups and among groups and between ideas and perspectives. Culture is concerned with identity, aspiration, symbolic exchange, coordination and structures and practices that serve relational ends such as ethnicity, heritage, norms, meanings and beliefs. It is not a set of primordial phenomena permanently embedded within national or religious or other groups but rather a set of contested attributes, constantly in flux, both shaping and being shaped by social and economic aspects of human interaction.

—Rao & Walton, 2004.

This paper engages the politics of media culture within the framework of the question of which ethic, between 'freedom' and 'regulation', should govern the media infrastructure in Kenya. The premise of the paper questions the reality and applicability of these terms in a conflict situation. The notion of a media culture of freedom and regulation is a myth that needs to be re-shaped and reconstructed to embed its current context(s). There is no authentic intention for media freedom or regulation. There is only safeguarding of the interests of actors in the game of politics of the event at play. Media regulate the news for the reader, thus denying the reader the freedom to make informed conclusions about matters affecting their daily lives. Freedom is about media providing readers with information for transformative opportunities of sustainable peace within the self, families, communities and nations. One role media can play is setting the 'table' from which people will choose what they need for empowerment. Empowerment in this paper then relates to people's ability to take charge of their own transformation.

Culture in this paper is understood as the way entities (the media, for example) choose to build a particular identity as an exemplar of specific lived experience. In this understanding, the notion of 'this is how we do things' becomes a marker for regulation and freedom for an entity like the media, with the result of upholding the status quo (portrayal of only official view, resistance to change for justice, no transformation), exclusion and silencing of some voices, and intolerance of diverse views. In addition, culture is contested, constantly in flux, and both shaped and being shaped by social and economic aspects of human interactions (Rao & Walton, 2004).

In view of the above, any culture talk (including that of media) needs to embody a critical and reflexive application of what is going on locally, nationally, and internationally. I argue that there is no media culture outside of other culture(s) and actors and everything/everybody is affected by everybody/everything–all of us are, and everything is, intricately entangled at a very complex level—in the power embrace that informs human interactions. In other words, media culture shapes structures, beliefs and behaviour and is supported and perpetuated by a web of relationships. These relationships are characterized by differences in power so that different groups benefit differentially from media cultural practices. According to Rao and Kelleher (2005), these same power relationships are used to change and perpetuate cultural beliefs and practices. It is within this complexity of issues and multiplicity of actors that the politics of a media culture of freedom and regulation needs to be engaged in order to see who is excluded and understand why, with the ultimate goal of ensuring all voices are heard and included. In other words: who is regulated and who has freedom to speak, to be listened to and to be heard?

This paper addresses freedom and regulation in the context of media coverage of peacebuilding initiatives in Kenya and Sudan. I use the condition of women and their roles in peacebuilding that is for the most part overlooked by the media. Women's experiences and contributions economically, politically and even in peacebuilding are erased by media practitioners in the way they choose to represent women, largely as victims. Media have the potential for being formidable agents of peace. However, this is impossible when certain voices are excluded and/or silenced. In addition, recognizing that women experience war differently from men would enhance media coverage of the same. This would call for re-thinking coverage of conflict sites by media in ways that use gender-sensitive lenses.

Lastly, this paper addresses the question of Western media reportage of the rest of the world—the question of the West and depiction of African issues in their media. Just like the media in Kenya and Africa take women for granted, erase them from any economic, peacebuilding and other development dialogues, see them as victims of war, and use a patriarchal lens when covering them in the media, the West uses an ethnocentric lens when covering conflict in Africa. Writers from the West reporting on Africa are cynical, base their analysis on myth, and largely misrepresent conflict or peacebuilding scenes altogether. I argue that both the local and international media do not embrace their freedom for the good—indeed media perpetrates the very violence they purport to be reporting objectively. I contend that by denying readers the opportunity to hear the voices of those on the ground, the media regulate the news for us, denying us the freedom to make our own conclusions about issues affecting us.

The challenge for an effective media that serves the interest of most people is to innovatively imagine and craft new ways and include new actors to re-negotiate different media culture dialogues and initiatives for freedom and regulation. These new ways are not only necessary but critical for an atypical media culture that embraces concepts of freedom and regulation that transcend and reconfigure the larger social frameworks that have constructed rigid media cultural identities in media sites.

Defining media culture, freedom and regulation

Media culture is understood in this paper as the mainstream, modernist way of media action. This is epitomized by a tunnel vision definition of media where a linear, top-down approach of news coverage and presentation is upheld, including maintaining the status quo where only men are seen as engaging in newsworthy events. In addition, media will quote only official sources, mostly men, and ignore the views of those most affected by violence on the ground, mainly women, youth and children. Furthermore, media will operate from the perspective of the owners and present the worldview of these powerful agents.

Media freedom and regulation need to be articulated within an analysis of not only the owners of media entities but also the question of 'freedom' for who and 'regulation' for what. When media houses cry foul at government attempts to regulate their 'freedom' (i.e., how far the media can go in criticizing the powers that be), the reasons behind these events need to be understood within contextual aspects such as politics, economy, ownership, culture, and so on. People should always be open to asking whose agenda is being pushed when these hot debates arise. Whose freedom is sought and who is regulating who and for what?

In the Kenya media context, operating from the premise of 'freedom of speech and opinion paradigm', one is bound to ponder the question: who will decide that a media story or broadcast is bad for the listener and that airing it warrants regulation? After all, what one person deems bad may be palatable for another. Who speaks for me: the government, the media, or myself? In a place like Kenya, the freedom of speech paradigm needs to be addressed with care. When people are prone to manipulation and misguided incitement by politicians, one has to be careful who speaks for another.

Media ownership in Kenya is an 'open secret.' In other words, it is not something that is openly talked about or highlighted in the media. However, a close scrutiny will reveal that powerful political personalities are aligned to certain television networks, newspaper chains, magazines and radio networks. There is a move towards media consolidation where a television network also owns a newspaper and a radio station. Repercussions of such consolidation mean that only ideas of the few media houses in Kenya will be presented to citizens, dangerously narrowing down options and ideas reaching the public. The need for establishing alternative media sources becomes critical.

Theoretical premise for understanding culture

The theoretical stance I take for my argument in this paper is based on critical theory. A critical approach stresses the importance of change and conflict in society. According to Martin & Nakayama (1999), the goal of this approach is "to understand the role of power and contextual constraints on communication in order to achieve a more equitable society. The approach emphasizes the unstable aspects of culture and society" (p. 8). Within this paradigm, Martin & Nakayama, (1999) point out, "reality is socially constructed, and the voluntaristic character of human behaviour is emphasized" (p. 8). This voluntaristic human behaviour is conceived of as "dominated by ideological superstructures and material conditions that drive a wedge between them and a more liberated consciousness" (p. 8). In view of this, studies undertaken within this approach are grounded on a belief in changing the uneven, differential ways of constructing and understanding other cultures. Culture is thus seen as a "site of struggle where various communication meanings are contested" (p. 8). This paper is based on a critical perspective because it is a social critique that attempts to bring to light the 'restrictive and alienating conditions of the status quo' in the media culture discourse. I focus on the oppositions, conflicts, and contradictions in the current media situation, and seek to point to emancipatory attempts that might help eliminate the causes of alienation and domination in media culture talks on the Kenyan and Sudan conflicts. Many definitions of culture exist. However, I use the following definition for this paper:

> Culture is about relationality—the relationships among individuals within groups, between groups and among groups and between ideas and perspectives. Culture is concerned with identity, aspiration, symbolic exchange, coordination and structures and practices that serve relational ends such as ethnicity, heritage, norms, meanings and beliefs. It is not a set of primordial phenomena permanently embedded within national or religious or other groups but rather a set of contested attributes, constantly in flux, both shaping and being shaped by social and economic aspects of human interaction (Rao & Walton, 2004).

Applying a critical lens highlights the challenge for an effective media that serves the people to innovatively imagine and craft new ways and include new actors who re-negotiate different media culture dialogues and initiatives for re-naming freedom and regulation. These new ways are not only necessary but crucial for an atypical media culture with concepts of freedom and regulation that transcend and reconfigure the larger social frameworks that have constructed rigid cultural identities in media sites. After all, freedom and regulation should not be about media only, but also about the freedoms enjoyed by every person living in Kenya—freedoms that must be premised on and promote empowerment and the human rights of the every citizen.

Culture in context

In situations of conflict such as the one enacted in Kenya in December 2007/January 2008 as a result of the disputed elections, notions of 'nation', ethnicity, religion, gender, class, power, and hegemony, are significant in understanding the whole picture of the conflict within which the media operate and name themselves. How do media for instance understand themselves as part of Kenya, a nation? Ono (1998) points out that peoples' or entity's sense of nation and national identity can vary enormously. According to Anderson (quoted. in Ono, 1998, p. 199), nations exist only in socially imagined spaces—in a fictional world ontologically distinct from the world in which we live our daily lives. If nations are "imagined communities", why is the world tearing apart in intense conflicts? And why do the media operate as if these national spaces are real? The answer to this question can be found in understanding how universal claims and assumptions have been made about how people/entities act (Ono 1998, p. 201) or ought to act.

Within the project of modernity human behaviour is seen as predictable and measurable; thus human beings act in rigid and predictable ways, and live in unchanging geographical spaces known as 'nation'. In this world view, culture is static and non-changing. It is therefore possible to presume conflict scenarios where human behaviour is perceived in determined and limited ways because each person is seen within a universal bracket of 'nation'. For example, in this thinking, as a Kenya, I am assumed to be like all other Kenyans, irrespective of the fact that I am a woman, a mother, a peace proactivist, a lecturer and I hold a PhD, among other attributes and identifications that I claim. But not every Kenyan woman is like me; indeed, none is. Definitely I am not like any Kenyan man. Universalizing people, entities and culture thus fails to take into account the unique identifications and experiences of people in everyday life—their contextually lived lives, where the scripts of who we are, are written.

People and entities operate and occupy both geographic and relational spaces. Geographic spaces are unchanging. However, relational spaces are fluid and can be enhanced in order for people to attain common goals. Recognizing and understanding the context within which life is enacted by people is a critical requirement for media, if they are to be effective agents of peace in the world.

Media coverage of events that focus solely on national issues and exclude people's experiences in everyday life does not do people or peace justice. For example, coverage of Kenyan's experiences of conflict as if everyone is affected by it in the same way fails to represent effectively the conflict situation and the condition the people are in. In addition, merely presenting the voice of the officials and government agents who may not be at conflicts scenes instead of highlighting the opinions and experiences of the people on the ground, especially women and children, presents a skewed representation of the violence.

In an unprecedented television coverage of the post election violence effect on displaced families, CITIZEN TV brought to the homes of Kenyans in February 2008 images of what life in internally displaced people's camps looked like. The channel also engaged the voices of survivors of the violence as well as families who had lost children and other family members. This enabled Kenyans to feel the pain of their brothers and sisters living as refugees in their own country. Kenyans then mobilized through churches, mosques, social groups, NGOs and the international community to get food, clothes and other necessities to the families living in the camps.

Mainstream peace processes and media coverage of the same focused on the 'unity of the nation,' premised on track one diplomacy, where only government officials and diplomatic personalities negotiate peace on behalf of the rest of the people. It was assumed for instance in the case of the 2008 post-election violence in Kenya, that government leaders and mediators knew what the rest of the Kenyan population needed, even though some of the government representatives at the peace table were suspected of having funded the violence. The diplomats are seen (or see themselves) as experts on Kenyan's peace needs. In track one diplomacy peace negotiations, people in conflict are not allowed to speak for themselves. They are spoken for. Their agency, ability to speak for themselves, is not recognized, and it is either taken for granted or ignored altogether. Speaking for the rest of the Kenyan population is based on the assumption that since Kenyan people belong to one nation, they want the same thing and have the same experiences. Individual interests at the level of everyday lived experience are lost in media coverage of people and their culture in these fixed, universalized, and essentialized forms.

The fixing of a people's culture and who they are is a colonial legacy— a product of 'project modernity'. The 'native' was seen as one entity, where everyone was undifferentiated and acted in the same way. Fixing people (stereotypes of women as accommodating and nurturers, or Africans are war mongers, for example) is safe, because they can be figured out and consequently controlled. In the context of the Kenyan conflict, fixing of people can be seen at two levels: Kenyans in the eyes of the regional (African) and international (rest of world) fraternity seen as 'war-mongers.' The rest of the population of women, children and youth is included in this categorization, yet they comprise the majority of the population of Kenya although they are not the ones who cause or perpetrate the violence.

When women create peace strategies, as was the case in Liberia, their approaches involve everyday life improvement for their families and communities. In Liberia for example, women chose to embrace child soldiers after the war ended in order to integrate them in the community (Personal discussion with Michelle Hovey, 2008). When women insist that they need to be covered by media or be represented in peace talk initiatives so that their voice is heard, they are essentially negotiating the old representation (Sorrells, 2003, p. 31) that depicts them as passive victims of violence as opposed to active agents of peace. Women have a different peacebuilding approach because their experience of violence is different from that of men. They have become targets of bullets, rape, displacement and so on. Getting this contextual aspect right when media are talking about freedom and regulation in the context of war would greatly enhance reviewing what has come to be called 'media culture.'

If media culture refers to doing business as usual, that is, maintaining the status quo—depicting women as victims of war, essentially erasing women from mainstream news, having 'experts' speak for them, and so on—then it is no wonder the print and mass media have not 'seen' what women are doing for peace in Kenya and the rest of Africa. Just like the media in Kenya and Africa takes women for granted, erases their voice from any political, social, economic, peacebuilding and other development dialogues, and uses a patriarchal lens when covering them in the media, the West uses an ethnocentric lens when covering conflict in Africa. They are cynical, base their analysis on myth, and misrepresent the conflict or peacebuilding scene altogether. Both local and international media do not embrace their freedom for the good—indeed, they perpetrate the very violence they purport to be reporting objectively. By denying readers the chance to hear the voice of those on the ground, the media regulate the news, denying them the freedom to make independent conclusions about issues affecting them.

The Sudan Example
In this section I demonstrate how the language used in the description of the 'failure' of the Sudan peace process indicates domination, power, gender insensitivity or lack of awareness, and a totally Eurocentric way of addressing the process. I note that the observers making the comments in the media are people from the West and as advisors of the peace process, they are utilizing a western mind-set to address issues about Africans, with no regard at all to the Afrocentric world view of the actors. According to Chuang (2003) this is perceptual imperialism understood as "the process of observing and interpreting "cultural Others" through "an underlying set of ideas based not so much on reality as on myth" (p. 26). In addition, discursive imperialism: language marked by ethnocentricism and hegemony (p. 26) and perceptions cultures as totalities (p. 27) are evident in the "Go to Hell" (Prendergast and Mozersky, 2003) article examined below.

The critique of the Sudan government leader's "Go to hell" speech by Prendergast and Mozersky (2003) in *The Observer* is illuminating. They begin by stating in very negative terms that "Sudan's peace process is *in trouble*" (p.1 italics mine), a very colonial way of looking at the Other which emphasizes "natives'" incompetence and hence failure.[1] The Sudan conflict is further described as "Africa's longest-running war" in the report, giving the reader the impression of the intractability of this conflict. The report goes on to say: "Until recently there was hope across Sudan that a peace *deal* (not a process) could be reached to end one of the *world's longest and most brutal wars*—the conflict between the *Muslim-dominated government in Khartoum* and *rebel forces of the Sudan People's Liberation Movement (SPLM)*. Here, once again we see the dichotomy of Muslim/Christian; Government/Rebel. The use of the word "rebel" calls to mind Mau Mau freedom fighters Kenya who were referred to as "terrorists" by the colonial government. The same colonial legacy is evident in the use of the term "rebel", a notion that essentializes the Other—the freedom fighter. According to Chuang (2003), such generalizing mutes voices of the Other who are not allowed to speak for themselves (p. 31). Knowledge of localized understandings and acceptance of a plurality of diverse language forms (p. 38) is absent in the article. The only way the writers make sense of the Other culture is through an "imperial and colonial gaze" (p. 38). In addition, perpetual and discursive imperialistic processes related to the argument on cultural hegemony and the idea of European superiority over African backwardness is evident here because the language used in the article ideologizes Sudanese knowledge and "imposes a variety of negative value judgments that people from a hegemonic culture tend to have toward people from less dominant cultures" (p.39), leading to covert ethnocentricism and cultural superiority (institutional knowledge of Other). For example the use of the words "... *one of the most brutal...*" creates an impression of these African brutes. Yet, while any people warring against each other exhibit the same brutish behaviour, media renditions of the US-executed war in Iraq for example depict the American military as "fighting terrorism", something that makes them 'heroes' and not 'brutes'.

Ethnicism is also promoted in this article. Defined as "a system of ethnic group dominance based on cultural criteria of categorization, differentiation, and exclusion, such as those of language, religion, customs, or world views" (Chuang, 2003, p. 38), the Sudan government excludes the South through religious oppression. There is also a sense of elite (mainstream, hegemonic) discourse that reproduces ethnicism (p. 38), where "power and ideology are embedded in the reproduction of ethnicism" (p. 39). The Sudan government exercises its power—"the types of control elites have over the actions and minds of other people" (p. 39). Although this control might be implicit, "it is usually explicitly implemented by decision making, use of special acts, and discourse genres" (p. 39)—as is evident from the government's refusal to accept the draft peace proposal because they feel it confers upon the South a lot of benefits. The government issued threats to return to war, which is a characteristic of those in power. The article states:

> last month President Omar al-Bashir told the Kenyan-based mediation team to "go to hell", *refusing to accept their draft peace settlement*. If the mediators didn't come up with a "reasonable alternative", he said, "they will have to *dissolve the document in water and drink it.*" SPLM leader John Garang has since warned that *if the government doesn't accept* the peace proposals, there would be a *return to war*. Hopes for a peace deal are not lost altogether, but *they are diminishing*. The issues important to the process are identified in this sentence: "Since the Machakos Protocol, the mediators have overseen further incremental successes on *power sharing, wealth sharing, security arrangements, and the administrative status* of the three contested areas of Abyei, the Nuba Mountains and Southern Blue Nile. (*The Observer*, 2003, p.2).

These areas of concern contrast drastically from the issues that Sudanese women focused on in their initiatives. U.N. Secretary-General Kofi Annan (quoted in Swanee & Posa, 2001, p. 3) described women as" instrumental in building bridges rather than walls." He further observed that women have been able to bridge the divide even in situations where leaders have deemed conflict resolution futile in the face of so-called intractable ethnic hatred. Referring to the role of women in peacemaking in the Sudan, Kofi Annan also noted that in the south women working together in the New Sudan Council of Churches conducted their own version of *shuttle diplomacy*—without the panache attendant to photo sessions while jetting between capitals—and *organized* the Wunlit summit in February 1999 to bring to an end bloody hostilities between the Dinka and Nuer peoples. As a result, the Wunlit *Covenant* guaranteed peace between the Dinka and the Nuer who *agreed to share rights to water, fishing, and grazing land*, which had been key points of disagreement. The covenant also returned prisoners of war and guaranteed freedom of movement for members of both ethnic groups. Likewise, an early goal of the Sudanese Women's Voice for Peace was *to meet and talk* with the military leaders of the various rebel armies. These contacts secured women's access to areas controlled by the revolutionary movements, a critical variable in the success or failure of humanitarian efforts in war zones. Women also worked with the military *to search for missing people*, a common element in the cycle of violence. In short through *moral suasion, local women* often have influence where outsiders, such as international human rights agencies, don't.

In rebel-controlled areas of Sudan women worked closely with humanitarian organizations to prevent food from being diverted from those who need it most. According to Catherine Loria Duku Jeremano (quoted in Swanee & Posa, 2001) of Oxfam: "The normal pattern was to hand out relief to the men, who were then expected to take it home to be distributed to their family. However, many of the *men did what they pleased with the food* they received: either *selling* it directly, often in *exchange for alcohol*, or giving *food to the wives they favoured*" (p. 3). Sudanese women worked closely with ethnic leaders and relief organizations to establish a system allowing women to pick up *food for their families* despite contrary cultural norms. The food element brings to the fore issues of femininity and masculinity—what women/men should do culturally. The peace process is opening ways that enable Sudanese women agency as well as challenge power imbalance, socialization of gender roles; the distinction between in-group and out-group members, and the level of commitment in the relationship [community] (Chuang, ibid, pp. 29–30). The peace process is changing the communication and cultural practices as negotiated arenas where "the convergence of communication style, group identity, and relational history may transcend cultural boundaries" (p. 30).

The discussion above was meant to illustrate how women is peacemaking styles are different from those of men and the mainstream's power centre. However, a media culture that dwells in the crevices of the dominant worldview covers only the mainstream view. The relegation to the sidelines of women in peace talks is in part structural because even though there are now more women legislators and soldiers, underrepresentation persists in the highest levels of political and military hierarchies, including the media. According to Swanee and Posa (2001) the presidents, prime ministers, party leaders, cabinet secretaries, and generals who typically negotiate peace settlements are overwhelmingly men. Also media practitioners will send men to cover war and thereby guaranteeing a relay of war narratives cushioned by male perspectives.

I have demonstrated how a (dominant or mainstream) men-oriented report on a peace process is articulated in a dualistic, patriarchal, power, dominating and gender-insensitive manner. Only one worldview and a dominant language (the male one, using militaristic terms) is presented. Furthermore, the worldview imposed on the government by a Western lens brought in by Western advisors and reporters compounds the challenge of attaining peace since the language tends to perpetuate the hard positions held by protagonists.

Women, on the other hand use words like 'covenant' (meaning: agreement, promise) and address issues of water, land, and food (basic needs)—aspects that affect everyone in the community. In the women peace initiative reported above, the women met and talked, while the male-oriented article talks of 'putting pressure' and making 'deals', using threats, and so on.

Transgressing media culture

To transgress media culture means seeking freedom from the bondage of this culture that blots out other views and perspectives apart from those peddled by mainstream media. In addition, media's recognition of their role in excluding the voices of women and other marginalized groups, and fighting to bring in those excluded voices, is a critical aspect of what media freedom ought to look like.

Before 1970 women were viewed by the UN system as entities or objects that needed the protection of the world community. In the 1970's, programs that were aimed at achieving women's integration into development began, where women were viewed as 'resources' whose contributions would improve the development process. In the 1980's, at the end of the UN Decade for Women, the

UN officially recognized women's equality and rights as critical in their own right and at all levels of the development process. Many analysts have noted the shift from seeking to integrate women in development to seeking to transform the structures and relationships which perpetuate the marginalization of women. The role of media in this regard is critical. The media need to highlight the structures and relationships which perpetuate the marginalization of women. A gender approach to media action is vital in order to attain this transformation in the structures that perpetuate exclusion.

The need to integrate gender considerations in the coverage of conflict and peacebuilding initiatives by media is critical for effective and holistic tackling of the causes and impact of conflicts on women. Integration of a media sensitive to gender issues and how gender impacts experiences of war by men and women would enhance holistic coverage of the impact of violence on women, an aspect largely missing in contemporary coverage of war. Holistic coverage here means uncovering the structural, institutional, economic, political and cultural factors that constrain women's contributions to sustainable peace and development in our communities and nations.

Media have the potential to be formidable peace agents. To attain this goal they would have to be aware of what dialogues on women's roles in peacebuilding are being advocated locally and internationally. Media in Kenya never brought home any good news of the Fourth World Conference on Women in Beijing in 1995 because President Moi just focused on the issue of lesbianism. Many other fundamental aspects of the conference and the benefits it brought to the women's movement were overshadowed by this short sighted and narrow view of the Beijing conference. For example, the conference called for increased access to conflict prevention and resolution mechanisms by women. It also raised the consciousness of international policymakers about women's role in peacebuilding and in creating conditions of trust and confidence among conflicting parties. The Platform for Action states that:

> In a world of continuing instability and violence... the equal access and full participation of women in power structures and their full involvement in the prevention and resolution of conflicts are essential for the maintenance and promotion of peace and security (Fraser, 2001).

Furthermore, Resolution 1325 (2000) of the UN Security Council reaffirmed that a gender perspective in conflict as well as its prevention and resolution, needs to include measures that support women's peace initiatives (Fraser, 2001). At the implementation level, the resolution calls for the involvement of women in all implementation mechanisms of peace agreements and ensuring human rights of women and girls. The significance of this resolution is in its bringing up at the UN level issues of how violent conflicts affect women. It acknowledges the need for greater attention to the needs of women caught up in warfare and to incorporate more women in peace and reconciliation processes. The resolution calls upon states and actors to ensure women's full participation in peace processes.

A critical aspect of women's participation in peacebuilding therefore, involves the nature of this participation. Within the mainstream conflict resolution and management approaches based on Western models, local communities' knowledge and input to peacebuilding were excluded and dubbed 'primitive.' Yet, these foreign approaches have had little success in attaining peace in many places in Africa, largely because they ignore the context within which the conflict is enacted. Inclusive approaches to peacebuilding anchored in indigenous and traditional approaches are ignored even though they are critical for successful peacebuilding interventions today. In addition, the root causes of the conflicts are hardly ever addressed, as is the case with the violence of 2007/2008 in Kenya. Even more tragically, in most cases the opinions of the people living with the consequences of the conflict are not consulted by the 'experts' sent to investigate the violence.

Media practitioners need to know that inclusive peacebuilding models, ones that enable incorporation and understanding of more comprehensive approaches to peacebuilding anchored in indigenous and traditional approaches, seem to bear more results than western, classical ones. However, our experience in Kenya is that there is no political will to change the old ways.

Paulo Freire (1970) introduced the concept of using conscientization, a process by which the learner advances towards critical consciousness and thus liberation, through education as communication. The approach was receiver-centred and helped oppressed people understand the ideological and social structures that maintained their domination. Communication became more of a dialogue in which the 'underdeveloped' person, group, or organization is an equal partner in the development process. This re-engagement of recipients in the process of self and social progress introduced conceptualizations that encouraged empowerment and integrated the effects of development on the environment, society, economy, and political structures. This participatory method engaged stakeholders in a dialogue that helped to define development needs and encouraged methods that were sensitive to historical and cultural factors that had proven to be barriers to communication in the past. The process also generated new knowledge and provided the tools for grassroots people and local leaders to take control of their own development efforts (Sen, 1999), including the right to communicate and to be covered by media. This approach attempts to inter-relate media freedom, political freedom, economic facilities, social opportunities, transparency guarantees, and protective security, to better understand the nuances of the development and communication theory and peace.

Women's involvement in media and peace talks and the issues they raise make visible the historically and socially constructed constraints of places and borders they inherit. Women's peace initiatives, their insistence on being at the mediation table and the impact they are making in Kenya today in the political, economic, and social spheres are acts of transgressing borders (Giroux, 1993)—in discourses of war and peace as well as politics and socio-economic arenas—by attempting to cross the border lands of a media culture premised on exclusion, sexism, patriarchy, gender insensitivity, and domination within existing configurations of power between media/media owners and citizens, men and women, governments and the opposition and so on. Women's initiatives provide us with possibilities of building strengths by recognizing their agency and capacity to reason in order to address war issues and their unique impact on women in day-to-day interactions. The reports on women initiatives show how cultural borders exist that are historically constructed and socially organized within rules and regulations that limit and enable particular identities, individual capacities, and social forms" (Sorrells, 2003, p. 30) some which we have called 'culture' and others that are hidden in so called media freedom and regulation. Media are a significant cog in this wheel of exclusion of some voices in Kenya. Media freedom in this context means uncovering this exclusion. If freedom and regulation for media means representing everyone's voice, such that everyone's freedom to speak for themselves is ensured and regulation to silence some voices is discarded, media will truly become the voice of conscience for social justice.

As the voice for social justice, the media are called upon to highlight women's peacebuilding initiatives at all levels—economic, political, social, cultural, environmental—and to uncover the ideological and hegemonic powers that continue to constrain these initiatives. Myths about what women and men can do and cannot do need to be unveiled. For instance there is the myth that since war is started by men, men should end it. UNIFEM Executive Director Noeleen Heyzer (2003) succinctly calls this myth to question when she observes that women are no longer willing to accept that the world expects war-makers to be peacemakers while women's perspectives, experiences and contributions to shaping a sustainable future are rendered trivial. Not only are women continuing to devise creative and effective strategies to advocate for peace, they are also bolstering international support for incorporating their perspectives in all areas of decision-making related to peace, including within the agenda of peace talks. Media should not only help challenge, cross and reconfigure the border of gender in peacemaking, but also recreate borderlands in which the very production and acquisition of knowledge is being used to rewrite people's own histories, identities, and learning possibilities (Swanee & Posa, 2001) with regard to how peace should be achieved in their society.

Swanee & Posa (ibid.) highlight the plight of women in times of conflict. They observe that women and girls are among those most affected by the violence and economic instability associated with armed conflict. They further observe that whether at home, in flight or in camps for displaced people, women are threatened by rape, domestic violence, sexual exploitation, trafficking, sexual humiliation and mutilation. Yet, when it comes to negotiating peace and facilitating the reconstruction of societies after war, women are grossly underrepresented, including in the media.

According to Swanee & Posa (ibid.), in traditional thinking about war and peace, women are ignored or regarded as victims, an oversight, they posit, that has cost the world dearly. This is so because the wars of the last decade have gripped the public conscience largely because civilians were not just merely caught in the crossfire; they were targeted, deliberately and brutally, by military strategists. In view of this, they contend that just as warfare has become "inclusive" (with civilian deaths more common than soldiers'), so too must our approaches toward (media coverage of conflict and) ending of conflict. From the foregoing we might argue that, today the goal of peace is not simply the absence of war, but the creation of sustainable peace by fostering fundamental societal changes.

In my view these fundamental changes will take place within a framework of Freire's (1970) conscientization—and the media must play the leading role in this campaign to change human thinking regarding violence in our societies. The first step toward this transformation is making human beings and their communities, rather than states, the point of reference for sustainable peace. In addition, our spring board for ending violence in our communities should be that of peace (a proactive approach) and not conflict resolution (a reactive approach). This approach focuses both on safety and protection, particularly of the most vulnerable segments of a population, as well as on providing people with correct information so they are able to make informed decisions concerning matters of peace that affect them. Those affected by a conflict must be involved in the processes that are geared towards ending the conflict and looking for the common goals that they want to advance as a community for sustainable peace. Media freedom entails bringing these new ways of thinking to the attention of readers. Media regulation demands a conscious effort on the part of media to self regulate in order to end impunity in reportage of events such as conflicts so that people are conscientized to create sustainable peace.

Conclusion

It is critical that we recognize that for our world to be transformed from a seemingly static conflict-ridden entity, spaces we occupy that we have embraced and refuse to let go have to be shaken up, broken up and re-negotiated. A volcanic event needs to take place to cleanse us and move us afresh to new ways of seeing, being, and doing. The violence that broke up in Kenya was one such opportunity. The media are not the only ones called upon to engage, re-member, reconfigure and transform. Each one of us is part of this transformation of the self, family, community, nation and Africa.

Media freedom entails bringing new ways of thinking to the attention of readers. Media regulation demands a conscious effort on the part of media to self regulate in order to end impunity in reporting events such as conflicts so that people are conscientized to create sustainable peace. The media can present news in context and ensure all sides are represented, all perspectives are given, and all voices are heard. Hopefully readers will then make informed decisions about issues important to them and critical for their survival.

Notes

1 Note that the Sudan Comprehensive Peace Accord (CPA) was actually signed in 2005

References

Chuang, R. (2003). 'A Postmodern Critique of Cross-Cultural and Intercultural Communication Research: Contesting Essentialism, Positivist Dualism, and Eurocentricity'. In W. Starosta & G-M Chen (Eds.) *Ferment in the intercultural field: International and Intercultural Communication Annual*. Vol. 26 (pp. 24–56). Thousand Oaks, CA: Sage.

Fraser, A. (2001). 'Becoming human: The origins and development of women's human rights'. In Marjorie Agosin. *Women, Gender and Human Rights: A global perspective*. New Jersey: Rutgers University Press.

Freire, P. (1970). *Pedagogy of the Oppressed*. New York: Continuum Books.

Giroux, H. A. (1993). *Border crossings*. New York: Routledge.

Heyzer, N. (2003). Women Making a Difference at the Peace Table http://www.unifem.org/search.php October 23, 2003.

Martin, J. N. & Nakayama, T. K. (1999). 'Thinking dialectically about culture and communication'. In *Intercultural Communication Association*. Vol. 9 (pp. 1–25). Thousand Oaks, CA: Sage.

Jeremano, C. L. D. (2001) Women Waging Peace http://womenshistory.about.com/gi/dynamic/offsite.htm?site=http%3A%2F%2Fwww.foreignpolicy.com%2Fissue_mayjune_2001%2FHunt.html, October 23, 2003.

Kofi Annan (2001) Women Waging Peace http://womenshistory.about.com/gi/dynamic/offsite.htm?site=http%3A%2F%2Fwww.foreignpolicy.com%2Fissue_mayjune_2001%2FHunt.html, October 23, 2003.

Ono, K. (1998). 'Problematizing "nation" in intercultural communication research'. In D. Tanno & A. Gonzalez (Eds.), *Communication and identity across cultures* (pp. 34–55). Thousand Oaks, CA: Sage.

Prendergast, J. & Mozersky, D. (2003). Five Minutes to Midnight in Sudan's Peace Process'. In *The Observer*. URL http://www.intl-crisis-group.org/projects/showreport.cfm?reportid=1038. October 23, 2003.

Rao, A & Kelleher, D. (2005). Human rights, institutions and social change. Paper presented at the Helsinki Conference. URL: www.genderatwork.org. October 2, 2009.

Rao, V. & Walton, M. (2004). *Culture and public action*. Stanford: Stanford Social Sciences.

Sen, A. (1999). *Development as Freedom*. New York: Anchor Books.

Sorrells, K. (2003). 'Embodied negotiation: Commodification and cultural representation in the US Southwest'. In M.J. Collier (Ed.) *Intercultural alliances: Critical transformation. International and Intercultural Communication Annual*. Vol. 25. (pp. 17–48). Thousand Oaks, CA: Sage.

Swanee, H, & Posa, C. (2001). Women Waging Peace http://womenshistory.about.com/gi/dynamic/offsite.htm?site=http%3A%2F%2Fwww.foreignpolicy.com%2Fissue_mayjune_2001%2FHunt.html, October 23, 2003.

Globalized Identity: Diaspora Kenyans and Local Conflict

KĪMANI NJOGU

Many people and forces are feeding Kenya's current crisis: politicians and their informal militias, intellectuals disseminating hate on the internet, police shooting at innocents, young men at road blocks killing people with machetes. Who will move the country back towards rule of reason, institutions and a civil national society?

—Jacqueline Klopp, (07 February 2008). www.opendemocracy.net

In all African countries a greater respect for due process and the independence of the judiciary, limits on executive power and action against grand corruption, as well as better design of electoral systems and electoral management, must contribute towards the creation of states in which all can be sure that their rights will be respected without the need to take up arms .

—Bronwen Manby (2009:160).

It is no longer debatable that we live in a world in which states are becoming increasingly connected through migrations, advances in information and communications technology, urbanization, concerns for security in the face of global terrorism, transnational infections such as HIV, swine flu or H1N1, the devastating consequences of climate change and food insecurity, and the global economic crisis. Cultures are being challenged and undone in fundamental ways as new alliances and identities are sought (Featherstone 1992; Appadurai 2006). There is 'enforced proximity' of people around the world (Tomlinson 1999:181). The problems of one nation have global implications and positive co-existence is viewed as crucial to peace not only within the nation-state but also beyond it. Evidently, citizens and leaders who focus only on their communities and country, despite their geographical location, limit their ability to contribute to human interconnectedness and advancement. They ought to be simultaneously global and local, serving and defending the interests of humanity within their communities and nation-states and at the same time transcending their geographical space to maintain global linkages. This would contribute to a reduction of conflict and enhancement of democratic practice and justice for all. Those who do not reach out beyond their boundaries and seek solidarity only with 'their people'—located within limited cultural, linguistic, and territorial spheres—open themselves to the possibility of contributing to the suffering of others through exclusion and balkanization.

Over the last fifty years, the world has experienced intrastate conflicts in which government harms its people, people stand up against government or people within the nation-state engage violently with each other. Whereas it had been anticipated by many that the end of the Cold War would lead to peaceful co-existence, it did not. Rather, it was quickly followed by the genocide in Rwanda and the devastating conflicts in the former Afghanistan, Yugoslavia, Somalia, Iraq, Ivory Coast, East Timor, the Democratic Republic of Congo, Sri Lanka, Sierra Leone, Liberia, Haiti, Sudan and Kenya. Moreover, threats of nuclear usage have been lingering in Pakistan, India, Iran and North Korea. We are also witnesses to globalized terrorist attacks, mainly under the hand of non-state actors who fight local conflicts, such as those in the Middle East, on the world stage.

Citizens in the diaspora quite often find themselves as active participants in homeland dynamics at least in four ways: individual remittances to homeland; political involvement in the homeland; civic-oriented involvement such as community activities and business investment; and lobbying in the host country over specific homeland matters (Mohamoud 2006:4). Their involvement is extensively facilitated by advances in information and communication technologies, including the internet and mobile telephony which make interaction instantaneous and money transfer speedy. By reducing time and space constraints, the technologies are transforming local conflict and globalizing it in fundamental ways through transnational solidarities, fast information exchange and financial remittances. Digital broadcasting has made possible the global expansion of news and current affairs TV channels by connecting the world at once, transcending linguistic and geographical barriers. Through *list-servs, blogs* and *chatrooms* citizens across the globe engage interactively; interpreting and shaping local conflict no matter their physical locale. Kenyans in the diaspora were no exception during the 2007/2008 election related crisis. The 'homeland' and the diaspora were connected in a significant way.

In this paper, I discuss ways in which local conflict finds expression in the global arena, especially among citizens in the diaspora. Drawing mainly from the experiences of the 2007/2008 election related violence in Kenya, I argue that ethnic solidarity in the nation-state manifests itself within the diaspora, at times shaping local conflict. Ethnicity is a form of identity driven by perceptions of shared values (language, ancestry and kinship beliefs, cultural practices); an active consciousness of collective selfhood through naming; and boundaries between the self and other (Young 2004:7). When moving from the homeland to a foreign state citizens do not delete their cultural solidarities and tensions; rather, they 'suspend' them momentarily and retain traces which can be activated during moments of anxiety, fear and crisis either in the homeland or in the diaspora. Apparently, there is never closure to ethnic identity but transformation and repositioning; continuities and discontinuities; presences and absences. After discussing the nature of a global identity and the diaspora, I explore how Kenyans in the diaspora 'participated' in the violence that peaked after the highly contested and controversial 2007 presidential elections in Kenya.

On being labelled

Events in one country are of interest around the world and the Kenyan election crisis was received in multiple ways by non-Kenyans and then replayed on Kenyans in the diaspora. Pointedly, certain non-Kenyans read the crisis only in ethnic terms and assumed that ethnic identification essentially translated into an unchallenged solidarity with a particular political position. In order to start thinking about the dilemma, anxieties and identity related issues facing Kenyans in the diaspora, let us visit a space on the internet occupied by *Mama Junkyard*. She says:

> In the wake of what can only be described as one of my country's darkest moments I have found that being a Kenyan abroad has generated a series of deeply troubling questions from *non-Kenyans* such as:
>
> *Oh you are Kenyan? So what tribe are you/What ethnic group do you belong to?*
>
> Or
>
> *You are from Kenya? So are you Kikuyu or Luo?*
>
> On the surface it is easy to view these questions as innocent enquiries from a non-Kenyan who wants to know more about where I am from. Given the manner in which ethnic differences crept into the dispute over the government's claim to power I know all to well that these questions are anything but innocent.
>
> The first question, in my view is a personal question and should have no place in a discussion between people who barely know each other. Furthermore it rests on the assumption that there is a simple response. For instance, there are many Kenyans who do not belong to one ethnic group or tribe and the question suggests that a single tribe response is the desired answer.
>
> In the case of the second question, it is equally personal but it is more offensive than the first because it reduces my country to a two-tribe nation. It ignores the existence of every other Kenyan who does not fall into either the Kikuyu or Luo ethnic group. It also assumes that one can not fit neatly into both ethnic groups.
>
> That said, what really angers me about both questions is that most people who ask will then use whatever response I give as a basis to project their own limited knowledge of the political and ethnic situation in Kenya.
>
> When I opt to answer these sorts of questions I simply state '*Kikuyu.*' Each time I have done so my response has been met with statements like:
>
> *You must be happy with the result then*
>
> Or
>
> *Ah! It is your man/brother who is in power*
>
> even this:
>
> *You guys really rigged this election.*
>
> In single sentence a person has taken *my* cultural/ethnic identity and formed an opinion about *my* political allegiance, placed blame upon *me* for the outcome of the election and worst of all suggested that despite the fact that *my* country is in turmoil... I am pleased. The most frustrating part for me is, I am still not sure who/what I should be angry at. (*www.beginsathome.com/2008/04/01/don't tell me who I am*)

The questions directed at Mama Junkyard point to an essentializing tendency often encountered by those in the diaspora. They also point to a simplification of complex issues related to identity. But it is not just in the diaspora. Simiyu Barasa, writing his obituary from Nairobi, urges his friends to read it as a love letter to a "country that has died in that critical moment when its dreams were giving birth to a beautiful bouncing future." Language abilities were used to 'identify' the 'other' and for those who are products of mixed marriages, such as Simiyu, the situation was quite complicated. He says,

> "My sister, Rozi, called me yesterday trembling with fear. She lives in Western Kenya, on the Eldoret/Kakamega border. They had taken a patient to Moi Referral Hospital Eldoret. On their way back, the ambulance was stopped by youths bearing all forms of crude weapons. They demanded to know which tribes everyone in the ambulance belonged to. The driver was of the local tribe, so he was told to step aside. As the others showed their National Identity cards, my sister realized that all around them were corpses of human beings freshly chopped to death. Her turn came and she said she was Luhya. They told her to speak in Luhya, but my sister doesn't know Luhya. "I really can't speak it because my mother is a Taita!" she pleaded. She had to desperately show a photocopy of my mother's National Identity card which she had in her purse, a photocopy my mother had given to her the previous week to use as a referee for the bank account she was switching to. That photocopy saved my sister. The only language my sister can speak, apart from English and the National Swahili, is Gĩkũyũ. The tribe the youths were targeting. My friend, I know no tribe. I only know languages. My mother is Taita, my Father is Luhya, and we were raised in Kiambu among the Gĩkũyũ." (http://liblit.org/2008/02/16 the obituary of simiyu-barasa)

Simiyu's sister is defined narrowly on account of her inability to speak a linguistic marker but is saved by her mother's identification card, intended initially for a financial transaction. Though the experiences of Rozi and Mama Junkyard are different contextually, they are similar to the extent that they both point to the dangers of ethnic stereotyping either within the nation-state or in the diaspora.

These reflections in *Mama Junkyard*'s site, comparable to *Diary 25: The Obituary of Simiyu Barasa*, written by himself in Nairobi and posted by Ory Okolloh in *kenyelections07*, raise important issues as we seek to understand the various positions taken by diaspora Kenyans in relation to the events before and after the 2007 General Election. On the one hand, they have to contend with non-Kenyans who seek to pigeonhole them through a questioning of their national citizenship. The 'look' of the non-Kenya fixes the diasporan 'Other' and attempts to situate them on the homeland in final, pure and simple terms. By assuming that ethnic identity is clear and uncontested, they force a narrow interpretation of national events, ignoring individual choice and agency and subscribe to a unitary consciousness among members of an ethnic group located in the diaspora or 'homeland.' It is important to appreciate that although diasporan Kenyans are connected to their kin and have relationships of solidarity, they are also individuals capable of disengaging with the 'happiness' or 'sadness' of their communities and to 'reach out' to others, which quite often they do. Indeed, while citizens in the diaspora may value their ethnic roots they are also subjected to a wide range of influences including race, class, profession, gender and political leanings and these influences could allow them to transcend one identity and to embrace other forms of belonging, including global solidarities.

On globalized identity

Whereas local identity (ethnic or otherwise) may be historically situated and viewed as expressing the most immediate reality and facilitating interpersonal understanding between local members, globalized identity refers to a deterritorized distancing which affirm a person's sense of self, transcending national boundaries. It is underpinned by certain attributes of our being; of convergences and divergences; of similarity and difference in the human species because every person is in certain ways like all other human beings, like some other human beings and like no other human being. Globalized identity is significantly deprived of strong affiliation to the particularities of ethno-linguistic heritage and content and relates mainly with human nature: our shared commonalities as human beings. The defining feature of globalized identity is identification with all peoples of the world, transcending immediate community and national boundaries. It is a diffuse concept and is based on common denominators of humanity, including our ability to use linguistic signs creatively. Socrates articulated his affinity to a globalized identity when he said: [I am] not an Athenian, nor a Greek, but a citizen of the world'[1]. By emphasizing that he is a citizen of the world, Socrates gave primacy to our shared humanity as a locus of identity and devalued an identity driven by ethno-linguistic and nationalistic considerations. This shared humanity would make us develop solidarity with others in the world irrespective of their territorial location, religious affiliation, racial or ethnic backgrounds. By invoking globalized identity we start appreciating that all of us have basic needs and rights and that we are part of a cosmos held together by gravitational forces.

Imagined more broadly and through an inclusive integral vision, globalized identity is identification with cosmic pluralism—a shared oneness between humans and other things on earth. Indeed, our efforts to understand the nature of life on earth and elsewhere are a quest to understand who we are. It is a recognition that human beings are dependent not only on each other but also on the physical processes of the solar system, planet Earth and its biosphere. Much as we may seek to celebrate our particularity, we are part of a mutually dependent whole with which we have a dialogic relationship (Bakhtin 1984; Njogu 2004). It therefore becomes imperative to widen the scope of basic moral philosophy so that normative claims can be generalized in a manner acceptable more broadly to humanity. A key feature of this vision is to see things from the point of view of others and to be ready to compromise and seek common ground. Heikki Patomaki (2008:13) has correctly observed that,

> ...a cosmic and planetary perspective clearly facilitates and encourages the adoption of such a moral viewpoint. The level of moral consciousness in turn is directly connected to identity formation. A possible and plausible argument for global morality and thus identity would involve an idea that we should work together as a species to preserve it on a cosmic scale.

This perspective allows us to extend our identification horizon to other humans and the environment. The globalized cosmopolitan identity opens a window for us to see more similarities between ourselves than differences; connections than ruptures. An important expression of globalized identity is the presence of many global activists who protest at the activities of the World Bank, International Monetary Fund and at the meetings of G8. Many of them are involved in the struggle for environmental protection and human rights and against nuclear proliferation in different parts of the world. Like a "neighbourhood watch" they have an associational relationship and as global citizens demand that national leaders behave in a certain way for the good of humankind. The possibility of a globalized cosmopolitan identity suggests that we are not prisoners to local identities but are instead capable of operating at levels which are unconstrained by time and space to create relationships of solidarity with people with whom we share a global philosophy. This view is not meant to underestimate the poignancy of national and more local relationships of solidarity in our midst. Rather, it is to suggest that local identities such as articulated by ethnicity and race, though real and relevant in our lives, can be transcended when other forms of the self are affirmed especially in the intensely interconnected contemporary world. National identities are constructed and historically situated from the shared memories and values of ethnic communities. But within a globalized identity cosmopolitan citizens, free from national limitations, can emerge. This cosmopolitanism would point to a cultural disposition freed, to a degree from immediate locality and embraces and integrates the concerns of humanity. It is a willingness to consciously engage with the 'other'.

It seems as if 'othering' is inevitable, even in the context of extensive globalization because uniformity of culture is virtually impossible because we are all products of history and culture. As Featherson (1992) has emphasized:

> It should not be taken to imply that the there is, or will be, a unified world society or culture—something akin to the social structure of a nation state and its national culture, only writ large. Such an outcome may have been the ambition of particular nation—states at various points of their history, and the possibility of a renewed world state formation process cannot be discounted in the future. In the present phase it is possible to refer to the development of a global culture in a less totalistic sense... (1992:114).

In relative terms, however, one can talk about the emergence of a globalized identity through the prism of transnational 'third cultures' (life styles, bodies of knowledge and practices) unconstrained by nation-states as well as the heightened knowledge of the globe through connectivity and a concomitant consciousness of particularity as boundaries between self and other are drawn. In a sense, therefore, despite efforts to entrench a globalized identity, arguments against cosmopolitan identity continue to gain currency because among other things human beings are relational and presuppose also negativity and differences (Patomaki, 2008). For example, in the post 9/11 world, religion has become the defining feature of global identity politics. It now dominates the discourse of identity politics as Islam and Christianity seek to deepen their roots around the world.

Is it possible to produce an alternative 'othering' through an invocation of critical distance from *what we used to be, what we tried to be, what we became and what we are?* That is to say, through critical distance from our past and present, can we create the possibility of ethico-political learning and normative improvement by individual and collective reflection? Can we change our position with regard to the values that exclude and which we currently hold? There is evidence of this possibility in post-1945 Germany after the Nuremberg trials concluded that Nazi Germany committed crimes against humanity. Since then, Germany has developed a post-conventional morality based on a universalistic and reflexive point of view. We have also seen that Truth and Reconciliation Commissions have been used around the world notably in South Africa, Liberia and Rwanda as a basis for democracy and justice and to enable moral learning and the creation of a 'we-feeling' across a society torn apart by violence. The Truth and Reconciliation Commission of South Africa, headed by Bishop Desmond Tutu, gave citizens a space to seek forgiveness over crimes committed during the era of apartheid and to embark on the construction of a new state based on democratic ideals. Equally, the Truth and Reconciliation Commission of Liberia and Rwanda sought to address those nations' violent past and to rebuild them. It seems that collective learning *via* collective criticism can lead to the location of negative otherness in every group and this may reduce bitterness and exclusion.

In a number of statements made by Kenyans in the diaspora, a sense of globalized identity is emerging although it has not solidified. Some, such as Ali Mazrui and Ngugi wa Thiong'o, share a strong identification with pan-Africanism, others refer to themselves as Kenyans principally and still others have strong ethnic fixation despite being away from home. Clearly, the energies of a globalized identity are released through the interaction between universality and particularity. Whereas universality 'dilutes' local identities, such as ethnic consciousness by spreading out its values and reducing ethno-cultural experiences, particularity penetrates universality by transcending its place of origin. How does this happen? Apparently, a globalized identity does not abolish cultural and historical differences, in spite of distance from the 'homeland'. Presences and absences will always be there and humanity will always have multiple identities which are given different weighting depending on circumstances. This tension was quite manifest among diaspora Kenyans during the 2007/2008 post-election violence.

Significantly, between global and ethnic identities lies an intermediate and bridging notion of self; a transformative identity which links universality with particularity. Thus situated, this intercultural identity can transform the local into the universal and vice versa and enhance intercultural interaction and co-existence. Intercultural identity results from a convergence of ethno-linguistic commonalities expressed linguistically and culturally. Cultural identity (Hall 1992) may be thought of in at least two ways. First, in terms of a landscape, experiences and cultural expression, a 'collective one' lodged among 'many other selves' with a shared sense of being; history, ancestry, codes and rituals which are points of reference and the construction of meaning. Secondly, it can be thought of in terms of 'difference'; 'what the self has become' over time and space and therefore an exploration of the ruptures and discontinuities of the collective being. Viewed as such, cultural identity is a matter *'of being'* and *'of becoming'*; a convergence of the past and the future made possible through contact and reflection. In a sense, then, communities are always 'becoming'; always in change and transformation. In its tolerant form, cultural identity reaches out and embraces 'otherness', embracing its impermanence and transitoriness.

Unlike globalized identity, intercultural identity can lead to greater understanding between ethnic groups in the homeland or in the diaspora. It can challenge ethnic nationalism through a conscious transcendence of ethnolinguistic boundaries. Intercultural identity is open to cultural otherness and is bi-directional, reaching out to particularity including individuality and cultural situatedness and extending towards a global identity enshrined in global ideals and values.

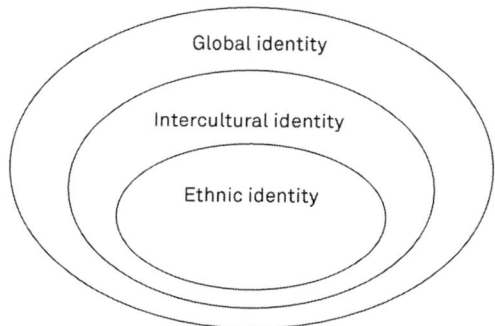

Fig: 1

National communities and identities are constructed but not out of nothing. They are the result of a collectivity of shared myths and legends, heroes, events, landscapes and memories disseminated through media—oral, print or electronic—in the creation of an imagined national community. When a national identity has not solidified, as is the case in Kenya, and in the context of intense competition for limited resources, power and representation, many citizens find more comfort in the ethno-linguistic affiliations even when they are located in distant lands. Cultural identities, as Stuart Hall (*Cultural Identity and the Diaspora*, 226), has observed:

> are the points of identification, the unstable points of identification or suture, which are made, within the discourses of history and culture. Not an essence but a *positioning*. Hence, there is always a politics of identity, a politics of position which has no absolute guarantee in an unproblematic, transcendental 'law of origin.'

Cultural identities have a dialogic relationship manifested in mutuality and interconnectivity with national and global identities as well as other forms of consciousness (professional, urbanicity, gender and so on). In moments of crisis, cultural identities can be immensely polarizing, including in the diaspora, possibly because they are the ones crafted at childhood through parenting and community socialization.

The nature of diaspora Kenyans

'The Diaspora' was at one time a concept which referred exclusively to the experiences of Jews, invoking their traumatic exile from Israel throughout many lands. In that sense, diaspora was associated with forced displacement, victimization, alienation, loss and a dream of return. These features led to the application of the term to Africans who were captured, enslaved and taken to distant lands. Derived from the Greek word for 'scattering of seeds', the term denotes a social condition, entailing a form of 'consciousness'; an identity.

The diaspora may be understood in terms of heterogeneity and diversity; a conception of identity which lives with and through, not despite, difference; by hybridity. For Stuart Hall (*Cultural Identity*, 235);

> The diaspora experience ...is defined not by essence or purity, but by recognition of a necessary heterogeneity and diversity; by a conception of 'identity' which lives with and through, not despite difference; by hybridity. Diaspora identities are those which are constantly producing and reproducing themselves anew, through transformation and difference.

The term refers to a process, a condition and a discourse: the unfolding and continuous processes by which it becomes possible, unmade and remade, the changing conditions of its existence and modes of expression and ways in which it is studied. The term also conjures images of time, space and cultural considerations, connections, and separations from the times, spaces and cultures of 'homeland'. The African diaspora of enslavement has been there for centuries and its connection to the homeland tends to be pan-Africanist but the diaspora of colonialism and neo-colonialism is less so and tends to be ethno-nationalist. Though important, dispersal is not a sufficient condition for the creation of a diaspora. A diasporic identity suggests a form of group consciousness and solidarity which is constituted historically through expressive culture (dance, music, art etc.), politics, thought and tradition and in which existential and representational resources are mobilized from the old and new worlds. It involves the mobilization of resources, for cultural production, people and places and their associated iconography, images, ideas and ideologies. Kenyans in the diaspora have occasionally shown this group consciousness as Kenyans, when convenient and as members of specific ethnicities present in the homeland at other times.

Zeleza (2005, 2007) has suggested that African migrations are on the increase and many of these migrants are constituting themselves into new diasporas, whose identities involve complex negotiations with the host African diaspora communities and their countries of origin. Moreover, Zeleza argues that if the diaspora of enslavement—the historic diaspora—had no choice but to see itself in pan-Africanist terms whenever it identified with Africa, "the diaspora of colonialism and neo-colonialism—the contemporary diaspora—is more disposed to see itself in pan-national or even pan-ethnic terms" (2005:212-213). Most Kenyans in the diaspora belong to the contemporary diaspora and are to be mainly found in the USA, UK, Canada and Australia. There are professionals, blue collar workers and students and their responses to events in the homeland are varied.

Generally, diaspora Kenyans exhibit a number of traits including the following:
(a) They have diverse social relationships resulting from history and geography and—many migrated voluntarily from Kenya to other countries in pursuit of education, professional development, economic opportunities, or exile;
— have consciously maintained a collective identity as Kenyans or members of an ethnic group and recreate "home" at parties and religious gatherings;
— have institutionalized networks of exchange and communication which go beyond territorial states and created new communal organizations in their host countries;
— have maintained explicit and implicit connections with Kenya;
— have developed relations of solidarity with co-ethnic members in other host countries;
— having not been fully accepted by host country, many suffer from feelings of alienation, exclusion, occasional superiority vis-a-vis those at home and a range of other forms of 'difference'.

(b) They exhibit tension of political orientation and participation because they would like to be involved in Kenyan politics from a distance. They are interested in being dual citizens and would like a stable nation-state so that they can invest in the homeland. While some are important individual actors in Kenyan politics, others engage national and local politics through collective associations such as the Kenyan Community Abroad and Kenya Diaspora Network. Moreover, still others function as lobbyists and fundraisers for politicians from their communities and regions or political parties with which they are associated. In addition, there are those who align themselves extensively to their ethnic groups and associations and perpetuate ethno-nationalism from far. They hardly reach out to Kenyans from other ethno-linguistic groups. This group carries the ethnic resentment in the homeland and will take the first opportunity to anonymously 'tell' authorities about the possibility of fellow Kenyans living 'illegally' in the host country.

(c) They participate in philanthropy and use economic strategies to boost the financial state of their families, communities and nation-state through pooling of resources, transfer of credit, helping out with student sponsorship ventures, investment of capital and provision of services to family networks, clans and ethnic group. These transformative philanthropic gestures are generally expected, even in situations of economic global down-turns, because the land yonder is viewed to have many opportunities not available in the homeland.

Some of these traits acquired significance during the violence experienced in Kenya after the 2007 elections. The diaspora was shaken in 2007 and the beginning of 2008 like no other time in Kenyan history.

Election related violence has recurred in Kenya since the re-introduction of multi-party politics and internal displacements have been experienced before and after general elections in 1992, 1997, 2002 (to a limited degree) and 2007. Although the violence tends to occur around national elections, it is in most cases a consequence of other matters, beyond the election, including the pursuit or retention of political power and instruments of the state, land allocation and use, youth unemployment, socio-economic inequalities and regional disparities, poverty, manipulation of ethnicity for political purposes, weak and ineffective institutions of governance and corruption. The election is used by a wide range of forces as an opportunity for the expression of other matters related to governance and citizenship. The 2007/2008 violence, though expected, was the most severe in magnitude, speed and viciousness. Given the centrality of Kenya in eastern Africa, the African Union and the international community quickly got involved in the pursuit of a solution to the crisis.[2]

It will be recalled that before Mwai Kibaki was declared winner on December 30, 2007 by the Chairman of the Electoral Commission of Kenya, amid closing of the gap between the two main contenders and claims of rigging, opposition leader Raila Odinga had announced his victory in a public briefing and the European Union observer team had openly expressed their dissatisfaction with the election results. The country was tense and ready for an explosion as the contest was replayed on live television and the internet and rumours spread around the country and beyond. When the Minister for Internal Security announced a ban on live broadcasts, Kenyans turned to other means of getting and relaying information, such as short message services (SMS) from mobile phones. Mobile phones were used to communicate locally and internationally and share news and feelings. The Ministry of Internal Security warned about circulating SMS that might cause public unrest and phone cards were also in short supply, suggesting that the ban led to a high demand for mobile phone communication. Social media tools like wikis, weblogs, Facebook, YouTube, and Twitter were extensively used to organize and share information about the crisis and violence and to raise funds[3]. While some discussion forums sought to promote peace and national unity others, especially in the diaspora, questioned national citizenship in the face of claims that a wrong person had been sworn in as president. Citizen journalism blossomed as Kenyans posted their thoughts online from the country and the diaspora.[4] Some politicians set up their own 'internet soldiers' who posted partisan opinions anonymously, at times carrying multiple identities. Ethnic tensions were heightened using new media.

Post-election violence and involvement of Kenyans in the diaspora

Kenyans in the diaspora were embroiled in the events back home and national tensions were replayed abroad. Mashada forum, Kenya's first online chat room, was invaded by war mongers. Expressing shock at the invasion, White African wrote:

> As you may know, I've been having quite a problem regulating mashada.com, despite having recently hired people to moderate the forums. It is starting to become a reflection of what is going on on the ground in Kenya. I'd hate for it to hinder our current efforts since I'm directly connected to it, therefore I am having to shut down the forums until further notice. Facilitating civil discussions and debates has become virtually impossible" (*http://whiteafrican. coni/2008/01/29/mashada-forums-kenyas-First-digital-casualty/* and quoted in *Tribal Hatred Claims Its First Online Casualty* on *www.politicsonline.com*)

The emerging diasporic identity had been challenged by ethnic solidarity being played out in the homeland. Later mashada.com was redirected to a new site appropriately called ihavenotribe.com which was meant to de-emphasize ethnic identity and to search for justice, reconciliation and peace driven by the issues at stake.

Kenyans in the diaspora use new communication technologies, notably the internet and mobile phones in order to stay connected with home and one notices on the internet and print media occasional tensions between them and those based in the homeland. Before the elections, conversations between the homeland and the diaspora had started. For example, in a *Commentary* 'Are the Stars in the Eyes of Kenyans Abroad Waning' (*Daily Nation 12/10/2007*) Rasna Warah says:

> Kenyans expect a lot from their diaspora. One, we expect them to send regular remittances to the motherland. Two, we expect them to acquire foreign nationalities so that they can become eligible to sponsor relatives who want to join them.
>
> Three, we expect them to lead the finest of lives, with posh cars, big houses and the latest gadgets. And last, but not least, we do not expect them to come back home for good.
>
> And the diaspora has not disappointed. It is estimated that Kenyans living abroad remit approximately $600 million to Kenya each year.

These 'expectations' point to a continuity of socio-cultural responsibilities unchallenged by distance. To generalize, just as it is in the homeland so shall it be in abroad. In a symbolic 'return' many Kenyans in the diaspora stay connected and recreate the memory of homeland through religious gatherings, evenings of *nyama choma* and Tusker get-togethers. Some insist on speaking their ethnic languages when they meet, listening to Kenyan music, watching Kenyan comedians (Redykyulass, Churchill Live, XYZ, Vitimbi and so on) online or during summer trips and replay the politics of ethnicity at home, even if there are pretences of having transcended it. When they send remittances home, it is to support and subsidize family members left behind or to invest in property or businesses.[5] Because it is assumed they have resources and connections in the North, they have been wooed by aspiring presidential candidates at every election since 1992 and the Kenya Community Abroad (KCA) has tended to be actively involved in national politics.

Others, especially the intellectual community, reconnect with the continent through a pan-Africanist approach continuing in the tradition of the late 19th and early 20th century in the production of knowledge about Africa. During the post-election violence in Kenya, however, pan-Africanism was occasionally challenged by some academics and the politics of exclusion invoked as more preferable. For example, at the peak of the violence on January 19th 2008, Maurice Amutabi writing in response to Abubakar Momoh argues that breaking up the nation-state may be desirable. He says:

> Your point on 'oneness' and its importance for Pan-Africanism is important, but I wonder if your point implies that small states or balkanization is bad. You seem to suggest that breaking up our nation-states which were colonial creations is dangerous...I would support the partition of Kenya, where Central Province becomes a separate state. There might be more peace given the tensions that have often played out between the Kikuyu and the rest of Kenya. That is why like many pramataists (sic), have always thought that it was a mistake for Yakubu Gowon to fight against the Ibo secessionist movement under Dim Chukwuemeka Odumegwu Ojukwu." (*Email correspondence titled The Haunting Demons dated January 19th, 2008 and copied widely*).

This Kenyan academic in the diaspora questions the concept of national citizenship and supports secession and balkanization of his homeland. By isolating one ethnic community as 'the problem' and 'the enemy' in the nation-state, he trivializes a national tragedy in which many people died, over 600,000 families were displaced, women raped, children killed and property and infrastructure destroyed. When entrenched, exclusionist and generalizing discourse from the diaspora is extremely dangerous and conflict enhancing and may lead to crimes against humanity or genocide if replayed at the community level in the homeland.

On Friday March 21 2008, Clay Muganda wrote about the diaspora in the *Daily Nation's Weekend Magazine:*

> ...their tribal footprints were all over the internet, all in the name of patriotism. With their much-touted knowledge, they forgot that, as somebody once said, patriotism is the last refuge of a scoundrel.
>
> When the chaos erupted—and you can even say they had a hand in it through their inflammatory advertisements—they went silent. Those of them who were on "holiday" boarded the first flight (economy class of course) to the Diaspora—or wherever else they have replaced dish-washing machines. Cowards!

These are harsh words directed at Kenyans who live far from home. Muganda suggests that despite being exposed to a global culture, the diaspora is still ethnically inclined and that it disengaged itself and retreated to safer ground. In responses to Muganda posted on the internet, especially *www.mashada.com*, Kenyans in the diaspora were most angered by the reference to the blue color jobs they do and few addressed the presence of ethnic footprints on the internet.

It may be assumed that the diasporic experience would lead to a dismantling of ethnic imperatives across identity and cultural narratives. Without doubt, identity choices of individuals and groups are broadened through migration and transnational movement. However, it is also the case that the diaspora can lead to ethnic fundamentalism because members seek to "compensate" for their absence; an absence that may be viewed as betrayal to the community. By compensating, diasporans may take radical positions that may present them as ethnic fundamentalists. In themselves, identities do not become politically salient until some political issue affects members of a group. When an identity is threatened, people may be forced to choose between competing identities and violent conflict may hence ensue, particularly if groups perceive they are in competition for access to the state or economic resources. Moreover, if political elites manipulate ethnic identity in order to attain or retain power, a trans-ethnic identity that may be found within the nation-state or the diaspora might be in jeopardy.

But some Kenyans in the diaspora worked hard to get the post-election violence story out. Ory Okolloh, David Kobia and Erik Hersman worked together to create www.ushahidi.com by combining Google Maps, which allows users to zoom in and view satellite images of Kenya, with a tool for users, via mobile phone or internet browser, to report incidences of violence on the map, add photos, video, and written content that document where and when violence occurs. The www.ushahidi.com was created to provide comprehensive reports of what was happening in Kenya with direct information from those who were affected where murder, riots, looting, rape and other forms of violence were taking place.

Ushahidi is part of Kenyan civic project that can be traced to around 2006 when Ory Orkolloh joined forces with an anonymous blogger known as 'M' to assemble *Mzalendo: Eye on Kenyan Parliament;* a website meant to assist Kenyan Members of Parliament become more accountable to their electorate. Kenyans in the diaspora initiated campaigns such as "Help Kenyans in Distress" at the peak of the violence some which leveraged SMS money transfer technology to support the Red Cross and the blogger Joseph Kaloki wrote about a young boy who was left crying when his mother was killed in Naivasha. He organized fund raising activities for "Baby Brian." Individuals and groups were seeking to find a solution to the crisis.

But it was Ushahidi that showed how diaspora Kenyans can use technology for the benefit of the homeland. Ory Okolloh on January 2, 2008 wrote in her blog:

> "Google Earth supposedly shows in great detail where the damage is being done on the ground. It occurs to me that it will be useful to keep a record of this, if one is thinking long term. For the reconciliation process to occur at the local level the truth of what happened will first have to come out. Guys looking to do something—any techies out there willing to a mashup of where the violence and destruction is occurring using Google Maps." www.kenya-pundit.com)

David Kobia and Erik Hersman heeded the call. They worked with designers and launched Ushahidi on January 9, 2010. The innovation has been extremely useful in documenting catastrophe.

> "An interactive map is a remarkably effective narrative tool for a transnational audience. Tragic violence calls for empathy and action, but it is difficult to feel a connection with a place one can't imagine." (Goldstein & Rotich 2008:6).

These tools allow cooperation on massive scale as they harness many people towards common goal. The Ushahidi experience was later to become immensely useful in dealing with the Haiti and Chile earthquakes. Ironically and unexpectedly, United States of America learnt from the Kenyan crisis how to map the various trouble spots.

Citizen journalism blossomed and Kenyan bloggers were instrumental in getting the story out, especially when live broadcasts were banned by the government. Radio broadcasters around the world started relying on bloggers for information. Mobile phones were used to circulate pictures outside mainstream media and mass SMS went out across the globe creating anxiety, anger and sense of despair. University Professors gave talks, or posted on list-servs and blogs. Many appeared on radio and television to explain the crisis to the world.

A number of Kenyans in the diaspora used their blogs to show the complexity of the Kenyan crisis and argued that the election was held against a background of mistrust, manipulation of ethnicity, existence of small arms, the majimbo (regionalism) debate, socio-economic inequalities, the greed for power, corruption, past impunity, propaganda and poor quality of national leadership. Their audience was mainly foreign (see for example www.matunda.org based in Toronto). In his blog Matunda sought to broaden the debate on the Kenyan crisis and to incorporate political and economic factors in a holistic manner.

Urging national dialogue and international support

While some of them mobilized resources and channelled them through the Kenya Red Cross and religious organizations, others called for a stoppage of the violence, urged the international community to intervene and national leaders and professions to engage in dialogue and reconciliation. There were peace rallies in Minnesota, Dallas, Washington DC, New York among other cities (*www.mshale.com*) and Ngũgĩ wa Thiong'o shared his views with the BBC World Service on 10th January 2008 (*www.news.bbc.co.uk/gov/pr/fr/-/2/hi/africa*). Ngugi raised three issues: that we needed to separate electoral injustice from the violation of human rights; that some of the violence may have been pre-meditated and taken the form of ethnic cleansing; and that the United Nations needed to investigate the violence. Ngũgĩ's decision to downplay the dispute in the election results and to focus on the violence in the Rift Valley was seen as an endorsement of Mwai Kibaki and he was widely rebuked and castigated on the internet by quite a number of diaspora Kenyans. He was seen as providing a Party of National Unity (PNU) perspective and was labelled a 'tribalist'[6] because at the time of his commentary the targeted community for displacement was mainly Kikuyu, his ethnic group. Disturbingly, it was almost as if members of that community were not supposed to talk about the violence and the crimes that were committed against fellow citizens.

In an interview with journalist David Ohito, Ali Mazrui suggested that considering that a civil war was in the offing, triggered by a combination of ethnicity, power, rivalry and economic deprivation, it was imperative that the international community takes action targeted at the political elite. Calling on more pressure and threats to be exerted by the international community, he suggested that Kenya's membership of the African Union and the Commonwealth could be withdrawn, bank accounts frozen and specific members of both the government and the opposition be deprived of visas to the western world if they are identified as extremists against the search for solutions. Whereas Ngugi was incensed by the wanton killing and destruction of lives, Mazrui's strategy was to get a political process on track to avert an imminent civil war. These approaches by seasoned academics in the diaspora were driven by a search for a peaceful resolution of the crisis and did not demonize whole communities.

Ethnic mobilization and hate materials on internet

In her essay 'Kenya's Path to Peace' (*www.opendemocracy.net*) on 7th February 2008, Jacqueline Klopp called for a political agreement, the laying down of arms, the settlement of internally displaced persons, healing and reconciliation as key in the resolution of the post election crisis. As she correctly notes "as people are forced to flee their homes to some imaginary 'homeland' they take their trauma and tales of terror." The 'return' also creates immense stress on resources and services leading to new tensions, feelings of rage and revenge attacks. Klopp called on Kenyans in the diaspora to 'stop hate speech circulating on the internet, to avoid lending resources to destructive politics and instead support the internally displaced and peace activities'. This call for positive solidarity was apt because writings by diaspora Kenyans found on blogs and list-servs during the post-election violence were principally ethnically grounded. According to Matunda Nyanchama:

> "What you don't see [when you look at *Africa-oped*] is what I see as the moderator. Something snapped in the minds of even the Kenyans who used to be fair before the elections. They have become ethnically abusive, degrading and outright offensive. You can't believe educated Kenyans living abroad can bend so low. (*www.pbs.org/frontline/blog/2008/04/kenya_the_onlin.html*)

Julia Opoti, editor of *Kenya Imagine*, an online discussion forum, expressed similar disbelief at some of the comments appearing on *Kenya Imagine* and posted by highly educated professionals she knows personally.

> It shocked me because these were people living in the United States and who made very educated arguments before the elections. We have seen people calling for violence by posting comments like, 'Why did they vote that way? They deserve to die.' We could not sit around and watch that happen (*www.pbs.org/frontline/blog/2008/04/kenya_the_onlin.html*).

In other words, the moderators had to edit out the poison that was being emitted by Kenyans in the diaspora. Other contributors acquired multiple ethnic identities and posted extremely polarizing statements. The situation was so bad that David Kobia the founder of mashada.com had to shut down the site because it had become virtually impossible to have meaningful debate and discussion. He had hired people to assist in moderating the site but it was impossible to manage the vitriol.

In frustration, Kobia said:

> New registration on the site has been disabled temporarily to control the recent space of rogue users inciting hate and violence. Some of this material has really been shocking, and mashada.com will not be vehicle that transports this abhorrent material. It is truly sad to see the estrangement this election has caused, which has rubbed off on the atmosphere of our forum. (*www.mashanda.com*)

To avoid suffering Mashada's fate of having to shut down, owners of similar online forums started policing comments on their sites. They discovered that although the Kenyan middle class and the diaspora were absent from the mayhem in the country's streets and farmlands, they were fuelling the wars online.

The church in the diaspora was not spared of the hate. Writing on the internet from Newark Delaware, Billy Machage, said:

> Kenyans living abroad, are we different? No we are not! The tribal hate I witnessed in my church shortly after results were released shocked me. I became resigned and detached from the reality but vowed to speak my mind and the truth. Some don't like it but tell you what "the truth shall free us" all!! Okongo, keep up the good work and the good Lord in heaven will bless your territory and protect you from your enemies. (http://homelandcolours.blogspot.com/2008/01lmashada.htmn"(http://whiteafrican.coni/2008/01/29/mashada-forums-kenyas-First-digital-casualty/)

The Gĩkũyũ, Embu and Meru (GEMA) Mt. Kenya communities in the diaspora started organizing themselves to respond to the violence. They sought the inclusion of two other communities namely Kisii and Akamba. In a sense therefore, GEMA included four communities: Gĩkũyũ, Embu, Meru, Kamba. But the Kisii needed to be included and this was done through the invocation of historical linguistics. The Mt. Kenya linguistic communities and the Kisii are related linguistically and are part of the Thagicu. Linguistic and cultural solidarities were being mobilized in the homeland and the diaspora to deal with the crisis. On 24th January 2008, GEMA ABROAD was launched and all adults from Mt. Kenya region were required to register with at least £50 and above. The Organization agreed to involve GEMA communities in USA and in other parts of the world "so that we can help their community who had 'become the target of the recent mass killings" (www.wanjuguna.blogspot.com/ 2008/01/gema-abroad). There was a veiled threat that those who would not register are of no value to the community and that members would 'monitor the progress of the registration and to know who is who'. GEMA ABROAD would have played a key role in resource mobilization towards the local conflict.

Around the same time, documents were circulating on the internet galvanizing the Gĩkũyũ community for an eminent war. One document purporting to be the declaration of 500 supporters of GEMA in the UK urged the community to provide funds for the war threatening "...if you don't join and register at this crucial time you are of no use to the community." Another document from

"Thagicu Renaissance Movement" names human rights activists as "traitors" to the community.

> "We have conceived and designed the formation of a Renaissance Movement and a Communal Defence Structure to protect and defend our people from genocide, our woman and girls from mass rape and our (sic) reclaim our property in Nairobi City;
>
> We are a renaissance movement and not a militia group; we shall not operate underground or use violence to achieve our aims; we are educated people, professionals in various disciplines, trades and investors and business people of repute;
>
> We shall only act in self defence to protect the lives of our people, our children and the dignity and honour of our women and girls or protect our rightfully owned property.
>
> We have identified the traitors of our communities and request you to spare them for now; we WILL take decisive appropriate action against them at an OPPORTUNE moment" (*www.jukwaa.proboards.com/index*).

A group referring itself to 'Kalenjin Online' (*http://geraldbaraza.blogspot.com/2008/01/ladies-and-gentlemen-gotab-kalenjin-html*) called for unity of the community against the 'enemy.' The statement said, among other things, "we urge our people to ensure that every family is fully equipped with our normal tools; if we can afford, ferry two warriors from upcountry fully armed and house them until we have this thing sorted out." Individuals from the community who would not cooperate were called 'traitors'. "If any of us (gotab Kalenjin), God forbid, betrays our course, we shall not only eliminate him/her, but their entire lineage. We shall invoke our Kalenjin CURSE in ensuring that the individual and all their generation shall not live." Modern technology and community belief systems were merged to create fear among those who may challenge an ascribed identity. It is not clear who were circulating these documents but they were intended to incite inter-ethnic hatred and violence.

Evidently, tension in the homeland would be squarely transferred to the diaspora. There were reports that the contact details of Kenyans living illegally in the USA were being circulated to American intelligence for action. The crisis in Kenya had started taking an international dimension.

Rationalizing the violence and urging partition of Kenya into ethnic enclaves
In an article published in the *Daily Nation* on January 14th 2008, Rasnah Warah sought to introduce class, inequalities, poor institutions of governance and the quality of leadership as factors in the post election. The main objective of her article, in my view, was to seek to see the violence in a broader sense beyond the

ethnic lens. The reaction to her article from Kenyan academicians in the diaspora was immediate and merciless. Maurice Amutabi of Central Washington University wrote on the same day in a listserv circulated widely:

> Rasnah Warah, or whatever the name is, is among those people who are not just getting it. They are wrong, and such shallow theorizing will not get us anywhere. Martha Karua, John Michuki, Uhuru Kenyatta, Amos Kimunya and other hardliners have one thing in common—they are Kikuyu—and nothing to do with class. To talk about class in Kenya before we even have a clear distinction between the bourgeoisie and the proletariat, where the middle class is not even distinct as a social group, is crap, and complete nonsense. It is absurd that Rasnah Warah thinks that every Kenyan has househelps, drivers, gardeners, cooks and watchmen, like her fellow Asians in Nairobi, who are in fact the collaborating group in Kenya's corruption history. The likes of her should simply shut up and enjoy their wealth in peace, instead of these empty rants and polemics.

Writing from Washington under the subject of *The Haunting Demons* on January 17, 2008 and circulating widely, John Mulaa, a columnist for a Kenyan paper introduced the possibility of armed struggle directed at a section of the country, partitioning Kenya and isolating Central Province. In his view, the regime in power is fascist and cannot engage with reason, negotiation and dialogue. He asserts:

> We should stop beating about the bush. We have to support an armed struggle leading to eventual partition of the country. We cannot forget or forgive what these guys have done. There is no guarantee they will not repeat it. It is in their DNA. Kenyans are paying the price for the pathology of a traumatized and untreated people. Central province was the scene of horrific bloodbath just before independence. The elites there never sought truth and reconciliation among their people. We are now witnessing the results of refusal to face up to painful acts. Let Central go and spend time exorcising its demons. It is a horribly disfigured place.

John Mulaa raises two vital questions worth brief discussion. First, is it possible that an ethnic community could be genetically programmed so that it cannot conceivably engage in dialogue or co-exist with other communities? Globally, which communities are so programmed and what should be done to them? Any claim that a community is genetically predisposed towards a certain behaviour is myopic and extremely dangerous. It erases any possibilities of personal choice and agency. Indeed, it lays the foundation for violence on a whole community on the basis of their predisposition. The danger with this position is made even more potent if extracted from the desk of an academician. Second, Mulaa makes reference to a bloodbath that took place in Kenya before independence. He neither mentions Mau Mau freedom struggle by name nor does he link the 'pathology of traumatized and untreated people' to the struggle for independence. The failure of Kenya to have a Truth, Justice and Reconciliation Commission at the onset of independence should be a source of shame for the whole country. Doesn't the failure of the nation to recognize that a region lost thousands of people in the struggle for independence constitute a historical injustice? Disturbingly, except for a few lonely voices from the homeland, nobody on the list-serv from the diaspora questioned Mulaa's statement.

A week later on January 26th, 2008, he revisited the subject and argued that the emptying of Kikuyus from different provinces should lead to the partitioning of the country. He wrote:

> The Rift Valley is being emptied of the Kikuyu, there is nary any Kikuyu in any other province, and the country has effectively been partitioned. That is the immediate term.
>
> The medium term is central and eastern provinces will have to confront massive overcrowding, food scarcity (they are basket case agriculturally), and, of course bickering among themselves.
>
> In the long term they will inhabit a failed statelet that cannot feed itself or govern itself.

Later on February 5, 2008 he was to write in reference to the Kikuyu, "We have called their bluff but they persist in their foolishness. We shall be left with no option [than] carry it to the logical conclusion, i.e. fight and defeat them on the battlefield and then invite them to choose between joining the rest of us in one country or go their way. I have never seen such a deluded group." It is often claimed—and the convictions of various individuals by the International Criminal Court (ICC) trying suspected culprits of the Rwanda killings have demonstrated the veracity of these charges—that religious leaders and educated individuals participated in the genocide in Rwanda. Therefore if anything is affirmed by the celebration of the 'emptying' and 'defeating' of communities that this highly educated diaspora-based Kenyan reinforces, it is the belief that formal schooling is not a sufficient condition for an individual to see the value of all humanity, irrespective of its cultural base. The structural problems of state formation and citizenship cannot, in all fairness, be attributed to any one community. Problems of a historical and constitutional nature can only be resolved through an entrenchment of democracy, the rule of law and human rights. Such an effort lies in upholding the rights of all citizens, the harmonization of citizenship rights with universal criteria as well as action towards equality and inclusion in the conduct of national affairs (Appadurai 2006; Manby

2009). These actions would demand the centralization of a global cosmopolitan identity, alongside other forms of belonging.

Conclusion

Cultural heterogeneity has existed since time immemorial although this has been accelerated through modern forms of globalization. In the recent past, especially with the rise of modernity and its emphasis on individualism and equality, cultural differences have become politically salient and subject to manipulation. Local forms of identity, such as ethnicity, have gained more salience because of the competition for resources and power, corruption and the crisis of governance.

Apparently, during times of national tensions Kenyans at home and in the diaspora pay most attention to a singularity of human identity for which we have no choice. But this, as Amartya Sen (2006) has shown, tends to diminish us all and make our neighborhoods more volatile. Where does the solution lie? It lies in the recognition and celebration of the plurality of our identities and the anchoring of structures that all citizens get a sense of belonging, irrespective of their territorial location. Our shared humanity is immensely tested and challenged when our differences are reduced into one system of categorization, defined ethnically.

While it is important to appreciate that it is through ethnic identification that competition for power in the state and in the allocation, management and use of resources becomes apparent in most of Africa sometimes exploding into conflict as happened in Kenya after the 2007 elections, ethnicity by itself is not a problem whether in the homeland or in the diaspora. Conflicts are about power and resources. Ethnicity may be constructed and anchored in order to conceal the repression and exploitation of citizens by a political and economic elite at the national or community levels and to suppress the possibility of building solidarities across ethnic and gender lines. It may also be emphasized in order to mobilise support for a declining political legitimacy aimed at acquiring power or maintaining it. What happened in Kenya was a political dynamic pinned on ethnicity and read as such in most of the diaspora. Similarly, solutions to those problems must be found in a reorganization of the political dynamics not in the demonization, exclusion and victimization of certain ethnic groups.

Evidently, the perception of diaspora as breaking the ethnic spectacle underestimates the unceasing attachment to the idea of ethnic particularity. There is no doubt that ethnic identities have provided social safety nets that have cushioned many Africans from poverty, disease and illiteracy in the faces of the excesses of globalization such as Structural Adjustment Programmes (SAPs) and economic difficulties ignited in the North. We also recognize that ethnic based movements can serve as counter-hegemonic forces to the centralizing and hegemonic ambitions of the modern territorial secular nation-state by localizing the struggle for citizenship in ways that create moral communities with shared problems, mobilize social capital and broaden the space for cultural citizenship in post-colonial Africa. But given limited resources, politics of exclusion, corruption, pursuit of power, weak governance institutions, mistrust and poor leadership, politicized ethnic identities can be intensely divisive and isolationist, either in the homeland or the diaspora. The diaspora, in view of its networks, can play a critical role in delineating the difficulties in the homeland and together with other agents of change contribute in coming up with ways of resolving them.

※

Notes

1 *Attributed to Socrates* (469–399BC) by Plutarch, *of Banishment*. www.quotationspage.com/quote/24177.html
2 The US government docket for foreign policy in Africa was at the time held by Assistant Secretary of State Jendayi Frazer. She took three positions on the Kenyan crisis which were replayed in the diaspora. First, she declared that the vote could not be reassessed through an independent tally; second, she claimed that there had been vote rigging from both sides of the political divide, and suggested that the true election results were extremely close and that perhaps Mwai Kibaki had won; and thirdly, she argued

that the two sides needed to compromise and share power. These position were to guide the National Dialogue process led by Kofi Annan and the eventual setting up of the Coalition Government with Mwai Kibaki as President and Raila Odinga as Prime Minister.

3 Kenya chat rooms include africaonlinekenyachat; club waudo Kenya chat and information; insight Kenya room; java beach Kenya travel chat room; kelele chat room; Kenyachat.com; Kenya message board; Kenyaniyetu.com chat room; Kenyans.com chat room; Kenyaweb.com chat room; Kenyasearch.com chat room; Kenyans soccer fans chat room; Kibarua.com chat room and discussion board; Kisumuonline chat room; mabeste.com chat room; mambogani.com discussion boards; mashada.com chat room; Mkenya.com chat room; Orientation Kenya chat room; SuperEva Kenya chat room; Urban Kenya.com discussion board and many others. It is believed that some politicians had 'internet soldiers' who posted partisan and ethnically charged opinions anonymously.

4 The development of the internet has increased the possibility for creating and maintaining multiple relationships and identities. In anonymity, users are able to say things they would not share in face to face interactions. For more on this tendency see Duncan Timms *Identity, Community and the Internet* www.odeluce.stir.ac.uk/doc/identity.

5 Some of the collective remittances are unfortunately key resources for conflict. This is especially so where the diaspora views its political involvement as best done through political channels and not civil society. The diaspora can contribute in bringing about peace and stability and can be key to providing policy directions that are accommodative and inclusive. However, the diaspora may seek solutions to political problems by supporting rival political groups engaged in a power struggle that shuts out reconciliation. In such cases, sections of the diaspora provide financial resources, networks and war materials to political groups in the homeland. The factional agendas may be detrimental to the national good.

6 Both in the homeland and in the diaspora, talking about the violence and displacement of citizens was viewed as sympathy for the government, until the reprisal attacks commenced in late January 2008.

References

Appadurai, A. (2006). *Fear of Small Things. An Essay on the Geography of Anger.* Durham: Duke University Press.

Aseka, E. M. (2007). 'History, Culture and National Development: The Role of Kenyan Diaspora in Constructing a New Politics of Culture and Identity.' *Paper presented at the International Conference held at Kennesaw State University, Georgia on the 'Role of the Kenyan Diaspora in Kenya's Development'* on March 24, 2007.

Bakhtin, M. (1984). *The Dialogic Imagination: Four Essays.* Michael Holquist (Ed). Austin, Texas: University of Texas Press.

Featherstone, M. (1992). *Undoing Culture, Postmodernism, and Identity.* London: Sage Publications.

Floya, A. (1998). 'Evaluating Diaspora: Beyond Ethnicity'. *In Sociology* Vol. 32 No. 3, pp. 557–580.

Goldstein, J. & Juliana, R. (2008). *Digitally Networked Technology in Kenya's 2007–2008 Post-Election Crisis.* In Internet Case Study Series. The Berkman Centre for Internet and Society at Harvard University.

Hall, S. (1992). 'The Question of Cultural Identity'. In S. Hall et al (Eds) *Modernity and Futures.* Cambridge Polity Press, pp. 274–316.

Kagwanja, P. (2003). 'Globalizing Ethnicity, Localizing Citizenship: Globalization, Identity Politics and Violence in Kenya's Tana River Region'. In *African Development XXVIII Nos. 1&2*, pp. 112–152.

Klopp, J. M. (2008). ' Kenya's Path to Peace.' Open

Democracy. http://www.opendemocracy.net.
Manby, B. (2009). *Struggles for Citizenship in Africa*. London: Zed Books.
Mohamoud, A. A. (2006). 'African Diaspora and Post Conflict Reconstruction of Africa.' Copenhagen: Danish Institute for International Studies, DIIS Brief.
Njogu, K. (2009). 'Narrative and Memory.' In (Ed.) *Healing the Wound: Personal Narratives About the 2007 Post-Election Violence in Kenya*. Nairobi: Twaweza Communications.
Njogu, K. (2004). *Reading Poetry as Dialogue: An East African Literary Tradition*. Nairobi: Jomo Kenyatta Foundation.
Patomaki, H. (2008). 'Is a Global Identity Possible? The Relevance of Big History to Self-Other Relations.' *Paper at the 49th Annual ISA Convention "Bridging Multiple Divides"*. San Francisco, March 26th-March 29th 2008.
Riggs, F. W. (2002, May 20). 'Globalization, Ethnic Diversity, and Nationalism: The Challenge of Democracies'. *Annals of the American Academy of Political and Social Science, Vol. 581; Globalization and Democracy*, pp. 35-47. Retrieved July 23, 2009, from www.jostor.org/stable/1049705.
Young, M. C. (2004). 'Revisiting Nationalism and Ethnicity in Africa'. *UCLA International Institute. Studies Center. James S. Coleman Memorial Lecture Series*. African Los Angeles: University of California. http://repositories.cdlib.org/international/asc/jscmls/Nationalism.
Zeleza, T. (2005). 'The Academic Diaspora and Knowledge Production in and on Africa: What role for CODESRIA' In (ed.) Thandika Mkandawire *African Intellectuals: Rethinking Politics, Language, Gender and Development*. Dakar: CODESRIA Books.
Zeleza, T. (2007). 'Journeying to Excellence: Knowledge, Diaspora and Leadership.' In (ed.) Onyekachi Wambu *Under the Tree of Talking: Leadership for Change in Africa* (pp. 231-251). London: Counterpoint.

Websites
www.beginsathome.com/2008/04/01/.
http://liblit.org/2008/02/16.
http://whiteafrican.coni/2008/01/29/mashada-forums-kenyas-First-digital-casualty/.
www.politicsonline.com.
www.mashada.com.
www.ushahidi.com.
www.kenyapundit.com.
www.matunda.org.
www.mshale.com.
www.news.bbc.co.uk/gov/pr/fr/-/2/hi/africa.
www.opendemocracy.net.
www.pbs.org/frontline/blog/2008/04/kenya_the_onlin.html.
http://homelandcolours.blogspot.com/2008/011mashada.
http://whiteafrican.coni/2008/01/29/mashada-forums-kenyas-First-digital-casualty/.
www.wanjuguna.blogspot.com/2008/01/gema-abroad.
www.jukwaa.proboards.com/index.
http://geraldbaraza.blogspot.com/2008/01/ladies-and-gentlemen-gotab-kalenjin-html
www.quotationspage.com/quote/24177.html.
www.odeluce.stir.ac.uk/doc/identity.

Intellectuals and the State: A Historical Perspective

VINCENT G. SIMIYU

All in all where the initial work of African intellectuals seems to have been mainly directed at fighting racism they soon established a more courageous position in opposition to the colonial state. As long as they were part of the nationalist anti-colonial movement they were viewed as patriotic by the majority of Africans.

Thus the activities and publications of people like Kwame Nkrumah, Jomo Kenyatta, Julius Nyerere, Walter Rodney, Frantz Fanon and Nelson Mandela among others were well received not only in Africa but also internationally.

Since ancient times intellectuals have played major roles in the development of societies the world over. Indeed it can be argued that societies have advanced in all fields of human endeavour due to mainly to the work of intellectuals. It is therefore a singularly tragic paradox that political leaderships, with only a few exceptions have loathed, curtailed, imprisoned and even killed intellectuals in the name of the advancement of the same societies. This apparent contradiction is perhaps the very nature of an intellectual, simultaneously positive and negative such that he has been described as controversial probably because it takes another intellectual to understand what the other one is saying.

Who then is an intellectual? He is one who is endowed with significant brain power and can understand in depth and then analyse ideas and facts before rendering them in a lucid manner that will allow ease of comprehension. However, the role of the intellectual does not stop at this abstract level. Contrary to the assertion by Archimedes that application of ideas is the work of inferior minds, the intellectual should enable society to embrace reality by conceiving mechanisms of practically implementing ideas. Akbar, one of India's great rulers and the founder of the Moghul Empire, always sought the counsel of intellectuals through frequent discussions with scholars.[1] We should also underscore the fact that intellectuals have occupied high political office; Thomas Jefferson of the U.S.A. and Napoleon Bonaparte of France are cases in point. Our concern, however, is whether such intellectuals have advanced the course of democracy or not. This chapter explores the role intellectuals have played in the advancement of democracy as a system of governance, first generally and then with specific regard to post-colonial African societies. We begin with a survey of ancient societies and then move to examine modern Europe before finally turning to interrogate the situation in Africa. The discussion is pegged on the principles of democratic discourse. This general framework proposes that the idea and movement of democracy, understood as rule by the majority for the majority of the citizens by consent, has been a long standing yearning by the people over the millennia. For many it has been a reality but for just as many it has also been an illusion. As a system of governance it has been condemned sometimes by rulers and their subjects. Plato condemned and blamed it for the execution of his intellectual mentor, Socrates. Two millennia later an American statesman Jefferson hailed democracy as the best and most appropriate system of governance. Democratic governance implies a just and prosperous society where leadership is responsible and accountable to the people.

When modern Africa wrestled political independence from European colonialists, the fervent belief was that African intellectuals who were associated with the push for self-determination subscribed to principles of democratic discourse that were to be translated into efforts aimed at the achievement of a just and prosperous society. The question then is how far has democratic dis-course advanced in Africa since independence and what role if any have intellectuals played in the achievement of that goal? It might be observed from the outset that whereas some intellectuals have influenced states to move towards democracy others have pushed their political collaborators in the opposite direction. How might this phenomenon be explained? We shall use democratic discourse as a prism through which we might be able to understand the relationship between intellectuals and the state, especially in Africa.

Imhotep

In ancient Egypt intellectuals like Imhotep played a major in various fields of human endeavour. Imhotep was an all-rounded individual who was endowed with enormous intellect and professional abilities: he was a physician, an engineer and an architect. He was the personal physician of Pharaoh Zoser of the Third dynasty around 2700 B.C. In medicine he wrote treatises giving instructions on the examination of patients, diagnosis and treatment. The first person to conceive and enunciate a professional code of ethics and an oath for medical doctors, he was indeed the actual father of medicine given that the Greek Hippocrates only came to access Imhotep's Memphis library two millennia later. In architecture he introduced the concept of vaults and pillars, structural components which today are almost taken for granted when putting up buildings. He also introduced the use of construction materials like sun-dried bricks which today are common place in buildings all over the world. This was the era of the Old Kingdom (2700–2200 B.C.) when the Great Pyramids were built and Imhotep did introduce the step pyramids whose architectural style is reflected in the mosques of medieval West Africa. As the Pharaoh's personal physician he was very close to the state. Indeed Pharaohs were already considered gods in Egyptian civilization and given his closeness to power Imhotep was later deified and a temple built in his honour near the city of Memphis.

Being so closely linked to the state he definitely played a role in advancing the interests of his country. Yet it is still necessary to ask if Imhotep helped advance democratic discourse. He did not. This need not surprise us given that the idea was not even there. However he participated in advancing the course of human civilization. In that civilization women had more freedom, status and rights than in any other society of the ancient times. As such women's rights for instance, which are an integral part of human rights, can be seen to have sometimes existed in circumstances which really had nothing to do with the active pursuit of democratic discourse.

K'ung-fu-Tzu and Master M'eng-Tzu

It is also worth looking at the situation in China where intellectuals were highly respected personalities in the society. Whenever an intellectual was invited by the emperor to visit the imperial palace, the emperor himself came out in person, broom in hand, to sweep the way before the scholar and welcome him into the palace. The rationale was that the scholar was considered to be a person of profound intellectual power and knowledge which he was going to impart upon the emperor. The scholars were highly paid either in kind or in money. They became very wealthy and constituted another class that was called scholar-bureaucrats, a very powerful class not only in the state but in the society as a whole. This was the case during the reign of K'ung-fu-Tzu, popularly known as Confucius, and M'eng-Tzu of the period of the Warring States of China. K'ung-fu-Tzu was the most influential philosopher in Chinese civilization; it was evident that intellectuals had had significant input in these rulers' understanding of social issues. The philosophy of absolute filial love and obedience to the father has remained one of the most important and enduring characteristics of the Chinese society. For a very long time Confucian classic thought was the pillar of the examination system for recruitment into the state's civil service; indeed, the Sung Dynasty of the 9th century A.D. declared it the official philosophy of the state. The philosophy of K'ung postulated the promotion of the general welfare of the people in society and he advocated a practical approach to issues of governance. He advised leaders to promote the welfare of their people. In line with Confucian thought it might be argued that intellectuals whose ideas help promote the welfare of the majority of the people are in line with democratic discourse.

Another Chinese intellectual who lived a hundred years after K'ung-fu-tzu and influenced the Chinese state was Master M'eng-Tzu. One of his most notable arguments was that all men are brothers and equal. This new is in the contemporary world one of the critical tenets of democracy. Writing on human nature he said: "The tendency of human nature to do good is like the tendency of water to flow downward".[2] It was this same philosophy that would be taken up by the

French intellectual, Jean-Jacques Rousseau, two millennia later in his classical work "The Social Contract" (1754) to which we shall return further below.

Socrates and Kautilya

Another example of a society with a deep-seated tradition of intellectuals engaged in publicly visible roles is the ancient Greek city states, with Athens being the ultimate illustration where intellectuals openly took various positions vis-à-vis the state. In Plato's *Dialogues* we read about the trial and death of Socrates, Plato's and the most forthright teacher of the fourth century B.C. Athens. Socrates was accused of corrupting the young and the religious beliefs of the Athenians who in the General Assembly sentenced him to death in 399 B.C.[3] The irony is that Athens was a democracy but through its democratic institutions it was collectively responsible for the execution of his intellectual master.

Elsewhere in India intellectuals played a big role in the advancement of the state by virtue of their close relationship with some of the most powerful and illustrious leaders. One of the greatest rulers of India and the founder of the Indian Empire was Chandragupta Maurya who seized power in 322 B.C. and founded the Mauryan Dynasty. His chief minister Kautilya was among the first intellectuals to write a major work of political philosophy. His *Treatise on Material Gain* propagated the philosophy of unscrupulous means for anyone who is interested in acquiring and preserving political power. This philosophy was later taken up by the Florentine Nicolo Machiavelli in the now famous classic, *The Prince* that has been hailed as the dictators' bible. In Kautilya's case we see an intellectual who is not only a scholar and writer but also a chief minister who was at the epicentre of state power. He advised the ruler to "facilitate mining operations", "encourage manufacturers" and give them tax exemptions.[4] Kautilya advised that prices should be controlled because "goods should be sold to the people at favourable prices". Indeed the Indian empire then became a wealthy and prosperous country doing trade with major centres of the world at the time especially China, Asia Minor and Mesopotamia. Most notably there were no famines in India then; a fact that testifies to the success of the intellectually-driven state programs.

Thomas Hobbes

The European period of Enlightenment also brought forth another set of intellectuals that was very aggressive, purposeful and articulate in the rendition of their ideas and philosophies. They either supported the state, especially the absolutist European state of the seventeenth and early eighteenth centuries as did Thomas Hobbes and Bishop Bossuet, or vigorously opposed it in the manner of Voltaire, J. J. Rousseau and Denis Diderot and thus paving the way for the modern democratic state. The absolutist state emerged in Europe in the wake of the religious wars and at the end of the Thirty Years' War in the first half of the seventeenth century. Bishop Jacques Bossuet was one of the key advocates of the absolutist regime. He published *Politics Drawn from Scriptures* urging for total respect for the ruler:

> the person of the king is sacred, and to attack him in any way is sacrilege ...the royal throne is not the throne of a man, but the throne of God himself ...kings should be guarded as holy things, and whoever neglects to protect them is worthy of death ...the royal power is absolute ...the prince need render accounts of his acts to no one."[5]

Here was a cleric and intellectual justifying a particular state on the basis of his interpretation of the Bible. He was very influential in the French state of that time because he was the tutor of the son of the most powerful head of state of France of all time, King Louis XIV, 'The Sun King' who declared, " *L'Etat C'est Moi*" (I am the State).

Another intellectual of this period who justified absolutism as a system of governance was the English man Thomas Hobbes in his famous work, *Leviathan* (1651). In this work Hobbes argued that human society is comparable to that of wild wolves and that left on his own man is naturally, "brutish, nasty and selfish" and he would devour fellow human beings. Accordingly people should surrender all their rights to the state, a powerful monster, the leviathan which would then rule absolutely. People, he argues, can only obey the state. Only other states can challenge the power of others.[6]

In the last two examples above we see that some intellectuals in history have used their intellectual prowess to justify regimes that would be fought vehemently today in the name of democracy. Indeed, in the same century in Europe other intellectuals challenged not only this thinking but the absolute state itself. This was the time of religious turmoil in Europe and certain ideas were considered subversive by the political authorities depending on whether specific countries were Catholic or Protestant. Many people held that kings should be deposed and even killed for their poor governance records. The first to argue thus was Marsiglio[7] of Padua who in his *Defensor Pacis* (In Defence of Peace) propagated the theory of people's democratic right to fight for their rights against both the papacy and the emperor. He argued for popular sovereignty not only in the church but in the state as well. He pointed out that the Pope should not involve himself in temporal matters and if he did so he would be threatening peace. Marsiglio further postulated that people have the right to revolt against a bad ruler and even kill him and that the role of legislators should be performed by the majority of the people who must also have the right to punish princes. He and two others including William of Occam were excommunicated in 1328, but their ideas were victorious because an increasing number of intellectuals and other people believed that the power of kings/states should be circumscribed and that kings can be deposed.[8]

Indeed this line of thought was popular amongst intellectuals across Europe as might be testified by among others the Englishman John Locke who argued that governance ought to be a covenant between the king/ruler and the people. Similar thinking was espoused by the Swiss-French intellectual Jean-Jacques Rousseau. This self-declared citizen of Geneva supplied the one of the most lucid definitions on the origin and role of the state. In his article in Denis Diderot's *The Encyclopaedia* entitled, "The Origin of the State and Inequality among Men", Rousseau argued that the state is an instrument of power and force conceived by the rich classes first to protect their wealth and second to oppress the poor. Implicitly he was saying that that there must be limits of the state in favour of the people. In another of his more widely known works, *The Social Contract*, Rousseau takes up and acknowledges Locke's argument of the covenant between the people and the ruler/state. By entering into a contract with the state people gave the ruler the right to rule according to the terms of a socially-binding contract and as long he did so the former are obliged to obey the laws made by the rulers. However if rulers broke the terms of the contract then citizens had the right to not only disobey but also to remove the ruler. At regular intervals the people must have the opportunity to renew the mandate of the ruler for another term in office. What might be deduced from this last point is the possibility of regular democratic elections.

To complete this panorama of Eighteenth Century European intellectuals' work on the state that of three Frenchmen—Baron de Montesquieu, Jean-Marie de Voltaire and Denis Diderot—is crucial. De Montesquieu is famous for his theory of the separation of powers of the state through his *The Spirit of the Laws*. According to him there ought to be three arms of government; the legislature which makes laws, the Executive which implements them and the Judiciary which adjudicates or arbitrates disputes between the other two arms or between them and the citizens. Montesquieu, intellectual-cum-aristocrat was very critical of the indolence of members of his own class. However more important for the present discussion is what might be construed as his argument against colonialism and imperialism. He held that a country's laws are specific to it because they are a result of many factors; the people's culture, customs and history, the economy, and even the geography of the land. As such the laws of one country cannot be exported to another country. On his part Jean-Marie Voltaire is considered the father of the right to the freedom of expression, vowing to defend the right to speech even for those he might disagree with. In virtually all his writing Voltaire propounded the principle of tolerance on the part of both the state and the people even if they were against some of policies and acts of the state. In *Candid* he has argued that what might appear valuable in one society may not be so in another. Voltaire advocated for the English-type constitutional monarchy as opposed to the continental absolutist state.

On his part Denis Diderot, a most radical intellectual, spent his entire life editing a major twenty volume work, *The Encyclopaedia*, which summarised the knowledge of European intellectuals up to that time. Whenever he took time off his lifelong enterprise he wrote letters denouncing the pre-revolution totalitarian French regimes. He published a letter, "Letter on the Blind to Those with Eyes to See" which earned him a two-year prison term at the Royal Prison of Vincennes in Paris. In another letter addressed to the Hottentots (Khoi of Southern Africa), he denounced European colonialism abroad, especially in Africa. He extolled the Khoi "to sharpen their spears and arrows and arm themselves and even poison the arrows because monsters" were coming from the North to grab their lands, forests and wealth. The Hottentots, he held, should kill every one of the monsters to ensure that none of them survived to go back to Europe to boast about the ruins they had occasioned in the native land of the Hottentots. He was not locked up for this letter but it marked a turning point in Diderot's philosophy. He had become openly materialistic in outlook. In addition the philosopher openly attacked the Christian church and therefore the royal state itself.

Karl Marx

In the Nineteenth Century, European intellectuals would challenge the state more openly and in even more radical terms. Early socialists like Saint-Simon and Proudhon wanted a system based on contracts between peoples rather than on laws and states.[9] Karl Marx went farthest among the European intellectuals who challenged the state. Proceeding from Rousseau's idea that the state is an instrument of force in the hands of the rich classes, especially the bourgeoisie in the nineteenth century Europe, he argued that with the advent of a workers' revolution and the eventual elimination of the capitalist class, the state would become redundant and wither away by itself. While it is true that in the Twentieth Century Marxist intellectuals carried out what they called socialist (i.e. workers') revolutions in many parts of the world the state never withered away because societies never achieved the communist mode of production predicted by Karl Marx and his lifelong colleague and friend, Frederich Engels. However, theirs might be considered the bravest intellectual attack ever against the state. A view contrary to that of Marx and Engels is held by Plamenatz who does not believe either in the Marxist theory that the state is an instrument of force for the rich classes or in the possibility of realizing a classless society."[10]

African intellectuals
If European intellectuals have played significant roles in furthering democratic discourse it is necessary to attempt an examination of how Africans have fared in that domain. In contemporary Africa intellectuals have played rather contradictory roles. During the colonial period African intellectuals spearheaded nationalist movements against colonialism. Indeed they had attended European schools and universities where they had witnessed firsthand the glaring contradictions between, on the one hand, some European states that had matured into democracies by the twentieth century and from which colonizers came and, on the other hand, the backwardness of the oppressive racist colonial states in Africa. Further, certain African intellectuals had been to some of the most remote and primitive parts of rural Europe and now helped demystify the image of a super developed Europe. Moreover, they wanted the same democracy and the limited state that prevailed in Europe to be installed in their countries. They also aspired to be the leaders of their own countries and people under the terms of government chosen by the people. As such it might be argued that one of the roles pioneer intellectuals played had to do with critiquing the colonial project. Colonialism had robbed Africans their values, history and heritage. They wanted their people to recover all these things.

The earliest and one of the most assertive movements in sub-Saharan Africa was the 1930s Legitimate Defence led by African students in France as a counter ideology against white racism. They launched the Negritude movement which was premised on an ideology of black pride. Intellectuals like Leopold Senghor, Aime Cesaire, and Alexander Dumas among others were key proponents of these ideas. In a way they were challenging the French colonial state which with its policy of assimilation (i.e. turning all their colonial subjects into French citizens) was suppressing African nationalist movements with significant success. Through assimilation the colonial state in Africa was being domesticated a policy that succeeded for some time as seen in the fact that French colonies, unlike English colonies, witnessed less militant agitation for independence. All in all where the initial work of African intellectuals seems to have been mainly directed at fighting racism they soon established a more courageous position in opposition to the colonial state. As long as they were part of the nationalist anti-colonial movement they were viewed as patriotic by the majority of Africans. Thus the activities and publications of people like Kwame Nkrumah, Jomo Kenyatta, Julius Nyerere, Walter Rodney, Frantz Fanon and Nelson Mandela among others were well received not only in Africa but also internationally.

When independence was achieved in many African countries from the early 1960s onwards the reins of power in the new state fell into the hands of the intellectual class that had fought against the colonial state on the platform of democratic rule and governance. The emergent African states were largely predicated on the powerful Westphalian state model. The core structures of the this model include an all powerful sovereign/head of state and or government, a powerful, almost semi- autonomous bureaucracy that also ensures the collection of taxes from citizens, fixed territorial and inviolable boundaries that are internationally recognised and respected by other states, sovereignty that is recognised by other states of similar nature and, critically, powerful armed forces whose commander-in-chief serves is the head of state and/or government. Whereas the evolution and maturation of a democratic practice in the West has domesticated many aspects of the Wesphalian model of the state in Africa it operates still at the raw level of the absolutist state of the *ancient* regime in the seventeenth and eighteenth centuries France: totalitarian, intolerant, oppressive and repressive. This situation might be attributed to the fact that the few (former) intellectuals who rose to power at independence simply inherited the colonial state and went on to perfect its protocols of repression; 'reason of state', 'act of state' and 'state security' became the popular vocabulary of governance.

In certain ways the intellectuals-turned-new rulers in certain ways outdid their predecessors, not least because they had learnt certain things from their former masters but also because they knew better the tenets of democratic practice. Here might be found an abundance of examples of which we shall only highlight a few and which vividly illustrate the ethic of anti-freedom. Intellectuals who have proposed either governance reform or democratic reform have been labelled 'subversive' to be detained or even physically eliminated. Given this context, the role of the African intellectual has become quite fluid. For the sake of self preservation some intellectuals have chosen a path of collaboration with the state but others have confronted it.

Julius Nyerere of Tanzania for instance earned the title of Mwalimu because he had taught in high schools in colonial Tanganyika before going into politics. When he became president he launched the socialist ideology through the Tanzania Revolutionary Party, better known by its Swahili name *Chama Cha Mapinduzi*. Under the leadership of Mwalimu Nyerere the political leadership of Tanzania attempted to domesticate socialism into an African mould. However, the most important aspect of that configuration was the partial disaggregation of the Westphalia state model into regions and socialist villages known as *vijiji vya ujamaa*. The model produced a highly politicised populace, very committed to 'African Socialism' as practised in Tanzania. However, whereas in theory it should have been possible to disaggregate more the colonial Westphalia type state, the political leadership developed acute hypersensitivity to criticism, starting with Nyerere himself. Anyone who espoused divergent views was dubbed a capitalist and a lackey of imperialism and harassed accordingly. The same type of treatment was unleashed against any intellectual, whether academic or not who even remotely suggested modifications of the state's ideology. Generally, however, academics in Tanzania have shared the ideology of the country's political leadership and as such there has been a collaborative relationship between intellectuals and the state in what the politicians sincerely believed was the right route to national development and industrialisation. Had the enterprise succeeded, it would have been a unique case in Africa; at least both the politicians and academics seemed to have been well-intentioned. The major pitfall with the Tanzanian experiment was the retention of the Westphalia type of state without the corresponding democratic institutions and processes at all levels of the society.

In neighbouring Kenya the scenario was quite different. Academicians were initially viewed benevolently by the state since there were very few of them during the early years into the independence period. As the years wore on academicians were seen as an ungrateful lot, always complaining about the state, general governance and the country's exploitation by foreigners through multinational corporations. Those who were more politically vocal in their criticism of the system bore the brunt of the first phase of state attacks and quite a number were detained by the Kenyatta regime. It was, however, the Moi state (1978–2002) that perpetrated the worst terror and most sustained forms of terror against academics. First their trade union (Academic Staff Union) was banned and then detentions of perceived left-leaning academics followed throughout the 1980s; considered 'subversive elements', the lucky ones fled the country as those left behind were sacked from their teaching positions. Those who were incorporated into the service of the state knew only too well the boundaries of their functions; the watershed of the incorporation started in 1987 when the then president Moi began appointing academicians to various state and government positions.

These plum appointments were meant at one level to act as a carrot to radical academics and as expected there arose a division within the academics in their relationships with the state. A majority of them joined the rest of the Kenyan people in struggling for what was dubbed the 'second liberation', fundamentally a push for the repeal of Section 2A from the country's Constitution to enable a return to multi-party politics which had been abolished in 1981. Some academicians sided with Moi in his resistance to the clamour for political reforms. The notable trend at this time was for academics from Moi's ethnic group to support his bid to remain in power while the rest generally opposed him. In this manner, wittingly or unwittingly, ethnicity took on perceptible patterns even amongst academics.

In Uganda, the flirting with African socialism by Milton Obote who followed in the footsteps of his ideological mentor Julius Nyerere, gave intellectuals a platform to discuss a lot of ideas, especially through the scholarly East African Journal. However with the advent of Idi Amin Dada's regime (1971–1980) this freedom was quickly lost. Intellectuals and academicians were specifically targeted for assassination but ironically a few of them thought they could safely be incorporated into the state.

The new role

How then do view positively role of intellectuals in the emerging new dispensation of democratic governance? The emerging Africa does not need dead heroes, intellectuals or otherwise. However, intellectuals are capable of designing for themselves roles that promote democracy, good governance and respect for human rights using the method they know best: discourse. They have the brain power to simplify complex concepts for 'ordinary' citizens to grasp and hopefully act on. For instance they might explain what leaders mean in real power relations when they talk of checks and balances. If we take a queue from Montesquieu about the principle of the separation of powers, an intellectual can explain that once Parliament (National Assembly) has passed a law, for example on the Constituency Development Fund or the School Bursary Fund, both cases of revenue expenditure in Kenya, the members of the legislature cannot be implementers of the same, whether directly or indirectly. Whatever law has been passed by the legislator can only be implemented by the Executive Arm of the government. Likewise, members of parliament cannot determine their own remuneration. Such acts have no checks and so they vitiate the democratic principle. Where the governance structure has an executive presidency, the power and authority of the National Assembly to defy the president acts as a check on the president because the two institutions counterpoise each other. Thus the critical issue is that the national assembly can successfully and legally overrule the president. An impeachment motion is another example of a check on the actions of the presidency. However when, as in the Kenyan case the constitution provides for the non-prosecution of the president for whatever misdeeds, criminal or civilian, there is neither check nor balance. In this manner the constitution sets the presidency above the law and yet in a democracy all are equal before the law irrespective of status or function.

It is also necessary to point out that Third World intellectuals, especially in Africa, have for a long time now been questioning the validity of the Westphalia concept and practice of the state. One of the ways in which they have been doing this is by taking up civil society work. Implicitly then given the multiplicity of modern non-state actors like Civil Society Groups, intellectuals have been directly and indirectly highlighting the fact that the modern state in its present configuration (social injustices and class fractures are paramount examples) is not tenable. What for instance might be done about the vestiges of the African pre-colonial state, and how might citizens cultivate a sense of belonging to a state that to all intents and purposes seems bent on catering for the welfare of only one class? After analysing and interpreting the trappings of the state, intellectuals are capable of proposing syntheses for the people to engage in meaningful debate without fear of victimisation. There is only one thing intellectuals cannot do: get into action and try to implement their own ideas. If they did so then they cease being impartial and begin on a slippery road where they have to perpetually defend their ideas even when these are either outdated or unworkable because they are too abstract or both. They are also likely to become intolerant like any other dictator and since they have the brain power they can become even more dangerous to society especially if they offer their services to a morally bereft political class. It was this kind of situation whereby even though Adolf Hitler was not an intellectual, many intellectuals participated in making his Third Reich work through their support and perhaps even formulation of Nazi policies. At Nuremburg trials their defence that they were only implementing the laws could not save them from conviction and the death sentence. In similar fashion those intellectuals who surrounded Uganda's Idi Amin Dada Uganda of 1971 to 1979 lived to regret.

Conclusion

This paper does not in any way suggest that intellectuals should not be actively involved in politics. We are arguing that they have a right like any other citizen to get into politics and rise up to the top. But they do that as citizens. As intellectuals they are free to engage in any discourse and those who read them should not assume that what they write or talk are the policies of the government or the states they run. The modern state is an autonomous entity that has its own life and no single individual, intellectual or otherwise just bend it to the ultimate responsibility of the misdeeds and of course enjoy the glory of the good deeds.

> In short, we are arguing that intellectuals are endowed with brain power which over the millennia has been put to use by the state. We have cited specific examples in history. In societies like China intellectuals were well-respected and highly remunerated to the point of creating a special socio-economic class called scholar-bureaucrats. In other societies they have generated ideas that have helped shape the modern democratic state, especially in the Western world. Yet even in such situations intellectuals' lives were sometimes redolent with irony; Jean-Marie Voltaire—he who expounded on the freedom of expression—owned property in French West Indies worked by slaves. Others were so radical in their critique of the authoritarian absolutist state that they simply had to be locked up for some time in state prisons. Other despots of the time, like Empress Catherine the Great of Russia, invited them to their courts as their personal guests for long spells of time. We have stated that African intellectuals were an integral part of the anti-colonialist movements and the revived integrity of the African civilisation. Patrice Lumumba's last letter to his wife Pauline promising that one day Africa would write its own history was a powerful message not only to African historians but to all African intellectuals. However, after independence, African intellectuals were either incorporated into the inherited colonial state and power structure where they could enjoy the goodies that the state could give them, or they were terrorised in person or through the forced separation of exile and others, such as Ken Saro Wiwa of Nigeria, were killed.

We have also argued that intellectuals can engage in discourses which propose the road map to democratic governance and respect for and promotion of human rights in their countries without antagonising the state, in itself modelled upon the state that emerged out of the 1648 Westphalia conference, which is still too powerful to challenge head on. Intellectuals as citizens have the right to vie for leadership in their countries but this must not be misconstrued to mean that they should implement their personal philosophies.

Notes

1 T Walter Wallbank. et al. *Civilization: Past and Present*, Harper Collins, 1992, p.116.
2 *Ibid*.
3 Plato, "The Trial and Death of Socrates", Dover Publications, New York, 1992.
4 T Walter Wallbank. et al. *Civilization: Past and Present*, Harper Collins, 1992, pp.107–8.
5 Jacques Bossouet cited in Wallbank. et al, "Civilization." p.475.
6 *Ibid*.
7 Also spelt Marsilius.
8 Bertrand Russell. 1975. *History of Western Philosophy*. George Allen & Unwin Ltd. pp. 459–61.
9 John Plamenatz. 1963. *Man and Society*. Vol. 2, London. Longman. pp 52–53.
10 *Ibid*, p.403.

Conflict & Reconciliation

The South African Truth and Reconciliation Commission (TRC): Lessons for Kenya

GEORGE GONA

It seems to me that what we are seeing in South Africa today is a return of past violence, a representation of the connections that bind history, past political events, and present reality: today's perpetrators of violence are following a script that was enacted during the years of apartheid... The shame and humiliation that propelled it then, in the years of apartheid, however, has not vanished with the advent of the "new" South Africa. ... For today's "re-enactors" of past trauma, the dignity and respect that was lost through the humiliation of apartheid has not been regained; while political change has given power and economic success to a few, they, the re-enactors, remain buried in the abyss of economic and psychological suffering. This plunges them back, as traumatic re-enactment so often does, into the vortex of violence.

—Pumla Gobodo-Madikizela, a TRC Commissioner and a practicing psychologist.

The use of truth and reconciliation commissions as part of transitional justice has become widespread notwithstanding doubts about their efficacy and the variations of their outcomes. Since the launching of the South African Truth and Reconciliation Commission (TRC) well over a decade ago, a number of truth commissions have been set up in countries as diverse as East Timor, Sierra Leone, Ghana and Peru. There have been over twenty truth commissions in the last two decades, an indication of the increasing popularity of this transitional justice mechanism in countries coming out of intrastate conflict. The South African TRC is so far the most celebrated and it has been an example for countries on the path of post-conflict peace building. For new commissions being formed the South African commission continues to hold a myriad of relevant lessons.

In the past, truth commissions were largely understood as investigative mechanisms with the primary aim of publishing an authoritative and factual report on human rights violations committed in a country.[1] A new trend has gained ascendancy in which emphasis is now on looking at the societal impact of gathering information with considerations being made for the varied impacts the TRC process has on individuals and society.[2] The social utility of truth commissions, and concepts such as healing and reconciliation, has become a core part of the critical discussion about the impact of such bodies. Whether transitional justice mechanisms—in this case, truth commissions—should be concerned with concepts such as healing is also a point for debate.[3] Nonetheless, a majority of the commissions have variously asserted healing and reconciliation as their stated goals.[4] It may be difficult to decipher why truth commissions are politically popular. It is puzzling that even when TRCs are questioned on their capacity to unearth the truth, promote healing and reconciliation, Kenya has taken this transitional justice mechanism. Even so, what lessons can Kenya's Truth Justice and Reconciliation Commission (TJRC) draw from the South African process? What is the magnitude of the task and are Kenyans ready for this exercise? There is fear in some quarters that the TJRC process may divide Kenyans and therefore not succeed in uniting or reconciling them.[5] The purpose of this paper is to provide insights into how issues of healing, forgiveness, reconciliation, which the TRC grappled with, may play out in Kenya and whether Kenyans can draw lessons from it.

How did the South African TRC work?

Generally, truth commissions include four elements: First, the focus is on the past rather than the present. Second, the commission attempts to paint the overall picture of certain human rights abuses over a period of time, as opposed to focusing on a specific event. Third, the commission usually exists temporarily and for a predefined period of time, ceasing to exist following the submission of a report on its findings. Finally, a commission is always vested with some sort of authority, by way of its sponsor, that allows it greater access to information, greater security or protection to dig into 'sensitive' issues, and a greater impact with its report than existing institutions. Lastly, commissions are best at telling the story of the past from the perspective of victims, allowing victims to tell their stories in an uninhibited fashion, explaining conflicts in broad causal terms, and assigning responsibility and accountability while leaving justice to the courts.

The South African TRC was established in December 1995 after combative debates. It comprised seventeen commissioners appointed by the recently-elected Nelson Mandela.[6] Sweeping across the country for 244 days, it received over 21,000 victim statements and more than 7,000 applications for amnesty. The TRC was the fruit of a political compromise whose terms both made possible the Commission and set the limits within which it would work.[7] The narrow remit of the TRC, as well as its political framework limited the possibility of a reconfiguration of the post-apartheid state. The compromise ultimately prevented the TRC from contributing to fundamental transformation because, among other issues, those responsible for apartheid were not held to account. The TRC's stated aims were to produce a record of the violations of the past and make recommendations to prevent them from ever happening again; to acknowledge the suffering of the victims and assist in their rehabilitation; to offer amnesty to past perpetrators; and to facilitate healing and reconciliation for the nation.[8] It is on these stated goals that evaluations on the "success" of the TRC process can be made.

It has been argued that the TRC had a number of unique features.[9] First, it gave priority to victims rather than perpetrators. The Gross Human Rights Violations Committee heard the stories of victims across the land. This committee ensured that people's suffering was heard, recognized, and referenced by the nation. Scores of hearings were held in city halls and rural community centres. The commission honoured the victims by going to them rather than calling them to a central venue. Through the Commission victims were empowered to speak-out; it was a therapy of healing the nation.[10]

A second unique factor in the work of the TRC was that victims on all sides of the struggle participated. The TRC's designers were determined that history would not be sanitized by the victorious side, and so those who suffered at the hands of the liberation forces were also invited to share their experiences. It so happened for instance, that a story of secret police torture was followed by a White farmer's story of how his wife and children were killed by an ANC landmine or by an account of abuses and torture in one of the liberation movement's training camps. These stories sent the important message that a morally justified struggle did not justify indiscriminate killing and deliberate brutality.[11] But the problem with this approach was that it tended not to draw distinctions between different kinds of violence: violence to support an iniquitous system is not the same as violence in the name of liberation. Of course, this complicates the question of violence, but it is an issue that cannot be ignored. Furthermore, by focusing primarily on individual acts of violence, the TRC managed only to make perfunctory analyses of the systemic problems undergirding that violence.

The Amnesty Committee, consisting of Supreme Court judges and lawyers, heard pleas for amnesty. The requirements for amnesty were clear. Only individuals—not groups—applied. For amnesty to be given there had to be full disclosure.[12] The abuses must have been perpetrated to further a political aim. At least to the Commission there were clear procedures for amnesty granting: If amnesty was granted, the slate was wiped clean. If not, then what was disclosed before the commission was not to be used in any subsequent court prosecution. Evidence was independently sought by the attorney general. A definite date (May 1997) was earmarked for perpetrators to lodge their amnesty applications. A further unique feature of both the Gross Human Rights Violations Committee and the Amnesty Committee was that all their hearings were public. This meant that perpetrators had to face the individuals they tortured or the families of those they killed.[13] While the TRC claimed to be victim centred, and much of the public hearings confirmed this approach, the Amnesty process in fact tended to be more perpetrator-centred.

A third committee was that of Reparations and Rehabilitation. The TRC was tasked with making recommendations on reparation measures to the president.[14] The president would then advise parliament on subsequent reparations regulations. Reparations were to be provided to those people designated as victims by the TRC. A person could be designated as a victim either by approaching the TRC to make a statement or by being referred to during an amnesty hearing. Urgent interim reparations (small payments) were provided relatively quickly, but the decision on final reparations was a drawn-out process that fostered significant frustration among victims. For a number of years, the government failed to respond to the TRC's recommendations on reparations. When a decision was eventually made by the government in 2003, the amount of individual reparation grants was much lower than that proposed by the TRC. This led to anger and disappointment among many of the victims. Since then, almost all of the 19,000 designated victims have received payment as reparations. Even where reparations were offered, the paltry 30,000 Rand for victims was to say the least a mockery of justice. For Tutu, the significance of the payment was in its symbolism since dead relatives cannot be returned to life.

The South African TRC: a brief evaluation
Public acknowledgement, breaking the silence of the past, creating an unforgettable record of the atrocities committed, and voicing of the past crimes were the TRC's greatest successes.[15] Even so, critics of the TRC have wondered whether the truth about South Africa's past was told, or whether healing and therefore reconciliation has taken place. South Africa's version of restorative justice emphasized reconciliation between perpetrators and victims built ideally on a perpetrator's repentance and a victim's forgiveness. Ultimately, it was hoped, the South African nation as a whole would likewise become reconciled. Although the TRC's task was not officially framed in religious terms, the dominant role of Chairman Archbishop Tutu meant that his theological view of reconciliation often triumphed other views. This was aided by the fact that a large number of commissioners who came from the faith community.[16]

It has been argued that two features of South Africa's religious culture supported the TRC's emphasis on forgiveness, rather than punishment: Christian theology and the traditional concept of *ubuntu*.[17] The Christian admonition to forgive one's enemies and embrace the sinner within the family of God was widely accepted among the largely Christian South African population.[18] Due in part to the considerable role many church organizations played in protests against apartheid the teachings of the church retained relevance for many South Africans.[19] The concept of *ubuntu* was also used to legitimize the TRC's call for reconciliation. In Tutu's words:

"We believe there is another kind of justice, based on something that we find difficult to put into English. *Ubuntu* is the essence of being human. It speaks of compassion and generosity, of gentleness and hospitality and sharing, because it says; 'my humanity is caught up in your humanity; I am because you are.' A person is a person through other persons."[20]

Thus, *ubuntu* emphasizes community over individual. As John Mbiti explains, "Whatever happens to the individual happens to the whole group, and whatever happens to the whole group happens to the individual. The individual can only say: 'I am because we are, and since we are, therefore I am.'"[21] This belief in the indivisibility of humanity, it is argued, creates a capacity for forgiveness. In Tutu's view, an offence breaks a relationship, ruptures interconnectedness, a harmony so essential for a full human existence. *Ubuntu* does not give up on the perpetrator and sees him with a capacity to change for the better and so *ubuntu* seeks to heal a breach, to restore relationships, to forgive and have reconciliation. However, complete assessments of the TRC will require extensive testing of the degree to which the Truth Commission resonated with South Africa's religious culture. Although Tutu invokes the African value of *Ubuntu*, ethnographic work by Richard Wilson in the local *lekgotla*—people's courts[22] establish an alternative notion of justice for the human rights abuses of apartheid, one that is opposed to the restorative kind advocated by the TRC and which emphatically calls for punishment and retribution.[23]

At the Human Rights Violations Committee hearings, a select group of victims testified publicly about how they had suffered. About one tenth of the 20,000 deponents testified—a very small number out of a national population of 43 million. Still, anecdotal evidence suggests that for many who addressed the commission, the value of telling one's story before a supportive audience was significant. Referring to the psychological value of testifying, one witness said: "When the officer tortured me at that time in John Vorster Square, he laughed at me: 'You can scream your head off, nobody will ever hear you!' He was wrong. Today there are people who will hear me."[24] Commissioner Mary Burton agrees that giving public testimony had some measure of healing for many survivors: "The right to be heard and acknowledged, with respect and empathy, did contribute to a process of healing in many cases."[25]

The Amnesty Committee held hearings for those who admitted having committed crimes. Approximately 7,000 applicants applied for amnesty. However, many were common criminals hoping to convince the commissioners that they had political rather than criminal motives, and only a few were top leaders of the apartheid system. Nearly half of these applicants were from the African

National Congress.[26] Contrition was not a requirement for amnesty, and indeed many applicants did not apologize for their actions. In the end, amnesty was granted to approximately 16% of the applicants.[27] Thus out of a population of 43 million people, only about one thousand individuals acknowledged their responsibility for apartheid's crimes, receiving amnesty and being allowed reintegration back into society.

Scholars debate the advisability of offering amnesty. In promising amnesty to apartheid killers, did the ANC expediency upon which to establish a new democracy on a flawed judicial response to a systemic crime against humanity? Mahmood Mamdani argues that the TRC resulted in "an institutionally produced truth, as the outcome of a process of truth-seeking, one whose boundaries were so narrowly defined by power and whose search was so committed to reinforcing the new power, that it turned the political boundaries of a compromise into analytical boundaries of truth-seeking."[28] It appears the government let off apartheid crimes so as to facilitate crime. That was the costly path that Tutu has always talked about.

In short, it should be cautioned that truth and reconciliation processes may not always have an independent influence on healing and reconciliation and especially on the likelihood of consolidating an attempted democratic transition. Indeed the political compromises during the transition period have led to the conclusion that the truth and reconciliation process in South Africa did indeed exert independent influence on the democratization process through its contributions toward creating a more reconciled society. However, there is yet to be scholarly research done that will establish a positive relationship between TRC processes and democratisation.[29]

Why reconcile Kenyans?
Perhaps there are lessons to be learnt from the South African TRC, particularly for those nations with wounded histories. Kenya is no exception. Graybill and Lanegran (2004) have observed that the South African case can provide empirical evidence to help scholars make more informed evaluations of transitional justice. However, such work will require identification of the means with which to assess the impact of the process. For example, how can we know whether reconciliation emerged from the TRC? What does reconciliation look like? Who becomes reconciled?[30] Even more importantly, why should there be reconciliation? A significant addition is that Truth Commissions have their relative merits

when adapted to the particularities of the context, and when instituted with appropriate and sufficient mandates, material and human resources and political support-which is regrettably rarely the case in low-income post-conflict countries like Kenya.[31] The South African TRC had ample resources. The Kenyan TJRC on the other hand seems to be lacking the requisite funding and support from the donor community. The government has not earmarked specific funds for this purpose.[32] Even if there was funding, another problem is whether the recommendations of the Commission will be acceptable to politicians. A poorly resourced Truth Commission whose recommendations are ignored by the political leadership, as in Haiti, can be worse than no Truth Commission at all. Likewise, trials sometime aggravate divisions between perpetrators and victims within society, at a time when reconciliation is sought.[33] As Alex Boraine has pointed out facile imposition of the experience of the TRC process in South Africa may be futile as much as it can be a good example for countries wanting to deal with their pasts.[34] In other words, contexts and histories of countries undertaking transitional justice processes like TRCs vary; so do eventual outcomes. The South African TRC was possible because there was a widespread belief, produced by what appeared to be mutual magnanimity between the apartheid state and liberation movements, that compromise and negotiations would produce reconciliation and nation building. As will be observed below, reconciliation conjured different meanings among South Africans and that it is a problematic concept that isn't easily measured. Whether South Africans were or are reconciled because of the TRC process is still a matter of contestation in the rainbow nation.

Nation-building was a primary objective of reconciliation in South Africa, and therefore of the TRC. It was supposed to be part of a collective effort, including negotiations and the new constitution, to give birth to a new nation. This was perhaps the main political objective of the TRC. There are mixed signals as to what the political objective of the Kenyan TJRC is. The political class have just woken up to the realisation that Kenya's past is replete with injustices and that if one will go by the post-election violence experience of early 2008, the possibilities of the same recurring in another election year is high. Perhaps politicians are aware of the serious problems past injustices pose for the country. And even more important they are aware that the often cited story of national building has been a mirage in the last 45 years of political independence (see Wafula, this volume). However, the manner in which the TJRC was quickly brought into existence smirks of a motive to circumvent the calls for post-election violence perpetrators to face justice in the courts of law or be tried at the International Criminal Court. For the suspected perpetrators (many of whom are perhaps politicians) the TJRC is a political safety net.

The decision by Kenya to confront its past through a Truth and Reconciliation Commission like South Africa is a bold step. It assumes that to undertake to unearth its past can help bring peace and democratic consolidation. It is possible that with the measured success of the South African TRC one can borrow something from it. For our purposes, looking at the South African TRC is an exercise not intended to detract from the successes of that Commission or the integral role it played in South Africa's historic transformation. Nor should it prescribe limitations on what a Truth Commission can achieve; but rather to identify some of the inherent pitfalls for forgiveness, healing and reconciliation that can result from unrealistically burdening a single institution with the mammoth and ongoing goal of reconciliation—a goal that may, from the experiences of either country, take a generation or more to fully consolidate. This reconciliation—or its quest—should not end when the TJRC's mandate expires; it should be a continuous process given the magnitude of the need to mend relationships.

The Kenyan TJRC was conceived after politicians associated with the key parties to the grand collation government (Orange Democratic Party and Party of National Unity) signed a document on March 14 2008 that paved the way for the formation of the Commission. It was formed to assess the history of human rights abuses in Kenya from independence in 1963 to February 28 2008. But the group agreed that that the period could be extended to allow for a greater understanding of the nature, root causes, violence or crimes that happened before that period. It was also agreed that the Commission would receive statements from the victims, witnesses, communities, interest groups, and persons directly or indirectly involved in the events. From this not-so-well defined mandate, the Commission seems to take a victims' perspective. Dealing with "other persons directly or indirectly involved" is vague and open to interpretation.

Unlike in South Africa where the chairmanship of Desmond Tutu was not in doubt and was not challenged even by the white population, the appointment of Chairman Bethwel Kiplagat to head the TJRC has come under critical scrutiny ostensibly on account of his having worked for the repressive Moi regime.[35] The argument of those opposed to his leadership is that he is guilty of being party to the "original sin" of partaking and abetting Moi-era excesses.[36] Indeed a group of former detainees have gone to court to challenge the appointment of Kiplagat to head the Commission. They have threatened not to participate in the process if Kiplagat remains the Chair.[37] Yet this reasoning has further been challenged as a bluff, for it is superfluous to generalise about people, including Kiplagat's 'sin' to serve under Moi. This is because practically every member of the Kenyan cabinet today worked for Daniel Arap Moi and by extension they too should not be serving in the cabinet. Aside from these arguments and for the purpose of this chapter, the challenges to Kiplagat's chairmanship succeed in undermining the process and significantly put to question his ability to midwife it. The TJRC is meant to find unity, heal people and reconcile them. The debate on whether Kiplagat should lead the way is healthy but divisive. In South Africa Tutu's anti-apartheid stance and endorsement that Nelson Mandela gave him moral authority across the nation; he was a rallying point around which a new hope for a better country lay. Unfortunately, Kiplagat seems to have none of these credits.

Truth and Reconciliation—Lessons for Kenya

What might be learnt about TRCs in general and the South African one in particular is that society is not merely a hypostatized entity that requires reconstruction after violent fragmentation, but instead nation-building is best understood as a process; a fragile undertaking that is never ending and shapes us as much as we shape it. The processes of truth telling and reconciliation are carried out through both public action and speech—"We humanize what is going on in the world and in ourselves only by speaking of it, and in the course of speaking of it we learn to be human."[38] Such an undertaking is first and foremost *political*. It rejects apolitical concepts such as compassion and love as the proper bedrock of social cohesion—the position of Desmond Tutu[39] and Miroslav Volf [40]—and instead focuses on the importance of worldly mediation between erstwhile enemies. Related to this overly stressed notion of restorative justice in which forgiveness is given prominence over retribution is the question whether Kenya is likely to suffer from the TRC's mandating of an all-too-speedy reconciliation, and its privileging of forgiveness as the highest form of ethical behaviour. It is not certain that this will happen but Bethwel Kiplagat's talk seems to point in that direction. The Kenyan TJRC should be sceptical of transcendental claims about moral reasoning, privileging in its place the contestability of opinions and the plurality of views about the past.[41]

In Kenya public debate was ignited when the government announced it was considering expanding the mandate of the TJRC to include prosecuting perpetrators of past human rights abuses. The Kenyan commissioners rejected this proposal arguing that prosecutions should be made by relevant qualified authorities. The TJRC seems to be wary of the South African case where the TRC was mandated to investigate but it did not have powers to prosecute. It is worth mentioning that other forms of transitional justice systems could be applied parallel to the TJRC process including using the ordinary justice system and traditional methods of conflict resolution process where applicable. Unlike the TRC where the choice to engage the process precluded the use of courts, the TJRC provides the possibility of recourse for other spaces for justice-seeking including the courts.

Just like in the South African commission, the Kenyan Truth Commission has consciously chosen to include the term reconciliation in its title, placing it as a central objective of the institution's work.[42] As already observed, the experience in South Africa demonstrated, however, that the word reconciliation is itself a contested one. For some, reconciliation was equated with theological notions of forgiveness as bestowed to the process. For others it was no more than the amount of political tolerance required to build a common national project and consolidate a democratic transition. There are also the various levels at which reconciliation must take place—individual, community, national and political. Each of these levels needs to be addressed for true reconciliation to occur, but not all can possibly be addressed fully solely through the work of a truth commission. In South Africa, debate continues more than a decade since the inauguration of the TRC over the question of whether reconciliation has been reached, and within this debate, the equally important question of what reconciliation should look like. Kenyans have not debated fully (if at all) what kind of reconciliation they expect in this process. There is no rigour in debates surrounding notions of reconciliation. These debates, based upon the South African situation around the issue of reconciliation and the fact that the concept has been viewed as an 'ideal' that is almost impossible to achieve and therefore measure, make it futile to include reconciliation as an objective of the TJRC process. It would be preferable that the objectives of the TJRC be confined, for example, to uncovering the truth and the persecution of perpetrators (individual and collective).

Unlike in South Africa where there was rigour in debating issues around the formation of the TRC and establishing its mandate, historically Kenya has lacked this critical approach. The debate has at times centred merely on the search for the "killers" of J. M. Kariuki, Robert Ouko and at times the atrocities committed on Mau Mau fighters by the British colonialists. While this will be part and parcel of the process, it nonetheless reduces the whole TJRC process to that of personalities rather than one for unearthing institutional rot in Kenya. Embarking on a national discussion or conversation early on in order to inform what the definition of reconciliation might mean in the Kenyan context would no doubt further the sensitization and outreach work of the Commission, establish clear criteria against which to assess the work of the Commission, as well as perhaps guard against unrealistic expectations of what the Commission can achieve. The issue of inflated expectations and the negative impact that they can have is perhaps one of the most important lessons learned from the South African experience.

Dangers of heightened expectations

Many survivors also came to the South African Commission in the hope of finding new truth about the fate or whereabouts of loved ones, vesting hopes in particular in the amnesty process which promised the possibility of amnesty for full disclosure of the details of the crimes committed by perpetrators.[43] This was not to be the case. Studies done among South Africans have found that many of those interviewed believed that the amnesty process had aggravated their suffering as it was unable to meet their expectations—that of revealing substantial new truth and holding all perpetrators to account.[44]

At an individual level, unrealistic and unaddressed expectations of the TRC sometimes resulted in an adverse impact on victims themselves. The assumption that healing would be the natural outcome of survivors' public recounting their stories proved not to be uniformly true. Trauma centres in both Johannesburg and Cape Town reported that some survivors who sought counselling in the wake of giving public testimony had been left traumatized by the event.[45] This is not to say that public testimony and acknowledgement cannot play a beneficial role in the healing process for many survivors, but rather to note that the expectations for healing should be informed by the reality of the different ways in which giving testimony may be experienced. There is danger in Kenya of adopting a similar attitude towards healing given the apparent assumption that healing will inevitably lead to reconciliation.

In South Africa limited new information was gained through the amnesty process.[46] Of the more than 7,000 applications for amnesty, the majority came from individuals already in prison for criminal offences. With nothing to lose and freedom to gain, these individuals attempted to retell their crimes through a political lens and therefore match the criteria for amnesty. Those that did apply for amnesty for political crimes were careful to ensure that the truth they disclosed matched the criteria required for amnesty and revealed almost no information on the organization of state violence and those who authorized it. Given that there has been some discussion in Kenya about whether to allow for amnesty similar to that aimed for in South Africa (offering amnesty for disclosure and remorse) it may be of value to bear in mind the difficulties encountered in urging perpetrators to come forward—even when encouraged by both the reward of amnesty and the threat of prosecution. Related to the amnesty process was apology and remorse. In South Africa, the TRC's use of a definition of reconciliation closely aligned to that of confession and forgiveness prompted expectations of remorse from those perpetrators who came forward. Again, in reality little genuine remorse was offered by amnesty applicants.[47] It is not clear whether in the Kenyan situation apology and remorse will be prerequisites for amnesty. It may well be that some applicants will feel that a display of the desired emotions would increase their chances of a successful amnesty application, which may later be revealed as having been an insincere apology.

The very drama and extraordinary nature of the TRC hearings allowed its truths to be compartmentalised and contained and suggested that apartheid was a "chapter of the past" that could be closed with a satisfying thump. Yet the hard questions–wearisome and difficult indeed–remained: What comes after the moments of revelation? How does one transform information into knowledge, emotion into insight, events into experience, and experience into meaning? How is the truth not merely recognized, but integrated into a new sense of self, into new social relationships, into new political structures, into the building of a future that is fundamentally different from (rather than an erasure of) the past? These were questions that in many ways were not answered during the TRC process. They are questions that the TJRC and Kenyans should be thinking about as they embark on this perilous journey. There could be hope that after testifying at the TJRC there will be those who will express a sense of a "new beginning", a "new man", "fresh start" and so on. Yet such statements are sometimes a reflection of the language of denial and not necessarily a departure with the past. These are the realities with which the South African TRC provided and which Kenyans should take note of. We cannot be certain that testifying at the TJRC would help victims break with the past.

Reliving the past and "closure"

So, too, should caution attend the incessantly optimistic notion of "closure."[48] In the South African situation apartheid was not the equivalent of an unhappy childhood or a painful divorce. To speak of closure in the context of systemic terror and degradation verges on obscenity. A quick look at some of the atrocities of apartheid learned through the TRC hearings can illustrate our point. There are South Africans who came to learn of the brutal nature through which their children met their deaths; a majority of those who died under apartheid died alone, naked and were tortured. Can these people "get over" and "move on"? It would be hard to say what kind of restitution should be offered to Nomatise Evelyn Tsobileyo; in 1985, a white policeman shot bullets into her vagina, which were still lodged in her body at the time of her hearing. Or of what healing would mean for Zahrah Narkedien, who testified about her solitary confinement: "I will never recover ... [T]he more I struggled to be normal, the more disturbed I became. I had to accept that I was damaged. A part of my soul was eaten away as if by maggots ... and I will never get it back again."[49] The broader point being raised here is that the TRC was perceived as a moment when South Africans as a whole could deal with the past and then move on. Despite its intentions the perception of the TRC in these terms has done enormous damage in the way that South Africans have turned away from the past and therefore are unable to properly deal with it. Likewise, we are suggesting that the testimony of, for example, a Nyayo House torture chambers victim may not necessarily make an individual "move on." The TJRC may only succeed to hype up emotions and expectations and not lead necessarily to "closure." Indeed, there are victims of the Nyayo era, including those tortured at Nyayo House, who have openly said they cannot easily move on just because Nyayo torture chambers were exposed or because the government has formed the TJRC.

What became clear from the TRC process—and is significant for Kenyans and the TJRC—is that souls can sometimes be reconstituted—though not easily, not in isolation, and with no guarantees. But this process has no connection to that of "getting over"; it demands, on the contrary, the recognition that what is gone cannot be retrieved; that what is done cannot be undone, that there are losses in this world that can never be redeemed. To know this is to enter into tragedy. The subsequent 'coping' is what Kenyans are not properly prepared for; that is the dilemma people have to grapple with.

The South Africa TRC was an important instrument in nation-building and a facilitator of the transition from a racist dictatorship to a multiracial democracy. It was not however, and was never intended to be, the sole instrument for furthering reconciliation or addressing the full range of social consequences arising out of the conflict of the past. New democratic institutions in South Africa such as the Land Commission, the South African Human Rights Commission, Commission for Gender Equality, the Jobs Equity Act, amongst others have all played a role in furthering justice and redress.[50] A Truth Commission such as TJRC cannot achieve its goals in the absence of democratic institutional infrastructure or by functioning in a vacuum, divorced from the broader realities of social injustice which are often the direct cause and consequence of the conflict being addressed. The challenge for Kenyans is how to put in place democratic institutions that can guarantee restitution and other forms of justice. For instance, there is at the moment lack of trust in government machinery including the police. The judiciary has been viewed as corrupt. Kenyans have lost confidence in the electoral system, particularly after the December 2007. Worse still, Kenya's history is replete with failed commissions, or most of whose findings have not been made public. Some commissions like the one probing the death of Robert Ouko were disbanded prematurely. Such a background does not augur well for confidence building in the TJRC. For Kenya's Commission to succeed citizens have to be educated on its difference with previous commissions in addition to putting in place democratic institutions that will supplement it. The Commission's work will significantly be boosted if there is in place an institutional framework that addresses distributive, legal and rectificatory justice issues.[51]

TRC and social justice

The TRC did not focus on social justice issues or the systemic violence of apartheid and therefore it never properly interrogated the underlying causes of the violence of apartheid, and the persistence of violence in the new South Africa. The TRC was established as a central tenet in the reconstruction of South African society, from a 'deeply divided past' to a more peaceful future.[52] Aside from unearthing the truth, the Commission viewed reparations and mechanisms defined by social justice as the principal means of building a new democratic society. While reparations promised a 'substantial impact' on victims' lives, progressive policies based on social justice could bring a sense of fairness and equality to a society based on socio-economic discrimination.[53] These hopeful visions have however been subverted by a lack of political will. Reparational assistance, recognised as an international right to victims of state crime, has been sidelined by the government. Linking up with the old beneficiaries of apartheid, the new ruling elite has restricted opportunities for societal transformation. While there has been a slow attempt to introduce some basic development in communities, this represents a slight challenge to the fundamental nature of apartheid. The lived experiences of those who bore the brunt of state brutality has not altered and with groups such as women and young people feeling excluded from developmental issues, prospects for future stability and equality in South Africa are bleak.[54]

There has been little government concern to fulfill its promise of reparational assistance for those directly victimised which means that broader societal transformation that challenges inequalities has become a distant possibility. The beneficiaries of apartheid have readily disconnected individual experiences of human rights violations from their own acceptance and encouragement of apartheid. As a group they have not acknowledged the links between violations and institutional practices or structural conditions. Given this stance, they have not pushed for change in the powerful worlds they occupy. Such lack of action has been unchallenged by the new ruling elite. This new 'petty bourgeoisie' have also compromised opportunities for societal transformation, making little attempt to radically alter forms of official policy-making.[55] The petty bourgeoisie phenomenon is not new on the Kenyan scene and its excesses have been evident in Kenyan politics for a long time. The likelihood of the TJRC becoming the shenanigans of this group is slim given their political and economic power.

Women and the TRC process

Equally the violence against women epitomises the phenomenon of violence re-enactment syndrome that post-conflict societies typically undergo. This is when people re-live their experiences of past violence by performing the same acts that their tormentors meted out to them. Pumla Gobodo-Madikizela, a TRC Commissioner and a practicing psychologist observes:

> It seems to me that what we are seeing in South Africa today is a *return* of past violence, a representation of the connections that bind history, past political events, and present reality: today's perpetrators of violence are following a script that was enacted during the years of apartheid... The shame and humiliation that propelled it then, in the years of apartheid, however, has not vanished with the advent of the "new" South Africa. What has disappeared is the container of the violent behaviour, the political purpose that provided the vital context. For today's "re-enactors" of past trauma, the dignity and respect that was lost through the

humiliation of apartheid has not been regained; while political change has given power and economic success to a few, *they*, the re-enactors, remain buried in the abyss of economic and psychological suffering. This plunges them back, as traumatic re-enactment so often does, into the vortex of violence.[56]

Such is the situation of the poor and more so for the women. This phenomenon resonates with the violence that has been witnessed lately in Kenya, including that performed by the Mungiki sect. It might be argued that economic marginalization of the youth has driven members of this sect to engage in violence against citizens. Be that as it may the TJRC appears to have its work cut out with regard to addressing violence in peacetime in Kenya.

One other area that the Kenyan TJRC can learn from that of South Africa is women's participation in the process. Women participated in the TRC process in large numbers by giving evidence of human rights violations in statements to the Commission; in fact, 54.8% of the participants were women. Of the participants who came to speak about their own experiences, the majority were men (56.1%), but a large number of women also did.[57] The TRC's official finding on women 21 reads as follows: Many of the statements made to the Commission by women detail the violations inflicted on others—children, husbands, siblings and parents—rather than what they themselves suffered. Undoubtedly the violation of family members had significant consequences for women. However, women too suffered direct violation of their human rights, many of which were gender specific in their exploitative and humiliating nature. The Commission thus found that: The state was responsible for the severe ill-treatment of women in custody in the form of harassment and the deliberate withholding of medical attention, food and water. Yet women who had suffered terribly underplayed their own experiences when talking about what had happened to men.[58]

It seems likely that many women were unwilling to go to the TRC to talk about their experiences for a range of reasons. One of the most important of these was the difficulty of talking about sexual abuse. The TRC referred to incidences of rape in 140 cases but it is highly likely that this reflects only a small number of the rapes that occurred in the period of the TRC's mandate.[59] Other reasons for women's silence included their unwillingness to betray comrades, their inability to face the pain of their experiences, their wish to move on, and, for some of the prominent women who were assuming important positions in the transitional society, fear that their stories would bring shame to them. Women tended to downplay or omit their own harsh treatment at the hands of the authorities when talking of their relatives.[60]

It will be worth watching how women's groups will engage the TJRC in probing gender-specific issues and ensure that women's own experiences are validated even where the evidence will not necessarily be meant for the formal purpose of defining them as victims. It will be interesting to see whether gender activists will engage Kenya's Commission and the media to highlight women's own suffering. In South Africa, the TRC responded in this aspect by encouraging women to talk about their own suffering when discussing what had happened to their loved ones. Some of the women were themselves victims according to the TRC's definition, since they were detained, beaten, and violated in other ways. However the final report has been criticized for what is seen as inadequate representation of women's experience under apartheid. This can be avoided in the Kenyan case if women's experiences are properly documented and acted upon but this will largely depend on how far women will feel encouraged to provide information to the TJRC.

In South Africa reconciliation was understood to be solely the mandate of the TRC. This has led to a somewhat blunted debate since the close of the Commission in 1998. The expectation that the TRC was the sole vehicle for reconciliation has led some to conclude that the closure of the Commission hearings spelled the end of the reconciliation process and by implication an end to the need to discuss substantive issues of redress. The TJRC mandate expires in 2012, a short period compared to South Africa's four-year lifespan. The TJRC should be seen as a long-term engagement with the past and a mapping of the future reconciliation. The end of its mandate should not be the end of the reconciliation efforts. This makes the need for public awareness an issue of paramount importance.

Bringing people to testify

One of the most disturbing issues in the reconciliation industry in South Africa was the deafening silences in the white population about their role in the apartheid system. There were few testimonies from this section of the South African population. Two things informed this silence. The explanation is partly offered in the play the "Story am about to tell" when one of the actors (who is white) dramatizes the point that there were no apologies to make for apartheid, that the white population did what it had to do, it was living a life.[61] This attitude irked a majority of Black South Africans who hold the view that one cannot reconcile with a people who think they did nothing wrong in the past. As late as the 2006 World Social Forum in Nairobi the feeling of "we can't work with them (white) because of their past deeds, which they have not acknowledged" still lingers in the Black population.[62] The White populations' silence undermined the TRC process since it was regarded largely as a Black's only exercise. This insincerity increased the already existing strain on victims and their families. Given the history of Commissions in Kenya, fear is that there will be South Africa-type silences from some quarters, particularly former politicians or those currently in high office. For our purpose the bigger picture should be considered and that is how to ensure that the high and mighty are also held to account and testify before the TJRC.[63]

Should Kenya use demonstrated remorse as a precondition for amnesty? It should be noted that issues of apology and remorse, particularly where incentivised by the promise of amnesty, can be fraught with psychological complexities for survivors. A lesson learned from South Africa and other Truth Commissions is the possibility of tying amnesty—with or without an apology—to a practical act of reconciliation.[64] The ability to contribute to individual reparations in a context of mass poverty may be improbable. Nevertheless countries such as Rwanda have tied their incentives for remorse and confession to the obligation to perform community service as part of the sentence—a practical act of sacrifice and symbolic reparations for victims.[65]

As has been observed above South Africans themselves are not reconciled for various reasons. The youth for instance are a disillusioned group. They envisioned life beyond reconciliation which they never saw as an end in itself. The disillusioned youth in the play "the story am about to tell" expresses the need for reconciliation to be achieved and translated into tangible things that the youth can enjoy and relate to; a reconciliation that would lay the foundation for the end goal of a society where the lived realities of all are improved and where the youth in particular are provided an environment in which they might explore and fulfil their own potential. Kenya is today facing the possibility of a youth rebellion and the possibility of social fragmentation if youth voices are not heard.

Violence and insecurity in any form stand as obstacles to sustainable reconciliation. The South African TRC provided an opportunity for South Africans to not only address the specific violations of the past but through its work contributed to the establishment of a shared condemnation of the use of violence in all forms and an embrace of the notion of "letting bygones be bygones."[66] However the end of violence and insecuritycan be one of the guarantees of reconciliation.

This vision speaks to the need not just for an absence of political conflict but rather one where human security is prioritized. In South Africa, as in many countries transitioning from a violent past, the gains of the new democracy have been tempered by new and continued forms of social violence which have persisted during the transition period. What this portends for Kenya's TJRC is that it should pave the road not just to an end goal of reconciliation but to an end goal of a shared development and human security premised on reconciliation. Only growing economic justice will allow ordinary Kenyans to experience some tangible rectification of the economic marginalisation that has marked the post-colonial state.

Conclusion

Transitional justice mechanisms the world over have provided opportunities to evaluate the past as well as future-looking mechanisms. As observed in the South African TRC forgiveness, healing and reconciliation are contested issues. The contestations make TRCs political and not moral projects. While the moral position taken by Tutu and his Commissioners may have carried the day it should not become a bone of contention in the TJRC. The TJRC should bear in mind the difficulty of heightened expectations and the changing and complex nature of survivors' needs. These issues serve but to give an indication of the magnitude of work that the Commission has cut itself.

The TJRC would learn from the South Africa TRC by defining terms in a precise way. The South African TRC was criticised for instance for working with ill-defined terms such as "victim" and "perpetrator."[67] The task of defining victims and perpetrators is a matter that could determine whether these categories of citizens would participate in the process. Since the Act establishing the TJRC is not clear on terms such as these mean it behoves the Commission to define them before it embarks on its hearings.

In the face of increasing public disillusionment arising from the slow pace of reforms in Kenya the TJRC has an uphill task of reassuring citizens that it is not merely another one of the many commissions whose reports have not been made public even after much hard work. It has a great responsibility of assuring the public that there is the possibility, through its work, for a new beginning, a renewed vigour, a new re-engineered culture of responsibility, accountability and fairness where impunity will be a thing of the past. This will depend on the way it will fashion its structures, how it will engage with civil society and generally carry out its business. Among the important things that Kenya can adopt from the South African TRC is the public nature in which the TRC conducted its affairs. One of the successes of the TRC was that almost everything was televised and open to the public. The TJRC process needs to do the same. The TRC also had a strong research component so that its findings were not only based on testimonies but also supported by a body of research. It will be interesting to see how much research informs the findings of the TJRC.

Notes

1 Brandon Hamber. 2003. "Rights and Reasons: Challenging for the Truth Recovery in South Africa and Northern Ireland, *Fordham International Law Journal*, 26(4).
2 Priscilla B. Hayner, *Unspeakable Truths: Confronting State Terror and Atrocity*, New York, Routledge, 2001, p. 252.
3 Hamber, "Rights and Reasons."
4 See Kader Asmal, Louise Asmal, and Ronald S. Roberts, *Reconciliation Through Truth: A Reckoning of Apartheid's Criminal Governance*, Cape Town, David Publishers, 1991, Alex Boraine, A. J. Levy and R. Scheffer, eds., *Dealing with the Past: Truth and Reconciliation in South Africa*. Cape Town, IDASA, 1994. Section 6(1) of the Sierra Leone Truth and Reconciliation Commission Act 2000 says its objective is "to promote healing and reconciliation", while The United Nations Transitional Authority in East Timor, section (d) says the Commission is grounded in "the desire to promote national reconciliation and healing."
5 *The Standard*, April 6, 2009.
6 For the full mandate of the South African Truth and Reconciliation Commission see the Promotion of National Unity and Reconciliation Act No. 34, 1995. A detailed summary of the SA TRC's mandate is also provided by Hayner, "Unspeakable Truths" footnote 1 and Alex Boraine " 2001. *A Country Unmasked: South Africa's Truth and Reconciliation Commission*.

New York, Oxford University Press.
7 Mahmood Mamdani, 2002 "Amnesty or Impunity? A Preliminary Critique of the Report of the Truth and Reconciliation Commission of South Africa (TRC), *Diacritics*, 32,3/4.
8 TRC Act
9 Peter Storey. 1999. "A Different Kind of Justice: Truth and Reconciliation in South Africa. *The Christian Century*, Sept. 10–17. Storey is past president of the Methodist Church of South Africa and of the South African Council of Churches. He was a member of the Selection Committee for the Truth and Reconciliation Commission.
10 Ibid
11 Ibid.
12 Mamdani, "Amnesty or Impunity?"
13 Storey, "A Different Kind of Justice," pp. 10–17.
14 TRC Act and the South African Interim Constitution.
15 See Hugo van der Merwe, Polly Dewhirst and Brandon Hamber 1999. "Non-governmental organizations and the Truth and Reconciliation Commission: an impact assessment *Politikon*, 26, 1, pp. 55, 79 cited in Brandon, 2003. "Rights and Reasons," p. 5.
16 Ibid.
17 Graybill and Lanegran, "Truth, Justice, and Reconciliation" p. 6.

18 Ibid.
19 Walshe, Peter. 1995. Prophetic Christianity and Resistance Movement in South Africa. Pietermaritzburg. Cluster. Cited in Ibid.
20 Desmond Tutu, April 2000 "Taking the costly path to peace," edited extracts from a public lecture, the University of Sydney gazette, pp. 2–13.
21 John S. Mbiti, African Religions and Philosophy, London, Heinemann, pp. 108–109 cited in Lyn Graybill and Kimberly Lanegran, " Truth, Justice, and Reconciliation" p. 7–8.
22 They are not just township courts and they are common in rural authorities.
23 Kevin Avruch and Beatriz Vejarano "Truth and Reconciliation Commissions: A Review Essay and Annotated Bibliography," The Online Journal of Peace and Reconciliation, 4, 2, pp. 43 (www.trinstitute.org/ojpcr/4_2recon.pdf accessed on 23rd March 2008. See also Richard A. Wilson. 2000. "Reconciliation and Revenge in Post-Apartheid South Africa-Rethinking Legal Pluralism and Human Rights," Current Anthropology, 41 (1) February.
24 Graybill and Lanegran, "Truth, Justice, and Reconciliation," p. 7.
25 Ibid. See also Brandon Hamber, 1999. "Past Imperfect: Strategies for Northern Ireland and South Africa and Countries in Transition." Paper presented at the Conference on the Truth and Conference: Commission. University of Witwatersrand, June 11–14. The author attended the conference and is in possession of the paper.
26 Tom Lodge. 2003. Politics in South Africa: From Mandela to Mbeki. Oxford. James Currey.
27 Approximately 7,000 individuals applied for amnesty and only 1, 160 were granted amnesty.
28 Mahmood Mamdani. 2000. "The Truth according to the TRC." In Ifi Amadiume and Abullahi An-Naim eds. The Politics of Memory: Truth, Healing and Social Justice. London. Zed Books. Pp. 177–178. cited in Graybill and Lanegran, "Truth, Justice and Reconciliation" p. 7.
29 James L. Gibson, 2004 "Overcoming Apartheid: Can Truth Reconcile a Divided Nation?" Politikon, 31, 2, pp. 129–155, this citation p. 141,150.
30 Grayhill and Lanegran, 2004 "Truth, Justice, and Reconciliation in Africa," p. 7.
31 Rama Mani. 2005. "Balancing Peace with Justice in the aftermath of Violent Conflict," Development, 48 (3) pp. 25–34, this citation p. 30.
32 The Standard, November 5, 2009.
33 Mani, "Balancing Peace With Justice" p. 30.
34 Alex Boraine. 2002. A Country Unmasked: South Africa's TRC. New York. Oxford University Press.
35 There was the big question of who should head the Commission should it be established. Every Kenyan seems to agree that we did not have a Tutu!
36 "Tainted by the Original Nyayo Sin" Sunday Nation, August 2, 2009.

37 The Standard, September 18 2009.
38 Hannah Arendt, 1968. Men in Dark Ages. New York. p. 25.
39 Desmond Tutu. 1999. No Future without Forgiveness. New York. Doubleday.
40 Miroslav Volf. 2001.Forgiveness, Reconciliation, and Justice: A Christian Contribution to a More Peaceful World." In Helmick, R. and R. Petersen, eds. Forgiveness and Reconciliation: Religion, Public Policy and Conflict Transformation. Philadelphia. Templeton.
41 There is the danger that the Chairman of the TJRC is invoking similar sentiments of the Christian moral position in the work of the commission. There are other faiths and even non-belivers that may not necesariely hold this Christian position.
42 TJRC Act, 2009.
43 For amnesty procedures see the Promotion of National Unity and Reconciliation Act No. 34, 1995 and the South African Interim-Constitution. Not all the truth was uncovered: Jonathan Klaaren and Howard Varney. 2000. "A Second Bite at the Amnesty Cherry? Constitutional and Policy around Legislation for a Second Amnesty" South African Law Journal 572, 593. Cited in Hamber "Rights and Reasons," p.6.
44 Brandon, "Rights and Reasons," pp. 6–7.
45 Nahla Valji, Presentation made to the Public Conference on the Liberian Truth and Reconciliation Commission co-hosted by the International Centre for Transitional Justice (ICTJ) and the Transitional Justice Working Group, 23 June 2006, Monrovia City Hall, Liberia.
46 The granting of amnesty itself was challenged in the Constitutional Court of South Africa where the Azania People's Organization and the families of Biko, Mxenge and Ribiero sought victim's rights to seek redress in the courts, which the National Unity and Reconciliation Act had barred them. Cited from Brandon, "Rights and Reasons," p.12.
47 Brandon, "Rights and Reasons," p.11.
48 www.bostonreview.net/BR25.3/linfield.html Accessed on 26th October 2008.
49 Ibid.
50 These Acts and Institutions buttressed the Commission's work in addressing specific past injustices.
51 For an excellent expose of these forms of justices corresponding see Mani, "Balancing peace with justice," pp. 34–36.
52 TRC Final Report. 1998. Vol. 1(5) p. 110.
53 Elizabeth Stanley. 2001. "Evaluating the Truth and Reconciliation Commission" The Journal of Modern African Studies, 39 (3) September, p. 539.
54 Ibid.
55 Patrick Bondo. 2000. Elite Transition. London. Pluto. cited in Elizabeth Stanley. 2001. "Evaluating the Truth and Reconciliation Commission" The Journal of Modern African Studies, 39 (3) September, p. 539.
56 Pumla Gobodo-Madikizela. 2003."The Dynamics

of Violence in Peacetime: Traumatic Continuities," Presentation at the 4th Annual DPI/NGO Conference, *Human Security and Dignity: Fulfilling the Promise of the United Nations*, September, p. 6.

57 TRC Report. Vol. 5 para.161.

58 Beth Goldblatt, "Evaluating the Gender Content of Reparations; Lessons from South Africa," p.54, see also TRC Report, chapter 10, p. 285.

59 Ibid.

60 TRC Report, Vol.5 Chapter 1, appendix 1 see also Beth Goldbath, "Evaluating the Gender Content of Reparations: Lessons from South Africa," p.54.

61 I watched the play in Johannesburg in 1999 at the Wits theater during the TRC Conference, University of the Witwatersrand, Johannesburg, June 11–14 1999.

62 Personal Communication, Themba Eduard, January 2006.

63 The recent assurance by Bethwel Kiplagat, the Chairman of the TJRC that no one will be spared the wrath of the Commission for refusing to appear before it is a good gesture of the seriousness of the process. However, whether this will be truly followed through is another matter altogether.

64 The debate about amnesty is intricate. The arguments are varied. See Jonathan Klaaren. 1999. "A Second Organisational Amnesty" paper presented at The TRC: Commissioning the Past Conference, University of the Witwatersrand, South Africa. June 14.

65 Mani, "Balancing Peace with Justice," p. 34–35.

66 Boraine "A Country Unmasked," and Tutu, "No Future without Forgiveness".

67 Mamdani, "Amnesty or Impunity? p. 33.

References

Arendt, H. (1968). *Men in Dark Ages*. New York.

Bond, P. (2000). *Elite Transition*. London: Pluto.

Boraine, A. (2001). *A Country Unmasked: South Africa's TRC*. New York: Oxford University Press.

Gibson, J. (2004). "Overcoming Apartheid: Can Truth Reconcile a Divided Nation?" *Politikon: South African Journal of Political Studies 31(2)*, November.

Gobodo-Madikizela, P. (1997). "Healing the Racial Divide? Personal Reflections on the Truth and Reconciliation Commission". *South African Journal of Psychology 27(4)*, December.

Gobodo-Madikizela, P. (2003). "The Dynamics of Violence in Peacetime: Traumatic Continuities." *Presentation at the 56th Annual DPI/NGO Conference, Human Security and dignity: Fulfilling the Promise of the United Nations*, September 8.

Graybill, L., & Lanegran, K. (2004). "Truth, Justice, and Reconciliation in Africa: Issues and Cases." *African Studies Quarterly. 8 (1), Fall*.

Hamber, B. (2003). "Rights and Reasons: Challenges for Truth Recovery in South Africa and Northern Ireland." *Paper presented at the Strategies and limitations of truth commissions: the cases of Argentina, Chile, South Africa and Guatemala Workshop*." Centre for International Studies and CISA: Peterhouse College, Cambridge University, UK, March.

Hamber, B. (1999). "Past Imperfect: Strategies for Dealing with Past Political Violence in Northern Ireland, South Africa, and Countries in Transition." *Paper presented at the Conference on the Truth and Reconciliation Commission: Commissioning the Past*. University of Witwatersrand, June 11–14.

Hayner, P. B. (2001). *Unspeakable Truths: Confronting State Terror and Atrocities*. New York: Routledge.

Helmick, R., & Peterson, P. eds. (2001). *Forgiveness and Reconciliation: Religion, Public Policy and Conflict Transformation*. Philadelphia: Templeton.

Klaara, J. (1999). "A Second Organisational Amnesty." *Paper presented at The TRC: Commissioning the Past Conference*, University of the Witwatersrand, South Africa, June 14.

Lodge, T. (2003). *Politics in South Africa: From Mandela to Mbeki*. Oxford: James Currey.

Mamdani, M. (2000). "The Truth According to the TRC." In Ifi Amadiume and Abdullahi An-Na'im (eds.) *The Politics of Memory: Truth, Healing and Social Justice*. London: Zed Books.

Mamdani, M. (2002). "Amnesty or Impunity? A Preliminary Critique of the Report of the Truth and Reconciliation of South Africa (TRC)". *Diacritics. 32, 3/4 Fall*, pp. 33–58.

Mbiti, J. S. (1969). *African Religions and Philosophy*. London: Heinemann.

Storey, P. (1997). "A Different Kind of Justice: Truth and Reconciliation in South Africa". *Christian Century 114, (25)*.

Tutu, D. (2000). "Taking the Costly Path to Peace." *The University of Sydney Gazette, April*.

Tutu, D. (1999). *No Future without Forgiveness*. New York: Doubleday.

Van de Merwe, H., & Polly, D. (1999). "Non-governmental Organizations and the Truth and Reconciliation Commission: An Impact Assessment." *Politikon: South African Journal of Political Studies, 26 May*, pp. 55, 79.

Volf, M. (2001). "Forgiveness, Reconciliation, and Justice: A Christina Contribution to a More Peaceful World," in Helmick, R. and P. Peterson, eds. *Forgiveness and Reconciliation: Religion, Public Policy and Conflict Transformation*. Philadelphia: Templeton.

Walshe, P. (1995). *Prophetic Christianity and the Resistance Movement in South Africa*. Pietermaritzburg: Cluster.

Wilson, R. (2000). "Reconciliation and Revenge in Post-Apartheid South Africa – Rethinking Legal Pluralism and Human Rights." *Current Anthropology. 41(1), February*, pp. 41–42.

Post-script—
Truth and Reconciliation: A Reflection

BETTY CAPLAN

Discussions with students in universities need to be opened to the public in order to fill in the gaps in the education they receive. But in order to successfully achieve the goal of training civic-minded students it is necessary that academics be committed to ideas that promote the greater social good rather than ethnic and class interests.

Regardless of the diversity and harshness of circumstances that one finds in the complex placements of contemporary life one important lesson is to never lose touch with one's humanity.

I am starting with a personal introduction as a way of invoking the idea of identity and practices related to it because the issue is the key and has predominated discussions of what happened both before and after the Kenyan general elections of December 2007. While not out to compare the Kenyan and Israeli situations I still believe that there are lessons to be gleaned from parts of the Jewish experience that might apply in Kenya's case as we seek to move towards healing the country.

I am a Jew born in Australia of Polish Jewish parents fleeing Nazi Germany. So I am Australian too. But I lived in the UK for over 20 years. I have been in Africa for 12 years, 10 of those in Kenya. So what has become of my Jewishness? Am I any less of a Jew for having nothing to do with a community in Nairobi which defines Jewishness as complete and uncritical support for Israel, including the injustices of the post 1967 occupation? What I am saying is that Jewishness is only a part of my identity which is a fluid, changing complex thing. It is accidental, and geographically complicated. People confuse Jews with Israelis and fail to understand they are not necessarily the same. Jews are a people, not a nation, with mixed origins. Some are religious and others like me secular, but they still call themselves Jews because they identify with the people and their long bitter history. The languages they speak (apart from their native ones) are Yiddish—originally a medieval German dialect spoken by the Jews of Europe for centuries—and Hebrew, a completely different tongue, modernized from the ancient texts of the Bible and related books like the Talmud which has its own script. Briefly that is how convoluted the story of my Jewish identity is.

The above narrative enables us to see how identity is socially and politically constructed and the fact that possession of land has been critical in its making. Indeed few people are able to look beyond geographical landscape in any attempts at defining identity. Thus as a girl, I was taught by my Zionist parents that the land of Palestine was 'empty' until the Jews turned it once again into 'a land of milk and honey.' I only learned the truth much later, when I had left home in my twenties. We see then that society and political practice construct particular truths according to the imperatives of the day. The truth, in relation to individuals, becomes subjective to them and consequently it is relativized. And this truth is conditioned by the perspective from which history is (re)told. Certainly the present story about historical injustices in Kenya needs deeper examination than it has received thus far, especially amongst the elite class.

What has happened during my time in Kenya is that the label of 'tribe', like that of Jew, has in some sectors of this country become a fixed and rigid thing and it has completely taken over any perceptions of individuals. That has been, as we know, for political reasons and it has affected the poor, the unemployed and the disenfranchised disproportionately. 'Tribe' too has become extremely valuable as a basis for rendering Kenyan history and individuals' narratives. Only one version of history usually circulates at any given time and it is usually promulgated by the victorious side in a battle. History books are full of stories of battles won, but they take a short term view. For instance looking back at Germany's history—I can't avoid doing this given that this was the launching pad of my personal wanderings—one notices that the Second World War grew out of the First. Nazis were able to feed off the discontent fostered by the political settlement at the end of the First World War.

The fact that more often (official) history is based on written rather than oral evidence has meant that women, peasants, the under classes, the 'silent majority' have been left out. In addition traditional forms of upbringing have generally encouraged those who have been left out to remain obedient; until relatively recently during the Moi years questioning the nature of things hasn't been a crucial part of Kenyan public culture. However, in the 2007 elections, in a perverted convergence of aims, these same dispossessed people willingly came out to commit atrocities in the name of their higher placed kinsfolk.

However beyond the finger-pointing it is necessary for us to assess where and how Kenyans took the wrong turn. The shock has not worn off—one doubts the usefulness of the claim that time heals—and it is far too soon to talk about reconciliation or justice, as the chaos during the 2008 Justice Kriegler Commission hearings prove. Yet there are good things that have emerged from Kenya's present nightmare: problems are being brought into the light and examined. The explosion of violence has freed some to speak the unspeakable. It has generated discussions such as have been taking place under the aegis of the Public Lecture Series at Goethe-Institut Kenya. Time and the right attitude are needed to heal these wounds. Some of us have chosen to express our feelings (some highly vituperative) on websites rather than the conventional news media. Naturally the events of December 2007 and the resulting conflagrations were the product of many things. Whatever these were, one must honestly ask whether the 2002 NARC-euphoria wasn't unrealistically based merely on the relief of having dethroned Moi's dictatorial and corrupt regime.

Did Kenyans get any real change in December 2002? The 'Moi way' template has hardly changed. For instance was the freedom of speech and association that we experienced not quickly curtailed under the Kibaki government? There have been long-held grudges about land distribution which haven't been addressed despite the existence of various reports. Even an apparently radical move like free primary education, while good in certain ways, was proven to be utterly undemocratic in that the teachers who were to bear the brunt of bursting classrooms were never consulted and not sufficient resources were allocated. It was yet another electioneering gimmick. Clearly there are many things about which citizens still have boiling anger and as such it is too soon to talk about reconciliation. This is especially so given that victims have never been formally asked what they feel towards those who perpetrated various violations against them. Indeed the hostility with which the Bethwel Kiplagat Truth and Reconciliation team was received casts serious doubts about whether this body will achieve much. At Kiambaa near Eldoret town people were burned alive in the church where they had gone to seek shelter. That evoked horrible echoes of the Rwandan genocide, but in a profound demonstration of callous inhumanity just because the victims were not from her community, a female MP from the Rift Valley is reported to have attributed the cause of the fire to a burst gas cylinder! Some bodies were lost in forests—some arenas of the killings had chillingly prophetic names like Burnt Forest—while others were disposed off in mass graves. In other words many people's lives have been shattered and will probably never be put back together again, as witnessed everyday by the case of those in internally displaced persons (IDP) camps and other numerous half way transit camps where those that were allegedly "re-integrated" hover between the closed-down IDP camps and their former homes on farms that their neighbors do not allow them to settle on. At any rate, the fear and suspicion between the Kalenjin and Kikuyu have not been addressed in any serious fashion by the politicians who carry most clout, the task having been left to committees of village elders (not the larger communal Elders' Council) who at the end of the day take directions from the more powerful political figures.

For reconciliation to happen, we must first agree that the victims' story in regard to the 2007/2008 atrocities has not been fully told. Where attempts to do so have been made, there are perceptible partisan slants and omissions based on the tellers politics. Second, the political class has to climb down the denial pedestal upon which they have perched since they were elected to parliament through the blood of the dead and the trauma of citizens who previously had proper names but whom we now collectively call IDPs. And when we attempt to heal Kenya, it must not be because we want to lure the tourists back to put money in the pockets of other foreigners who own hotels at the coast but rather because we owe it to Kenyans—all those people now living in the very depths of the despair that is their shattered lives. The rapacity that drives the political class *en masse* to refuse to pay their full share of taxes coupled with the conceited vanity that makes most of them to consider riding in brand new government-issue Volkswagen Passat instead of Mercedes Benzes to be both demeaning and punitive is something to be addressed if Kenyans are going to enjoy their rights in a more just society. Only a 'leader' with a perverted sense of entitlement would be haggling over reasons as to why s/he shouldn't ride in the "type of cars driven by teenagers" (i.e. less than 1800 cc) while IDPs from Kĩrathimo in Limuru, fed up that the government has refused to afford them transport to take up land in Laikipia offered them free by a private citizen, decide to trek to the promised land and in the process a few of them die of pneumonia. It is not idle to ask: if in protest the rest of Kenyan society refused to pay taxes that sustain a mannerless political elite, would the political leadership have any moral grounds to send the tax man after them? Is it that citizens pay taxes for the sole reason of sustaining the opulent lifestyles of the politicians? Most Kenyans see clearly now that this class is a key obstacle to reconciliation and justice in society.

As Kenyans experiment with the idea of a reconciliation commission it has been fashionable to cite the South African Truth and Reconciliation Commission. This might be inspirational but it is necessary to underscore the fact that the South African situation was unique in that it provided a different model of healing altogether based on the psychological reality that some victims of crime can be helped by bringing a victim face to face with his persecutor. The set up was far more egalitarian than the old-style court hearings at Nuremberg in that the perpetrators are given a chance to show their humanity. There have been cases where mothers of murdered children have asked to meet the killers so that they can together come to terms with what has happened and why. This takes enormous courage. But in the Kenyan case it is going to be vastly more difficult to bring closure to families that can't trace the bodies of members who were killed during the 2007/2008 mayhem.

Looking at the contemporary South African situation where racial tensions seem to have been exacerbated by the lack of meaningful economic opportunities for the majority Africans even with the establishment of the Black Economic Empowerment program (BEE), one must ask how helpful the TRC was in the country's 'healing'. Economic injustices are as much a barrier to the achievement of social justice as is the removal of a government based on an ideology of race. In Kenya's case, how willing or ready are citizens to get rid of ethnicity as a basis for thinking about elections, government and their place in society? At any rate, within the context of what happened in 2007/2008, it is worrisome about the prospects of achieving reconciliation when prominent politicians from the Rift Valley—the central arena for the violence—traipse across the province demanding reconciliation even without first stopping to acknowledge their role, if any, in the election-related fractures. What truth, justice or reconciliation can be achieved while victims of the aggression, a great number of whom previously led economically self-reliant lives, languish in IDP and satellite camps or on tiny plots of land acquired through compensation money pooled together to buy five acres off a rich man? Some of these people owned land from which they were evicted yet even as the government engages in cosmetic 'resettlement' exercises like 'Operation *Rudi Nyumbani*' (Homecoming), ODM-allied Kalenjin politicians are not saying whether the constitutional guarantee for anyone to own land anywhere in the country is no longer part of the country's laws. Otherwise why has the property belonging to Gĩkũyũ, Kisii and Kamba land owners in the Rift Valley been expropriated? The possibility for Kenya's attempt at truth and reconciliation becoming a window-dressing exercise seem pretty high.

There is an important role that academics can play in these efforts. It is their work to provide critical analyses of the deep-seated issues that led us to this state. We need to have discussions in public fora but also on the internet; perhaps this is a good way of by-passing print and electronic media which, being owned mainly by rich (old) men, seem to be driven solely by the agenda of gerontocracy. For instance, discussions with students in universities need to be opened to the public in order to fill in the gaps in the education they receive. But in order to successfully achieve the goal of training civic-minded students it is necessary that academics be committed to ideas that promote the greater social good rather than ethnic and class interests. In this sense one must ask why academics took sides with various political actors for nothing else other than ethic affiliation; it is true that there were concrete grievances but one might wonder whether the high-sounding arguments that were marshaled in defence of particular positions were not in fact an attempt to legitimize whatever violence that might befall 'opponents' in the event that the presidential election outcome didn't go in a desired way. After all, looking at the context of Nazism with which I began these reflections, it mustn't be forgotten that the task of legitimizing Hitler's odious actions was left to highly educated people of whom Josef Goebbels—holder of a PhD in Literature from Heidelberg University—and the medical anthropologist Doctor Josef Mengele stand out spectacularly. It is thus necessary to ask what the role of education is in shaping socially responsible citizens. In this art—its various media shape the intellect in such subtle ways as to have fundamentally greater power than politicians' demagoguery—can offer us a critical lesson, which I draw from my own native Australia. Furthermore the lessons from art are also simple enough to be comprehended by anyone with the will to do so, and through it the Australian example might illustrate how intellectual work might be used to say sorry in a manner that enables action and change.

There is a moral victory to be seen in the fact that in places like Australia descendants of colonists who have benefited from high standards of living as a result of their fore bearers' decimating native populations now see the need to make amends for their ancestor's actions. For this alone, an apology was long overdue and it is proper that one was recently issued in Australia. In itself this gesture might be considered inconsequential since those who issued it were not personally responsible either for the killing of Aborigines or for the atrocities committed against the "Lost Generation" where children were taken away from their families and 'adopted' by white families in order to assimilate and thereby 'civilize' them. However the gesture's real value lies in how it demonstrates what enlightened leadership might be and what it can achieve. For years money has been thrown at Aborigines without producing any tangible solutions to their myriad problems precisely because a majority of the white Australian population has little if any understanding of these people or their needs. Instead, the constant failure of these interventions ended up confirming racist attitudes about Aborigine's supposed savagery and incorrigibility. This certainly was the basis of John Howards' refusal to even acknowledge Aborigine's grievances when he was Australia's Prime Minister for ten years (1996–2007). It is therefore relevant that one of the first official acts by then newly-elected Prime Minister Kevin Rudd was the issuing of an apology to the country's Aborigine population through a motion that was unanimously passed by the Australian legislature on February 13 2008 (ironically around the same time Kenyans were still busy devising and executing methods of annihilating both neighbors and nation).[1] Furthermore in the broader scheme of things it was necessary to apologize in order to set in motion mechanisms for meaningful redress of these past wrongs. In this regard The Prime Minister spelt out his government's agenda for talking some of the problems related to Aborigine marginalization. At another level it has come to be recognized that Aboriginal art constitutes a critical part of Australian history and identity. For instance Aboriginal paintings are now prized as a superb way of immediately coming to grips with a wholly different view of the world. Books, poetry, fiction, plays, films have all helped to bring to the national fore discussions that might lead to an honest examination about tangible grievances that have clear historical background and that continue to be manifested in many ways in contemporary society. No matter how limited these discussions are they are not so 'small' as to be inconsequential. They have given the Aborigine a voice and are helping the country to come to terms with a distinctive part of its identity, one that was hitherto lacking and suppressed. There could be lessons in for Kenya in that.

The Aborigine's woeful situation is obviously much direr than that of marginalized Kenyans given that the former are a dying minority in a vast, wealthy country that does not need or want them (for the most part.) That is fortunately not the case in Kenya. If truth and reconciliation are to do their proper work saying "sorry" to those who have been victimized in various ways by either the state or individuals must be accompanied by a concerted effort to address the problems that over time led to the sorts of fractures that were witnessed in 2007/2008–poverty, drunkenness, unemployment and unemployability, and alienation between leaders and the led, and the institutionalization of violence among others.

The personal story that links me to Germany, Poland, Australia, the United Kingdom and Kenya tells me that difference is inescapable and can be manipulated for all manner of reasons. Regardless of the diversity and harshness of circumstances that one finds in the complex placements of contemporary life one important lesson is to never lose touch with one's humanity. Thus given the fact that ethnicity—one of the key themes that comes up in relation to the period under discussion—isn't something that can be gotten rid of or wished away Kenyans must devise ways of managing difference in a manner that in the end does not prevent them from leading productive lives. That way there will be space for all to work at achieving a better society.

Notes
1 See http://news.bbc.co.uk/2/hi/asia-pacific/7242057.stm for the full text of the apology. Retrieved November 14, 2009.

Notes on Contributors

Betty Caplan is a journalist and teacher of English. / *George Gona* teaches in the Department of History and Archaeology at the University of Nairobi. / *Frederick K. Iraki* teaches in the Department of French at United States International University, Nairobi. / *Karambu Ringera* teaches in the School of Journalism at the University of Nairobi. / *Kĩmani Njogu* is a Director, Twaweza Communications and CEO, Africa Health and Development International (AHADI). / *Mbũgua wa-Mũngai* teaches in the Department of Literature at Kenyatta University Nairobi. He researches on urban folklore, popular culture and disability in culture. / *Peter Wafula Wekesa* teaches in the Department of History and Political Science at Kenyatta University. / *Pius Kakai Wanyonyi* teaches in the Department of History and Political Science at Kenyatta University. / *Ruth Wangeci Ndũng'ũ* teaches Linguistics in the Department of English at Kenyatta University. / *Sophie Macharia* formerly taught in the Department of Literature at Kenyatta University and is currently a full time consultant and researcher. / *Tom Odhiambo* teaches in the Department of Literature at the University of Nairobi. / *Vincent G. Simiyu* is Associate Professor of History at the Department of History and Archaeology, University of Nairobi.

List of papers presented

18. 06. 2008
Session 1: Identities—Between Ethnic and Civic Nationhood
Introduction: Johannes Hossfeld, George Gona,
Wambũi Mwangi
The Architecture of Ethnicities: Pius Kakai
The Political Economics of Identity: Onyango Oloo
Iconic Representations of Identity in Kenyan Cultures:
Mbũgua wa-Mũngai
Chair: Wambũi Mwangi

25. 06. 2008
Session 2: Memories, Narratives & Debates of Nationhood
Gerontocracy & Generational Competition: Tom Odhiambo
Negotiating Kenyanness: Peter Wafula Wekesa
Engendering & Power(lesness) in the Kenyan Political
Economy: Sophie Macharia
Chair: George Gona

09. 07. 2008
Session 3: Healing the Wounds
Recasting the Land Question(s): Between Repossession,
Dispossession and (Re)distribution: Karuti Kanyinga
Truth & Justice: Lessons from South Africa's TRC: George Gona
Kenya's Truth and Reconciliation?: Betty Caplan
Chair: Mbũgua wa-Mũngai

16. 07. 2008
Session 4: The Media, Ethnicity & Politics of (De)Regulation
Media Culture: Freedom and/or Regulation: Karambu Ringera
From Hate Media to Bloodshed: Citizen Ethnicization:
Levi Obonyo
Cross Media Ownership Monopolizing Public Spaces:
Frederick Iraki
Chair: Zahid Rajan

17. 09. 2008
Session 5: Thinking for the State?
Intellectuals under Siege:
Gatekeepers, Censorship & Boundaries: Okoth Okombo
Global Identity: Diaspora Kenyans and Local Conflict:
Kĩmani Njogu
The Academic and the State: A Historical Perspective:
Vincent G. Simiyu
Chair: Felix Kiruthu

24. 09. 2008
Session 6: Conflict Cultures
Renting Mobs: Militias—vs—Armed Forces: Kenneth Ombongi
Training Violence: Ideas and Practices in Socio-cultural Contexts:
Ruth Ndũng'ũ
Chair: Garnette Oluoch-Olunya

15. 10. 2008
Session 7: Memories and Narratives of Nationhood
Memories in Popular Culture: Gachanja Kĩai
Ethnic Stereotypes: Private/Public Self-Otherness:
Kibe Mũngai
Narratives of Survival: The Last Villains of Molo: Kĩnyanjui Kombani
Chair: John Mugubi

22. 10. 2008
Session 8: Healing the Wounds II
1. Achieving Social Justice: Othieno Nyanjom
2. Ending the Culture of Impunity? Political, Economic and other Crimes: Alice Nderitũ
3. Forms of Governance: Rethinking 'Democrazy': Katumanga Msambayi
Chair: George Gona

The sessions were held at Goethe-Institut Kenya

Lightning Source UK Ltd.
Milton Keynes UK
173978UK00006B/6/P